Old Ways for New Days

As Pagans, the Sabbats move us deeply. This book recognizes the profound spiritual connection we feel to the change of the seasons . . . and it shows how to intimately live that connection through meaningful ritual and craft in which even non-Pagan family and friends can participate.

This book does not intend to abolish the old ways. On the contrary, it seeks to blend the old with the new and offer creative ways for modern Pagans to observe the ancient holidays. It recognizes the natural atavistic tendencies in all people, and shows how to express those primal feelings in meaningful and satisfying ways that connect us to the changing seasons and the turning of the Wheel of the Year.

Not only will *Sabbats* help you gain the continuity with the past that comes from a deeper expression of the seasons—it provides a firm foundation on which to build cherished celebrations that will become new traditions for the future.

About the Author

Edain McCoy was born to parents from diverse backgrounds who always encouraged her to explore the history of religious thought, and to draw her own conclusions from those studies. As a teenager she began seeking the roots of her birth religion. Eventually that search, and her increasing feminist outlook, brought her back to the Old Religion. A chance meeting with a hereditary witch at a *ceilidh* (Irish Dance) in Houston led her to study the Irish Tradition of the Craft. Though she prefers to practice as a solitary, she has been part of several Texas covens, and she is always anxious to meet with like-minded persons.

Edain was born August 11, 1957, and describes herself as the "quintessential Leo." She numbers among her colorful ancestors Sir Roger Williams, the seventeenth century religious dissenter who laid down the principles of separation of church and state which govern the United States, and the infamous feuding McCoy family of Kentucky. A graduate of the University of Texas, she now lives in the Midwest where she is continuing her formal graduate studies in cultural history. She is a member of the Indiana Historical Society, the Author's Guild, the Wiccan/Pagan Press Alliance, and is active in her local Irish Arts Association.

To Write to the Author

If you wish to contact the author or would like more information about this book, please write to the author in care of Llewellyn Worldwide, and we will forward your request. Both the author and publisher appreciate hearing from you and learning of your enjoyment of this book and how it has helped you. Llewellyn Worldwide cannot guarantee that every letter written to the author can be answered, but all will be forwarded. Please write to:

Edain McCoy
℅ Llewellyn Worldwide
P.O. Box 64383, Dept. K663-7, St. Paul, MN 55164-0383, U.S.A.
Please enclose a self-addressed, stamped envelope for reply, or $1.00 to cover costs.
If outside the U.S.A., enclose international postal reply coupon.

SABBATS

Other Books by the Author

SABBATS

A WITCH'S APPROACH TO LIVING THE OLD WAYS

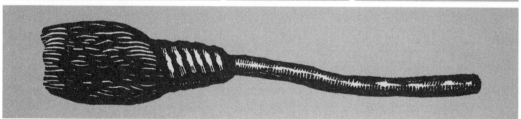

EDAIN McCOY

Llewellyn Publications
St. Paul, Minnesota

FIRST EDITION
Ninth printing, 2005

Cover Design: Kevin R. Brown
Interior Illustrations: Silver RavenWolf and Susan Van Sant
Book Design and Layout: Pamela Henkel

Library of Congress Cataloging-in-Publication Data
McCoy, Edain, 1957—
        The Sabbats: a new approach to living the old ways / by Edain McCoy.
            p.   cm.
        Includes bibliographical references and index.
        ISBN 1-56718-663-7
        1. Sabbat. 2. Paganism—Rituals. 3. Religious calendar—
        Paganism. 4. Witchcraft.   I. Title.
BF1572.S28M33 1994
299--dc20   94-29602
                                                                    CIP

Llewellyn Publications
A Division of Llewellyn Worldwide, Ltd.
P.O. Box 64383, St. Paul, MN 55164-0383
www.llewellyn.com

Printed in the United States of America

Table of Contents

List of Recipes

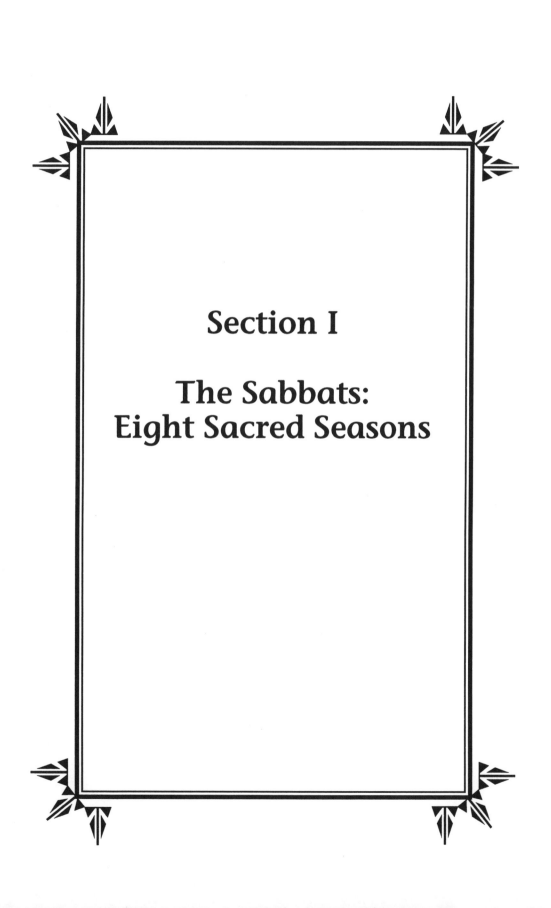

Section I

The Sabbats:
Eight Sacred Seasons

⇥ 1 ⇤

The Pageantry and Meaning
of the Sabbats

Modern paganism is a rich tapestry of interwoven traditions, ideas, and orientations. The eight Sabbats which are now known to Western pagans were not always the eight Sabbats of a single tradition, nor were they all a part of the popular Norse, Teutonic, or Celtic traditions which adopted them. They were not all even represented in the Roman or Greek pagan past. Each of the numerous solar festivals around the globe contributed to the amalgam, lore, and practice which has become our bounteous pagan heritage of today.

It is estimated that the Sabbats have been observed in various places and in various forms for at least 12,000 years. Originally these fire festivals were agricultural dates which marked planting, tending, and harvesting times. Today farmers still sow and reap by these dates and carefully consult farmer's almanacs which outline the best times for each of their crops, though they may not be aware they are following a very ancient tradition.

As civilizations became less nomadic and not solely reliant upon hunting and herding for their sustenance, the Sabbats became religious and celebratory holidays. The Vikings planned their raids and voyages around these dates. They planted just after Ostara, left on raids, returned for the harvest, and went out again only to return for the all-important Yule celebration, when they honored their reborn God. In Celtic lands the Sabbats not only marked planting times, but also the seasons, and told them which

3

deities were at their peak of power. Samhain marked the beginning of the old Celtic New Year, and Bealtaine the summer.

The Roman, Norman, and Nordic invaders had a profound influence on the prominence and significance of Yule in Britain and Ireland. In the Teutonic tradition, Yule was the Sabbat of central importance and it hailed the New Year for the ancient Norse and Germanic people in the same way that Samhain marked the New Year for the Celts.

To both the Celts and the Teutons, the "day" began with sundown the evening before. This idea originated in India and the Middle East, and even today the Jewish and Islamic calendars count the beginning of each day in this way. This idea no doubt spread west and north with the ancient Aryans and became a part of our pagan ancestors' world view. For example, in Western paganism, the beginning of the Samhain Sabbat officially begins at sundown on October 30, rather than at dawn on the 31st.

Long before the eight great pagan Sabbats met and melded in the well-known traditions of northern and western Europe, pagans world-over celebrated many of their solar holidays and festivals at times that roughly corresponded to the modern Sabbats. The chart on Page 5 shows which ancient cultures celebrated pagan solar festivals on or near these dates.

The word "Sabbat" comes from the old Greek word "sabatu," meaning "to rest." Since performing an act of magick is work (much more so than many often realize), it is customary that no magickal working be done on a Sabbat unless there is a pressing or life-threatening need. Spells were often performed just prior to the Sabbat in order to take advantage of the waxing energy caused by worldwide pagan anticipation of the day, but it was believed that one should never do magick on Sabbats except in an emergency. Sabbats are for relaxing, enjoying friends, feeling part of the season, and celebrating the lives of our deities and their earthly incarnations. Most modern pagans adhere to this old custom.

The eight solar Sabbats represent the turning of the Wheel of the Year, and each honors a stage in the eternal life cycle of the Goddess and God. Many pagans see time as one eternal whole which is forever turning, returning always to beginning and starting anew. The God is born, dies, and is reborn. The eternal Goddess goes from childhood to motherhood to cronehood and back again in an endless cycle of change and renewal.

The Sabbats and their lore as we know it survived thanks to a handful of hearty pagans who refused to turn their backs on their beloved religion, even when faced with persecution and death from the Church authorities of

Culture	Samhain	Yule	Imbolg	Ostara	Bealtaine	Midsummer	Lammas	Mabon
Aboriginal	X	X				X		
African, Central		X		X		X		X
African, West		X				X		
African, South		X		X		X		X
Anglo-Welsh	X	X	X		X	X	X	X
Aryan		X		X		X	X	X
Celtic	X	X	X		X	X	X	
Chinese	X			X		X	X	X
East Europe	X	X			X	X	X	
Egyptian		X		X			X	X
Greco-Roman		X	X	X		X	X	X
Iberian	X	X	X	X		X		X
Japanese		X				X	X	
Native American, North		X				X	X	X
Native American, South	X		X			X		
Russian	X	X	X	X	X	X	X	
Semitic		X			X			X
Teutonic, Northern	X	X	X	X		X		X
Teutonic, Southern		X	X	X	X	X	X	X
South Pacific	X	X			X	X		

Europe who sought to stamp out all vestiges of the Old Religion in favor of their new one. The word "heresy" had its meaning altered; it came to mean "a crime punishable by death." The word comes from the Greek word "hairesis" which means "a school of thought," not a "false doctrine," as the Church fathers led us to believe. Pagan deities were identified with the devils and demons of the new religion, and their images became associated with evil. The best example of this was the demonization of the Great Horned God of Europe, one of the most widely worshipped pagan deities, who became Christianity's horned devil and anti-God. No amount of logic could convince these witch hunters that pagans never had a devil and do not believe in one; he is wholly a construct of Christian theology. But pagans died horrible deaths fighting for the truth of the faith.

The Wheel of the Year

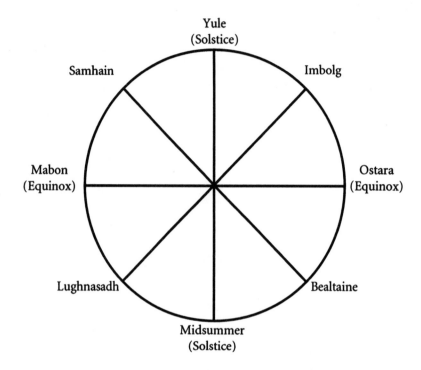

Each Sabbat's opposite festival falls directly across from it on the wheel. For example, Yule begins the waxing year and across from it, Midsummer begins the waning year. And both Ostara and Mabon are days of balance, but one moves toward darkness while the other moves toward light.

At this time of transition in the Church, pagans went into hiding. They met at night, used everyday implements as ritual and magickal tools, and also began the task of veiling the ancient folklore and stories of the old deities in nursery rhymes and folk tales.

But not everyone could completely ignore the old holidays, even Christians. So when the Church's distortions, threats, and coercions didn't achieve the destruction of the old practices, the Church decreed new festivals to coincide with the Sabbats in order to supplant their influence and prominence in the popular mind. It is no secret that the birth of the Christian God, Jesus, was deliberately placed near the time of the birth of the pagan Sun Gods, or that St. John's Day, celebrated with bonfires in Celtic lands, was set up to take the place of the Midsummer Sabbat.

Even in the face of this adversity, the old pagan ways refused to die. They are still celebrated by both pagans and non-pagans around the world, and the ancient folk ways, folk stories, nursery rhymes, and fairy tales have contained and preserved for us the hidden lore of our ancestors for more than a thousand years.

Basic Tools of Paganism/Witchcraft

Paganism and Witchcraft are not quite synonymous terms, though they are often used as such, a trend which may indicate a continuing blend of beliefs among pagan peoples everywhere. Pagans are followers of any and all nature or earth religions. The term comes from the Latin "paganus" which means "people of the earth." Witches are followers of the Celtic and Anglo traditions of the Craft (another name for paganism). Their name comes from the Anglo-Saxon word "wicca," meaning "wise one." Throughout this book, the terms will be used interchangeably for the sake of convenience.

The traditional pagan ritual tools used almost universally in Western paganism came to us from Ceremonial or High Magick, a highly codified ritualistic magickal practice based on the structure of Jewish and Gnostic Christian mystic texts known as the Kaballah. Ceremonial Magicians use lavish ritual adornments of the body, and have a distinct set of ritual tools (called "weapons" in their craft) to represent each of the four elements. Specially-colored robes, advancement along a hierarchy to various degrees of practice, a copious written body of secret knowledge, compulsory enslavement of spirits to do one's bidding, and specific head gear and jewelry are standard paraphernalia and ideas of Ceremonial Magick. Pagans, who have always valued a more simplistic and gentle approach to magick, have rejected most of this pomp and circumstance. However, the idea of specific ritual tools took hold and have become a standard part of neo-pagan practice.

The melding of ideas between these divergent paths is believed to have occurred in the late fifteenth century, when Spain initiated its Inquisition, aimed at ferreting out non-Christians and "devil-worshipping witches." After 1492, many of Spain's pagans, Jews, Moors, Gnostics, and other non-traditional believers fled the Iberian Peninsula under fear of death. Kaballists and pagans alike now believe that a great body of knowledge was shared between these two refugee groups. One tradition of Wicca, the Alexandrian (named for founder Alexander Saunders), successfully combines practices from both paths.

The ritual tools we adopted from High Magick are used to help us focus and direct our own inner energies. They are an extension of the witch and have no inherent magick in their own right, though they do eventually absorb a certain amount of magickal energy or vibrations from repeated use. Basically we use one tool to represent each of the four directions and their corresponding element. Each element has its own sphere of influences and correspondences when working magick, and these should be studied before you attempt to do magick spells. Check the Bibliography in the back of the book for the names of works which can steer you in the right direction.

In most traditions of Western paganism, the north corresponds to the element of earth. It is usually represented on the altar by a lump of clay, stones, a bowl of earth, a piece of wood, or a pot of salt. Earth is a feminine element and relates to matters such as fertility, growth, and prosperity.

The west is the realm of the element water, and is symbolized by a chalice, cup, pitcher, or cauldron. This tool is representative of the womb of the Mother Goddess and is the other feminine element. Water relates to matters such as psychicism, childbirth, and spiritual cleansing.

The element of the east is associated with either fire or air, depending on which tradition you follow. Some equate the east with fire because it is the direction of the rising sun, and others with air, because it represents the newness and freshness of each day. For either element it can be represented

Element	Color	Season	Direction	Tool	Character
Earth	Green Brown	Autumn Winter	North	Salt, Stones, Clay, Soil	Cool, Moist, Stable, Fertile, Feminine
Air	Yellow Blue White	Spring Summer	East South	Knife, Wand, Staff, Pipe, Incense	Intelligent, Changeable, Masculine
Fire	Red Gold Orange	Summer Spring	South East	Candle, Knife, Sword, Wand, Staff	Hot, Dry, Transforming Masculine
Water	Blue Aqua	Winter Autumn	West	Cauldron, Cup, Chalice, Pitcher	Feminine, Mysterious

by the ritual knife of paganism known as the athame, which is a double-sided knife resembling a small dagger, or by a sword, a wand (one to three feet long), or a staff (four to six feet long). The element of air can also be represented by incense, a feather, or a smoking pipe. Air is a masculine element and concerns itself with the intellect, communication, and travel.

The south is the realm of either fire or air, depending again upon your tradition. Some associate it with fire because of the heat of the sun, and some with air because of the balmy southern winds which warm our seasons in the northern hemisphere. South can be represented for either element with the athame or sword, or the wand or staff; for fire it can be represented by a burning candle. Fire, the other masculine element, is associated with fiery matters such as war, transformation, and protection.

Any of these ritual tools may be either found, made, or purchased, based on your personal tastes and circumstances. The Resources Guide (Appendix IV) in the back of the book lists mail order businesses which handle pagan supplies if you cannot find what you want locally.

Before using any ritual tools, they should be cleansed and blessed. This is especially important when you do not know the history of the item you now own and have no idea what negative influences it may have come in contact with.

To cleanse and "reprogram" a tool, sit down with it and visualize it being filled with your own energies, driving out all previous ones. See it filling with your own essence as the old energies are harmlessly absorbed into the ground, while focusing on your intent to use it only for positive purposes. After you have done this, it is traditional to pass it through the smoke of a purifying incense such as sage, rosemary, or frankincense.

As you pass your tool through the smoke, you can say:

> *May this* (name tool)
> *Be an instrument for my spiritual growth,*
> *An extension of my personal energies,*
> *Used for only positive ends in worship, in ritual,*
> *And in magick.*
> *May the Goddess and God* (or name of deities)
> *Bless my work with fruition and abundance,*
> *And my life with their love and peace.*
> *In accordance with the free will of all...*
> *So Mote It Be!*

After the ritual cleansing, it is important to spend time handling your new tool. Get comfortable with it and, more importantly, let it get comfortable with you. This will be your working partner for a long time to come, and the two of you should be familiar with each other.

After you have all of these items (or as many as you want), they should be arranged on an altar in their corresponding directions. For example, your earth tool should be placed on the north of your altar, the water tool on the west, and so on.

An altar is a place where deity is honored, a resting place for the powers of the macrocosm to exist in the microcosm. It is a place to set out and arrange items of power, or items which honor the deities, and it is a fitting centerpiece for ritual. Altars also create an easy and accessible workplace. It is a place where magick spells can be laid out, and where the power of the elements can safely reside.

Anything can become an altar, even a special spot of ground. Use a flat stone, a table, a portable cloth, a box—whatever you need to place your working tools and spells upon inside your circle. Druids used stone altars called dolmens, and the Norse often used wood from their warrior ships as altars. Later, small tables or flat stones were used as individual or family altars, and altars were viewed as a more permanent fixture in a home or community. During the Burning Times (witch persecutions), family altars which appeared to be for the new religion were actually disguised altars for the old. At each Sabbat they were decorated with the bounty of the season just as they are today.

Some pagans leave a permanent altar within their homes year-round, and others bring one out only on ritual occasions. An altar can be large and elaborate and can hold other items like Tarot cards, statuettes, stone collections, cauldrons, ritual oils, seasonal decorations, offerings to the deities, incense burners—whatever you feel ought to be there. Or it can be very simple, holding only one or two working tools.

It is traditional to orient your altar to one of the cardinal directions; which one is up to you or your tradition. North is the most common orientation, but some witches who follow the Alexandrian Tradition prefer the east, and the Irish tradition faces west. All are correct.

Ritual dress is another idea that came into pagan prominence through Ceremonial Magick. Some traditions claim that their ancestors always went skyclad, or nude, during their rites; others claim simple robes or even everyday garb was the norm. But the idea of having a special type of clothing for

A typical pagan altar. On it are the Goddess and God candles, a bell, a candle snuffer, and four items (also called ritual tools) which represent each direction and its corresponding element.

these special times is also a very old one. Stepping into clothing used only for magickal and ritual purposes signals your deep mind that you are about to shift consciousness from the everyday world to the magickal world, also called the astral world or the spiritual world. Even in the patriarchal religions, the clergy dons robes as vestments of spiritual power. Repeated studies have shown that when Western people are asked to describe their deity, an overwhelming majority—ninety-five percent—view their Goddess or God as a robed figure.

Most covens, and even some solitaries, choose to wear robes for their rituals which are worn for no other purpose. Robes can be of any color the witch chooses and can be either elaborate and of costly fabric, or can be simply cut from plain cotton. Black is the traditional color, as this was the color that best blended in with the night back in the days when witches had to sneak away to their gatherings under the cover of darkness. Now many colors are used, and often they vary according to tradition, the personal

Figure 1

taste of a solitary or a coven, or according to what particular spell or rite is to be enacted. Some choose green for its association with Mother Earth, and others like red or gold for its association with the sun Gods. What you pick is a personal choice. Whatever you're comfortable with is right. You should not let yourself be swayed by the personal choices of others which may hold little or no meaning for you.

Robes are fairly easy to make if you are reasonably handy with a needle. The following is a step-by-step guide to making your own. You will need several yards of fabric, a needle and/or a sewing machine, pins, matching thread, scissors, chalk, and a partner to help you cut your pattern.

1. Measure yourself from head to toe and then purchase two times that amount of durable, washable material, such as corduroy or broadcloth. For instance, if you are 5 feet 4 inches tall, you would need 10 feet and 8 inches of material (approximately three and one quarter yards of fabric). A sales clerk in any fabric store can help you convert the measurement to yards.

2. When you get home, iron the fabric and cut it in half so you have equal amounts in each section, i.e., two sections that are 5 feet 4 inches each.

3. Take one of the sections and lay it flat on the floor, a table, or on any other hard surface that can support your weight. Make sure the wrong side of the fabric (the underside of the cloth) is facing down. Then lay the other piece on top of this with the wrong side facing up, making sure they are as even as they can be.

4. Pin the two pieces together so they won't slip and so they will be easier to cut out later.

5. Lie down in the center of the fabric and have your partner trace your out-

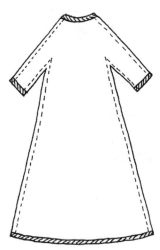

Figure 2

line with chalk. Make sure you trace somewhere between 5 and 7 inches away from the body to allow for the fabric to meet around you and to allow for seams. Larger people will need to allow more room and very petite people will need somewhat less. Do not trace the head or the hands. Your outline should look something like the outline in Figure 1.

6. When you are satisfied that you have drawn a pattern which will fit you, cut both pieces out.

7. Turn the pieces so the right sides (the outer part) of the material are facing each other and pin them together about two inches from the edge.

8. Sew the two pieces together, leaving a seam of about ½ to ¾ of an inch. Be sure not to sew over the neck hole, arm holes, or across the bottom. See Figure 2.

9. Hem the neck and arms with a needle and thread by turning the edges in about a quarter inch and stitching. The bottom can be turned up and hemmed either by hand or machine. Have your partner pin up the hem for you at the proper length.

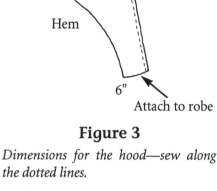

Figure 3

Dimensions for the hood—sew along the dotted lines.

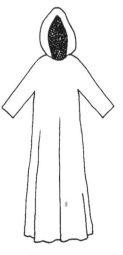

Figure 4

10. You may also want to make a hood. Lay out two pieces of fabric and pin them as you did in Step 3 above.

11. Cut two pieces that look like those in Figure 3.

12. With the right sides together, sew up the long side, curving over to the pointed edge.

13. Hem the part that will be around your face by turning it under by about ¼ inch.

14. Sew the end of the long part into the back neckline of your robe. The finished product should resemble Figure 4.

While most of the items one is told to gather to become a pagan are not completely necessary, one is of initial importance. This one requirement is a Book of Shadows, sometimes called a Book of Lights and Shadows. This is not really a magickal tool, but an indispensable working guide. The book, whose origins date from the late middle ages, is a bound collection of the way one individual witch or one coven works. It is a diary, recipe book, dream record, and a complete chart of progress and insights which outlines the witch's or group's spiritual career. In it are the texts of seasonal rituals, various spells and herbal recipes, a table of astrological times, outcomes of spells, weather reports—anything that may affect the outcome of any ritual or magickal working. Traditionally these books were written in a secret alphabet in case they fell into the hands of witch hunters, and were covered with black or dark wood covers. Many such books have been published, old and new, and are for sale in some of the most mainstream bookstores.

The name of the book is thought to have two derivations. One is that the book had to be hidden in the shadows, just like witches themselves, to avoid detection by witch hunters. Others say it represents that spells and rituals not enacted are without form and, therefore, are merely shadows.

All new witches are encouraged to keep such a book for themselves to chart their growth in the Old Religion and to record rituals and spells that have been particularly meaningful or successful. It should be thought of as a witch's personal diary, and as such, its privacy should be respected. The book doesn't have to be an expensive black-bound one. Mine is in a loose-leaf notebook. I prefer this method so I can change the format at will, or add and delete pages as needed.

All magick and ritual work should be done inside a circle. A circle is cast by directing energy that is commonly visualized as an intense blue-white light growing in size and intensity as more energy is poured into it. Often the circle is physically outlined with stones, herbs, or incense sticks, but it is the witch's own energy that creates it anew each time it is needed. Another way to mark a circle that has ancient origins is to light the boundaries with fire. Candles at the cardinal points are often used in Wicca (English and Welsh tradition) and in the Celtic traditions; the Norse usually use torches which are ritually carried to the circle site and erected. Torches used to light outdoor festivities are easy to obtain during the summer months at large retail outlets, or at camping centers and sporting goods shops.

The first use of the circle is protection. Many entities—human discarnates, elementals, faeries, and others of dubious intent—are wildly attracted by the vibrant energy of ritual and magick. A circle keeps them out. When the ritual is over and the energy is grounded, the uninvited entities will usually disperse rather quickly.

The other use of a circle is for containment. A witch wants to raise and store energy until it is ready to be sent out towards its goal. The "force-field"of the circle holds it in until it can be directed outward.

Some new witches will often not see the need for a circle of protection for simple spells and will even try to fumble through a ritual without one. This is a serious mistake! As you improve in your visualization and energy raising skills, your higher vibrations will attract an increasing number of entities which will come to feed upon your energy. This draining of your power will diminish the efficacy of your spells at best, and could cause you psychic harm at worst. Working with smaller circles at first will aid you to feel when you have accomplished your task. Increase their size as you become proficient at raising energy.

A circle is not to be broken once cast, and though some traditions allow that cutting an opening in the energy field with an athame will allow one to pass safely in and out, it is best not to go in and out of the circle unless absolutely necessary. How and when to leave and enter a cast circle is a matter for each individual or coven to decide for themselves. For reasons unknown, animals and small children can move freely in and out of a circle without ever disturbing the energy or risking harm to themselves and others. This may be attributed to the fact that children and animals have not learned to divide their thinking into the supposed real and unreal. They naturally see and feel psychic phenomena every day and are comfortable with it. Their minds see a magick circle as an everyday occurrence, part of the natural order of the universe, and they can move freely through it without disturbing its subtle energies.

It is important to cast a fresh circle each time you begin a ritual of any kind. To cast your own circle select a tool to help you, or choose instead to use the forefinger of your dominant hand (the one you write with). Stand quietly for a moment in what will be the center of your circle, making sure first that all the things you will need for your working are present. When you are ready, raise your arms skyward and feel yourself filling with life energy. Walk to the edge of your circle at any point you choose to begin (again, this is usually dictated by your tradition) and point your finger or tool at the ground. The object used may actually touch the ground if you wish, but it is not necessary.

Visualize energy coming from the end of your finger or magickal tool and creating a wall of intense blue-white light. For persons psychically sensitive enough actually to see the subtle body of a magick circle this is the color they report it to be. Continue around clockwise until you are back at your starting point. Move slowly, visualizing the circle building around you. Feel it! If you can do that, then the circle is there. Spend a few moments visualizing the energy surrounding you and know that you are protected. If you wish, you can further strengthen and purify the circle by going around it again with each of your tools, or with some special incense or liquid mixture (usually salt water or ritual oil) you have made for the occasion.

Take your time casting your circle until you are used to doing it and feel sure of yourself. The circle is not some cute bit of hocus-pocus, but a very real and essential magickal tool.

At the end of any ritual or spell you should ground your circle. This is done by reversing the process you used to create it. Moving counterclockwise, feel the circle's energy dissipate and sink into the ground.

The Role of Ritual

Rituals were used in the Old Religion to observe the Sabbats, the Esbats (Full Moons), to perform magickal spells, to mark human rites of passage, to heal, to divine the future, and to worship the deities. Modern pagans use ritual for these same purposes.

Ritual is always symbolic in content. Its function is to trigger responses in the deep mind which which will have a positive and lasting effect on both the physical being and the spirit being of a person. Ritual by its very nature has to involve a certain amount of repetition, but it need not be slavishly repeated to the point of mental numbness. There should always be something new and meaningful added, even if it is only the addition of one word, poem, gesture, song, or dance step.

Rituals can be group affairs, but they are also highly personal acts, reflecting the worshipper's feelings about their God/dess and their place in the universe. Even group rituals (good ones, that is) make allowances for everyone's self-expression so the working is deeply meaningful for everyone involved.

Sabbats in old Europe were times when entire communities came together to celebrate the season, and many of these old customs have not been entirely forgotten by even the most mainstream people. Though the names of the feasts may be different now, in many villages the Sabbats are still celebrated with much of their old symbolism well intact. For example, many communities in Britain and Ireland still have a May Pole dance at Bealtaine while being fully aware of its fertility symbolism. At the old Sabbats bonfires were lit, and the people feasted, danced the old dances, and celebrated their old deities. Life cycle events such as Paganing (dedicating a new life to the deities), Coming of Age (age thirteen for boys and at the first menstruation for girls), Handfasting (pagan marriage), and Passing Over (death) rituals were events commemorated at the Sabbat gathering.

The purpose of a Sabbat ritual today is specifically to honor the deities, ensure fertility, and to acknowledge and celebrate the continuous turning of the Wheel of the Year, though other events can be added.

Other rituals may be constructed around magick or a rite of passage, or just because the mood to worship and meditate strikes, but a Sabbat ritual is purely for worship and for achieving a deep connection with the meaning of the season. But worship need not be a wholly somber event. It is a celebration of life, death, and triumph over death by rebirth. Approach it joyously!

No ritual is ever wholly right or wrong, and none are sealed in blood. They are—or should be—flexible and can be changed as you change. There are, however, elements which are recommended in ritual construction, and these can be found listed in Appendix I in the back of this book. You can also glean ideas for ritual construction if you study the rituals in this book and other books on pagan practice.

Every coven or solitary is encouraged to write their own rituals to reflect their own needs and level of spiritual attainment. Names of personal deities should be added where appropriate, as should any other name referring to something in one's own tradition or personal worship habits, such as the names for the land of the dead or for the underworld. Repetitions of gestures, the number of candles, and number of herbs in the incense can reflect the sacred numbers of your traditions. In the Celtic tradition three and its multiples is the number of sacredness and completion, in the Norse traditions it is the number eight, the Fairy tradition uses five, the Native Americans four, and the Russians seven. No part of any ritual is ever cast in the proverbial stone, and none are better, or more correct, than any other. Some covens rewrite their Sabbat rituals every year, keeping what they love and in doing so creating their own traditions while keeping their rituals fresh. Others cling to the familiarity of the tried and true. The point is to write a ritual which you feel best represents the meaning of the Sabbat, and the ritual which you feel best gives love and honor to the deities.

Pre-ritual preparation for these festivals was as important as the rituals themselves. They were often approached by our pagan ancestors with fasts and purification rites. These should be observed as your tradition or inner guide directs you.

Any fasting should be done with careful consideration and possibly in consultation with a physician. Individuals whose jobs require great physical exertion, or those with diabetes, hypoglycemia, ulcers, and other physical ailments should never, under any circumstances, attempt to fast. Fasting has been used for religious preparation for more centuries than humans have recorded, and it has the effect of centering the body while expanding the consciousness. A modified fast which works just as well for today is one which eliminates all animal products and salt—especially salt, as it has a grounding effect on the psyche and tends to close down the psychic channels.

Purification techniques are as varied as pagan traditions. The most widely-known method of ritual purification is the Native American Sweat Lodge where people preparing to go on a Vision Quest (a spiritual seeking of visions) go to purge their bodies of impurities and negative influences just prior to their quests. A modified version of this can be done in your own bathroom either by taking a long, hot shower, or by soaking in a hot tub for a prolonged period. Usually in the Native American tradition, a purifying incense of sage, sometimes called a smudge stick, perfumes the air.

Other incenses which have been said to have a purifying effect are frankincense, cinnamon, basil, and black pepper. Dousing yourself and your ritual space in any one of these smokes will purify you and help open the psychic channels. As you stand in the smoke, visualize yourself purged of all negative energies—forced out of you and soaked safely into the ground.

Water is another time-honored way of personal purification, and is probably the best known among Western pagans. Water with a bit of salt added can be used to anoint and cleanse your chakras or energy centers. These are the palms of your hands, the top of your head, the forehead, throat, between the breasts, the solar plexus, just below the navel, the genital area, and the soles of the feet. As you anoint each area say something like:

> *Water and Earth, cleanse my hands that*
> *they might be open to the unseen world.*
> *Water and Earth, cleanse my head that*
> *it may be opened to the unseen world ....*

Purification baths have gained popularity among pagans over the last decade because of the ease and privacy they afford. In your own bathtub (or any small pool of water) add some purifying herbs or a few drops of purifying oils such as sandalwood, basil, pine, or mugwort. Avoid harsh oils and herbs such as cinnamon or thyme which can burn or damage skin and other delicate tissues. Tie loose herbs together in a cheesecloth to make them easier to clean up and so they won't clog your drains. As you bathe, visualize all your negative thoughts and energies being drained away from you into the water, and then either being swept downstream or down your drain. Feel your purified self poised on the edge of the world of form and spirit. Let the natural purifying energies of the herbs you have chosen cleanse you inside and out.

Pray to your deity(s) as you do your purification ritual and ask their help and strength as you pursue your goals.

Today's Sabbat Celebrations

Modern pagans often agonize over the Sabbats either because they work alone and would rather be part of a coven, or because they don't like the way their coven operates and would rather be solitaries. Others loathe the negative publicity some of the Sabbats, such as Samhain, garner, and others get much too serious about the whole thing and forget to have fun. Still others are so worried about doing the wrong thing (something which is virtually impossible), or so concerned with faithfully recreating the past that they do nothing at all or, if they do, they fail to feel the joy and beauty of the holiday.

The Sabbats were happy occasions for our ancestors, times when entire villages and communities left their work-day world behind and got together to honor the old deities and the old ways. They exchanged news, played games, made wedding plans, showed off new babies, and told jokes and stories, as well as worshipped and had a religious ritual. So worry less about what someone else tells you is ritually right and more about what you feel is best. This is especially true when it comes to ritual nudity, a choice some feel should be forced upon new pagans. If you are uncomfortable with ritual nudity even when all alone, then don't do it. Certainly there is little evidence to suggest this was ever a part of ancient pagan practice. And if you don't like ritual tools, but want instead to celebrate with one single lit candle, that too is perfectly acceptable and certainly much truer to the old ways than the formal tools of neo-paganism are. If you prefer to be alone, then be alone, and if you want to be part of a group celebration but know no other pagans, then throw a party to honor the day. No one but you needs to know just exactly what you are celebrating.

Due to the complexities of modern life, it is no more a given that pagans will be free to celebrate the Sabbats on their correct date than it is reasonable to assume that other people are always free for Christmas, Passover, etc. It is the acknowledgment of the season and its meaning which are important, the celebration of the turning of the Wheel of the Year of which we want to be a part. If you cannot celebrate Samhain on October 31, then celebrate it when you can, even if you can only devote a few moments to its observance. It is best to plan your observance date just prior to the Sabbat in order to take advantage of the waxing energies created by the anticipation.

The old ways are a guide, not a law, and they should be used as such. Religions, like people and ideas, evolve over time, and many of the old ways—such as live sacrifices—are concepts we do not want to revive.

About This Book

The eight Sabbats of Western paganism are ancient, with fragments of the observances, symbolism, and ritual practice coming down to us from those times, carefully preserved and passed on by those who would not cast aside their beliefs in the face of persecution or even death. So why, one might ask, do we need a fresh approach?

This book does not intend to abolish the old ways. On the contrary, it seeks to blend the old with the new and offer creative ways to observe the ancient holidays which are easily kept by modern pagans, some of whom may have few, if any, pagan contacts. It seeks to keep the old ways alive by keeping them fresh and spontaneous and by offering new approaches to old rituals which have added meaning for today's pagans. It recognizes the natural atavistic tendencies in all people, especially in pagan people, and shows how to connect with those primal feelings in meaningful and satisfying ways which put us in deeper touch with the cycles of the seasons and the turning of the Wheel of the Year.

In this text the Sabbats are referred to by their Irish names, but the most familiar of each Sabbat are given for easy reference. Each Sabbat is given its own chapter that includes information about its origins, history, and old traditions, and then gives fresh ideas for games, crafts, gatherings, foods, and ritual ideas for both solitaries and groups, and ideas for joining in celeration with non-pagan friends and family members who may or may not now of or share your religious views. These are only outlines, and everyone s encouraged to use them as blueprints for creating rituals and observances neaningful to them or their traditions. Take the craft and party ideas and xpand and mold them to fit your circumstances and lifestyle. But most of ll, feel the turning of the Wheel of the Year, and approach its celebrations oyously and with delightful anticipation.

Feel free to alter the printed rituals by adding deity names in place of the eneric "Goddess" and "God," and to flesh them out with any special read-ng, words, or gestures you love. And don't be disturbed if some of your rit-als look vaguely like modern, mainstream, religious practices. Remember nat the old ways have been so smoothly adopted by the patriarchal religions nd cultures that it is often startling when we analyze their origins. Sabbats vere appropriated by the early Church in order to supplant the old pagan olidays, and therefore there are many creative ways to celebrate these ncient pagan days, all of which are correct, meaningful, and positive.

May all your Sabbat celebrations be joyful!

⇚ 2 ⇛

Samhain

October 31

The Sabbat called Samhain (Sow-in, Sah-vin, or Sahm-hayn) has many meanings. Among these, it marks the end of the third and final harvest, it is a day to commune with and remember the dead, and it is a celebration of the eternal cycle of reincarnation.

There are two possible sources for the origin of the Samhain Sabbat's name. One is from the Aryan God of Death, Samana, and the other is from the Irish Gaelic word "samhraidhreadh," which literally means "the summer's end." Samhain marked the end of summer and the beginning of winter for the Celts, with the day after Samhain being the official date of the Celtic New Year. The reason the Celts chose this point in time as their new year rather than Yule, when the rest of Western pagans celebrate it, was because the sun is at its lowest point on the horizon as measured by the ancient standing stones of Britain and Ireland.

In the European traditions, Samhain is the night when the old God dies, and the Crone Goddess mourns him deeply for the next six weeks. The popular image of her as the old Halloween hag menacingly stirring her cauldron comes from the Celtic belief that all dead souls return to her cauldron of life, death, and rebirth to await reincarnation.

Unfortunately the Crone Goddess has been an object of fear and revulsion in modern societies, and this was definitely not the way our pagan ancestors viewed her. The crone was always revered as a woman of power whose vast stores of wisdom came with her great age and the life-long practice of her many skills. She was both the destroyer and the healer, and the grandmother and the eternal womb of rebirth. Her cauldron is deeply a part of the Samhain mythos representing the great cosmic womb in which all things are conceived, grow, and are born.

The cauldron became a popular tool among European witches because, unlike many pagan ritual tools, the cauldron was an everyday object needed for household chores such as cooking and cleaning, and could not be held up in the ecclesiastical courts as evidence of witchcraft. In some pagan traditions the cauldron replaces the cup or chalice as the ritual tool representing the water element.

Samhain is popularly known today as Halloween, a contraction of the words "Hallowed Evening," and it retains much of the original form and meaning it had long ago in Celtic lands, despite the efforts of the Church to turn it into an observance of feasting and prayer for their vast pantheon of saints. The Church began by calling it Michaelmas, the feast day of St. Michael, but the old Samhain holiday proved to be too potent a drawing card for one lone saint to combat. So it was renamed the Eve of All Saints, or All Hallows Eve, which precedes All Saint's Day, and is still one of the holiest days in Catholicism.

But even after all this effort, so much Samhain lore and practice remained within the popular culture that the Church was finally forced to diabolize Samhain into a night boiling with evil spirits. According to the church, these baneful creatures were dispelled only when morning broke on All Saint's Day to the ringing of the church bells. The 1940 animated Disney classic, *Fantasia,* presents a lavishly-drawn sequence set to the music of "A Night on Bald Mountain" which clearly illustrates the early Church's position.

When the Church diabolized paganism and its deities, they began a successful campaign of fear among Christians concerning Samhain. Even today in many parts of rural Britain and Ireland, leaving the safety of hearth and home is discouraged on this night. Unfortunately, the idea of Samhain being a night of unleashed evil took hold in the collective mind, and now all manner of mayhem and violence occurs around Samhain, though these terrors have absolutely nothing to do with the original meaning of the pagan holiday. Instead these horrors are the creation of modern humanity's all too vivid imagination. Pagan author and high priestess, Laurie Cabot, wrote of modern Halloween violence in her book, *The Power of the Witch,* "Is there any better proof [for those who doubt the efficacy of witchcraft] that mental projections become real?"

The cauldron was a popular tool among European witches.

For pagans who wish to help combat negative Halloween images, contact Laurie's organization, the Witches' League for Public Awareness. The address is in the Resources Appendix in the back of this book.

With all the inevitable negative press about paganism at this season of year, it is a not only a good time to throw your energy into an anti-defamation effort, but you might also consider joining the fight to preserve the integrity of whatever rights of free speech govern your country. This basic freedom, taken for granted in so much of the West, has come under serious attack in the last decade by those in power who wish to prevent us from disseminating information on any topic not in line with their narrow world view. Needless to say, paganism is high on their list of no-no's.

The pagan Samhain is not, and never was, associated with evil or negativity. It has always been a time to reaffirm our belief in the oneness of all spirits, and in our firm resolution that physical death is not the final act of existence. Though death is very much a part of Samhain's symbolism, this Sabbat also celebrates the triumph of life over death.

The idea that evil spirits walk the earth at Samhain is a misinterpretation of the pagan belief that the veil of consciousness which separates the land of the living from the land of the dead is at its thinnest on this night. This does not mean that hordes of evil entities cross this chasm. Some pagans believe this veil is made thin by the God's passing through it into the

A highly imaginative, but completely fictional, version of a Witch's Sabbat, complete with the conjuring of demons. From a seventeenth century woodcut by Hans Weiditz.

Land of the Dead, and that he will, for the sake of his people, attempt to hold back any spirits crossing into the physical plane whose intent it is to make trouble. In nearly all the Western pagan traditions, deceased ancestors and other friendly spirits are invited to join the Sabbat festivities, and be reunited with loved ones who are otherwise separated by time and dimensions of existence. All these spirits, especially those of the recently departed, are asked to help in divinations and ritual, and it was considered a propitious time to strengthen karmic ties with those whom you wished to be with again throughout another lifetime.

While it is true that Samhaim is no more evil than any other holiday, it is also a fact that evil does exist, and pagans have always been aware of this. Our ancestors sought to protect themselves on this night by carving faces in vegetables to place near windows or at the perimeters of their circle. These were the forerunners of our present day jack-o'-lanterns. These carved pumpkin faces are probably relics of the even earlier custom of placing candles in windows to guide the earth-walking spirits along their way. Today it is still a custom in Ireland to place candles in the windows on Samhain night and to leave plates of food for the visiting spirits. These are simple, but ancient, pagan ideas which can be easily incorporated into today's Samhain observances.

Window candles are commonly sold from September through January for use at Christmas, and they can be purchased rather inexpensively. Because they are electric you avoid the risk which fires present, while still maintaining the feeling and warmth of candlelight. Food can be left out for ancestors and other spirits by arranging it on a small tray or plate and placing it outside one of your lighted windows. It was this custom of leaving out food which evolved into our modern trick or treat.

The Samhain observance may deal with the uncomfortable subject of death, but it is not entirely a somber occasion. This is also a time for harmless pranks, lavish feasting, circle games, and merrymaking which can be teasingly blamed on nearby spirits. The best known pagan prankster is the Lord of Misrule, a personification of the spirit of fun and hedonism who invades the circle creating pleasant havoc and reminding us that even in the face of death, there is reason to rejoice. His job is also to keep the circle from becoming melancholy at the thought that summer is at an end and the harsh days of winter lie ahead. In other traditions this Lord of Misrule is called the Abbot of Unreason, the King of the Bean, the Jester, and the Master of Merry Disport. In the Norse tradition this is the time when the power of Loki, the trickster god, reached its peak. He is a god who delights in playing tricks on humans, animals, spirits, and other deities.

In Rome, Samhain was a day on which everything was turned upside down, when kings were slaves and slaves were kings. This was done in honor of the Apple Goddess, Pamona, whose sacred holiday this was. At night they lit fires in honor of the next day's festival, the Festival of Fortuna, the Goddess of Wealth and Luck. Feasting and drinking to her honor, as well as performing rituals so that she might favor the petitioners, were all a part of the observance. Pamona and Fortuna were thought to be able to go into the Land of the Dead together and bring recently departed relatives back from the spirit world to join with their living families for the celebrations.

Mexico, a land thoroughly immersed in patriarchal religion, nonetheless maintains many small ties to its pagan past. Two days after Samhain they celebrate El Dia de Muerte (The Day of the Dead). This is a time to honor one's ancestors with drinking and feasting, and to toast the personification of Death who was once believed to take this day as his one "day off" for the year. Businesses and schools close on El Dia de Muerte, and picnics are packed and taken to graveyards, where families sit near their relatives' markers and share their feast with them. Individuals dressed as Death dance among the revelers, and convivial mariachi music is always played nearby.

Chocolate is a delicacy traditionally served on El Dia de Muerte. The idea that candy should be a part of this celebration may have come from a long forgotten pagan observance of wishing the dead a sweet return to life in their next incarnation.

The most popular way to to serve chocolate in Mexico is as a frothy, hot drink laced with tequila.

Chocolate de Mexicanos
(Serves four)

4¼ cups milk
4 ounces semi-sweet baking chocolate, melted
5 tablespoons sugar
½ teaspoon cinnamon
½ teaspoon vanilla
⅛ teaspoon allspice
1 shot tequila

Place all ingredients in a large saucepan and bring to a boil. With a hand-held mixer or a traditional *molinillo* (a wooden beater resembling a honey dipper), beat the mixture until it stops boiling and becomes slightly frothy. Stir in tequila. Serve immediately in mugs garnished with cinnamon sticks.

Samhain bonfires, called balefires in paganism, were once lighted on every hilltop in Britain and Ireland as soon as the sun set on October 30. The word "balefire" comes from the word "boon," which means "extra." The fires serve the purpose of containing the energy of the dead god, lighting the dark night, warding off evil, ushering in the light of the New Year, purifying the ritual space or home, and being the focus of ritual. In many parts of the British Isles these balefires are still lighted on Samhain to honor the old ways. Unfortunately, in the United States the custom of community Halloween bonfires died out as fear and violence pushed celebrations indoors. For a glimpse at this custom and how it was practiced in America a century ago, get a copy of the 1944 MGM musical *Meet Me In St. Louis.*

An old Celtic custom states that one will have good luck all year if a dark-skinned visitor is the first caller of the new year. This was probably one of the earliest attempts at reverse psychology on record. It was hoped that any ill-meaning spirits coming toward a house would see a dark presence already upon it and not want to bother it further. The fair-skinned Celts also believed that dark-skinned individuals were gifted with special occult powers. As Samhain marked the beginning of the new year it was a certainty that on November 1, the darkest people in town were paraded around the countryside to fool the baneful spirits, and perhaps to divine their host family's future.

Pets played a role in even the earliest of human societies, and as winter forced people and their animals to seek shelter together indoors, pagans soon realized that they could form working partnerships with them. These working partners are called Familiars, and are deeply associated with witches both in fact and fallacy, with the most popular conception of them being the ubiquitous black cat.

Familiars are not just pets, but highly psychic animals who let it be known that they wish to help with magick and ritual. For example, I have owned many dogs, and none of them was ever interested when I began to do a spell or ritual. And since I was not overly interested in having a Familiar, this disregard did not bother me. But now my five-year-old sheltie is my working partner. He let me know this was what he wanted by showing an immense interest whenever I opened my magick cabinet and began removing items for specific rites. He would insist on being inside the circle when I worked, and had an uncanny sense of its boundaries. When I meditate he lies nearby—usually between my legs—and acts as my look-out. I can both see and feel his interest in what I do, and I can sense his added energy when he is near.

Occasionally a pagan will ask how he or she can find a Familiar. The best place to start is with your own beloved pet because you already have a relationship with it based on love and trust. Let it know you want it to work with you by having it near when you fashion magick, rather than banishing it to the backyard. Allow it to smell your herbs and oils, and to get a close-up look at your tools and altar. Its energies can never harm your working implements in any way. If your pet is interested in being your working partner, it will find a way to let you know.

It is unethical to get a new pet just to have a Familiar, especially since there is no guarantee that the new animal will want any part of your work.

The jack-o'-lantern is one of the most common symbols of Samhain.

If you really feel you want a Familiar, you can make a charm to attract one out of orange cloth stuffed with catnip, valerian, and rosemary that can be hung in various places in your house. Mentally send out a call for a Familiar and see if any animal answers you. Be open to whatever comes your way. You may not get a domestic animal, but a wild one who always manages to wander into your yard when you begin a ritual or spell.

The humble autumn gourd known as the pumpkin has become the most prevalent symbol of Samhain for both pagans and non-pagans, mostly due to the practice of carving them into jack-o'-lanterns. The jack-o'-lantern is at least two thousand years old. The first were made in Ireland, and were simple faces carved in turnips which could be easily carried if one needed to travel during the night. They were designed to frighten away evil spirits who were following deceased loved ones and blocking their way into the Land of the Dead, and also to protect the living. Today, jack-o'-lanterns are still usually carved with leering faces, and are seen as offering protection through the dark October nights.

Faces—rather than other available and more abstract designs—were not chosen at random to be carved onto the jack-o'-lanterns. The ancient Celts considered the head the most sacred part of the body, and at one time, even held a cult-like veneration for it. In battle the Celtic warriors would take the heads from their enemies and mount them on top of poles to guard their villages and encampments. For them, the head was not only seen as the center of learning, but also as the seat of the immortal soul, and therefore a repository for all knowledge. In death, as in life, it was believed that the attributes of a person of strength and agility (such as a warrior) were able to be used as a continual protective force.

The most famous head of protection was that of the Celtic God, Bran the Blessed, whose noble noggin was mounted high on the site where the infamous Tower of London now stands. As insurance against future invasions, he was turned to face the English Channel, from where the greatest threat to the islands always came.

But despite these ancient beliefs, all jack-o'-lanterns do not have to have faces with eyes, nose, and mouth. There are many creative uses for the pumpkin, and a variety of unique ways to carve them. Visit any craft store or seasonal display area of your supermarket in October and you will find an array of intricate carving tools and patterns for putting detailed pictures on your pumpkin. Many of these are very pagan, with drawings of Death, flying witches, and smiling ghosts the most popular patterns.

Even if you don't have the time or interest to devote to these detailed carvings, you can still make your jack-o'-lantern a little different. Try carving stars, hearts, interlaced knots, or pentagrams instead.

Luminaria can light up the way for trick-or-treaters in your neighborhood.

You can cut the top off smaller pumpkins and gourds and use them as candleholders in your home, circle, or for a party. Medium-sized pumpkins can be turned into lovely luminaria to light party guests' or trick-or-treaters' way to your door. Luminaria, a Latin word meaning "lights," are usually seen at Christmas and are made by placing candles or other lights in paper bags. Both of these luminaria have the same function—to light the way for night travelers and friendly spirits.

To make luminaria, instead of opening your pumpkins from the top, open them from the side by carving a wide circle in them. Scoop out the insides as you would for a regular jack-o'-lantern. Cut a few small holes in the top to let the heat escape and place a small votive candle in the center. Set these outside with the open sides shining over your walkways. (Be sure to blow them out before you go to bed!)

As part of the harvest feast, pumpkins are served in many forms: cakes, cookies, casseroles, puddings, and breads. But the best-loved and most familiar is the scrumptious pumpkin pie which adorns the harvest tables of both pagans and non-pagans from Mabon to Thanksgiving.

Granny McCoy's Pumpkin Pie
(Makes two nine-inch pies)

    3 cups cooked pumpkin (canned is fine)
1¼ cups evaporated milk
2½ cups granulated sugar
    ½ heaping teaspoon ground nutmeg
    ½ scant teaspoon salt
    ¼ rounded teaspoon allspice
    ½ rounded teaspoon cinnamon
    4 well-beaten eggs

Preheat oven to 375° F. Mix all ingredients thoroughly and pour into two deep, unbaked pie shells. Bake for about 50 minutes, or until a knife comes out of the center clean.

Not all of the strange faces seen on the streets at Samhain belong to the jack-o'-lantern. Odd collections of children and adults are seen wandering around the most mainstream places—even in the lobbies of large banks—sporting bizarre clothing and masked faces.

Masks are one of the oldest body adornments known to humankind. All body adornments once served ritual purposes and, in fact, masks are the ancestors of our present-day cosmetics. They have been used ritually in all cultures of the world to invoke animal or totem energies, to aid sympathetic magick, to raise power, and to imitate the deities. The first known mask dates from the Paleolithic period and is represented in a cave drawing in southern France.

The tradition of masking one's face at Samhain goes so far back in history that it is difficult to know just what the original significance may have been. Some pagan scholars believe it was originally a form of sympathetic magick. Whenever masking represents a particular goal, it is considered to be sympathetic magick. For example, if your goal was to have a successful hunt, you would mask yourself as your prey and seek to think like and become that animal. It is conceivable that the earliest Samhain masks were of game animals, so that the hunters would be able to catch the desired game and feed their clans and communities throughout the harsh winter ahead.

Making a Mask

Some modern scholars claim that Samhain masking was a ploy to scare away faeries and other mischievous spirits, but it has overtones of being a custom of a much later period, perhaps one which grew up around the Burning Times. During the Burning Times, masking and dark clothing hid the identities of witches going to their covens so that they might escape detection. The mask also had the added benefit of frightening away any inquisitor who might happen upon a lone figure in the night woods.

Many masks are available commercially in October, including some that might interest pagans. Or you can make your own. There are many methods to use and some are so simple a child could make them. Almost everyone has made a mask in elementary school by using a paper plate with eyeholes cut in it and a rubber band to hold it in place.

More elaborate masks can be made from papier-mâché. This requires cutting strips of newspaper which will eventually form the shape of your mask. To bond them, you must immerse them in a bowl which contains a thick paste made from water and flour. Begin with three cups of flour and one and a half cups of water. Mix these together, varying the proportions slightly, until you achieve a thick consistency.

This is the oldest known representation of Europe's Great Horned God. It dates from the Paleolithic period, and was discovered drawn on a cave wall in southern France.

    As a base for the papier-mâché mask, you might try a small cardboard box, a large balloon, or a broad-based wig stand. Any of these things will be large enough to allow you to place your head in them. Be sure to cut eye holes first and any holes you need for breathing, and work your paper strips around these openings. Once the paste dries, it will be virtually impossible to cut holes.

    You can shape the mask any way you like by molding and building the strips of paper. The elderly and dying Great Horned God, with his proud stag's antlers, is the god form honored at Samhain, and you can make a Horned God mask by taking two sections of rolled newspaper and placing wet papier-mâché strips around them. Then you can add more wet strips to attach the horns to the body of the mask. For other masks, you can build the forms you need in the same manner.

When you have finished with the body of the mask, you can add facial features, color, words, symbols, etc., with acrylic craft paint. You can also glue on sequins, beads, buttons, hair, or any other decoration you like.

The Witch's Besom

Another indisputable symbol of Samhain is the witch's besom. The besom is the witch's broomstick, and though it is not a tool of paganism in the modern sense, it was often utilized in the magickal practice of the Middle Ages. Like the cauldron, the besom was an everyday household object and could not be held up as a sign of witchcraft in the courts. This fact elevated their prominence as magickal tools, often taking the place of wands and staves.

Because of this association it is not surprising that they quickly became objects of magickal protection. Besoms were often placed near the hearth of the home to protect the opening, and many pagans still believe a besom at the fireplace will prevent evil from entering. If negativity is a problem, just take your besom and visualize yourself sweeping these feelings out the door. Using the besom to sweep away negativity from a circle site was common practice, one still observed by many pagans.

Placing the broom you jumped over at your Handfasting (pagan marriage) under your bed is not only protective, but is said to perk up waning sexual appetites. And for those who wish to be married, a strong act of sympathetic magick is to jump a broom each morning upon arising and each night before going to bed from the new to the full moon. Ashes collected for spellwork were thought to work best if first swept up by a magick besom, rather than an everyday cleaning broom which might negate the beneficial energies of the ashes.

The besom is a phallic symbol and was used by female witches in fertility rites, and it is from this that the idea of the Halloween witch riding around on a broomstick also may have materialized. The sweeping end was usually made of the European broom herb, a feminine herb. Thus the broom was complete as a representation of the male and female together.

At Halloween we are bombarded with images of the demonized Crone Goddess riding her broom across the moon. The idea that witches could fly on broomsticks may have been a misunderstanding of astral projection, a sending forth of one's consciousness to other places. An old untitled English nursery rhyme, which has no doubt been altered over the years, may have once shielded Samhain pagan lore about the Crone Goddess from the witch hunters:

There was an old woman tossed up in a basket,
Seventeen times as high as the moon,
Where she was going I couldn't but ask it,
For in her hand she carried a broom...

The besom-style brooms, structured differently in shape from the flat ones sold today, are round on the end, and have a smaller sweeping surface.

Making a Besom

If you would like a besom of your own, they are fairly easy to find in craft stores, country markets, or folk art fairs. You can also invest your energies into making one, a good idea if you wish to use it in place of a wand or other ritual tool.

To make a besom you will need a four-foot dowel one inch in diameter, a ball of twine, scissors, and straw or other long strands of pliable herbs.

Take the straw, or another herb you have chosen for the bristles, and allow them to soak overnight in warm, lightly salted water. The water softens the straws to make them pliable, and the salt soaks out former energies.

When you are ready to make your besom, remove the straws from the water and allow them to dry a bit, but not so much that they lose the suppleness you will need to turn them into your besom.

Find a work area where you can lay out the length of your dowel, and begin lining the straws alongside the dowel. Starting about three inches from the bottom, lay the straws, moving backward, along the length of the dowel. Begin binding these to the dowel with the twine. You will need to tie them very securely. You can add as many layers of straw as you wish, depending on how full you would like your besom to be.

When the straw is secured, bend the top straws down over the twine ties. When they are all gently pulled over, tie off the straws again a few inches below the original tie. Leave the besom overnight to allow the straw to dry.

The dowel part of the besom can be stained, painted, or decorated with pagan symbols, your craft name, or any other embellishments you choose. Examples of possible symbols appear in Appendix VII: Pagan Symbols. Dedicate your finished besom in your circle as you would any other ritual tool.

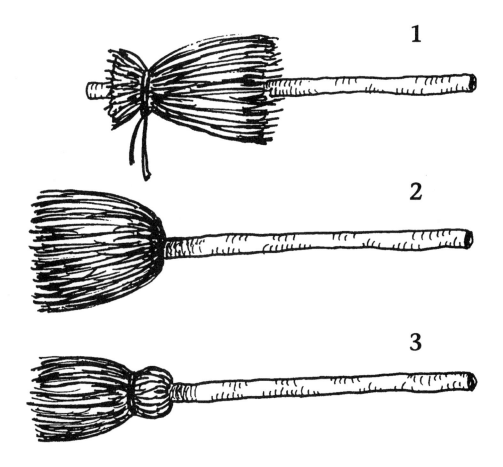

The three steps to making a besom: 1) Lay out the straws and tie them together. 2) Fold the straws over the tie.   3) Tie off the straws again just below the fold.

Samhain Feasts

With winter imminent, European pagans sought to stockpile food for the harsh times ahead. In every known culture in western Europe, fresh meat was always a part of the Sabbat feast. The predominantly herding cultures of Britain and eastern Europe slaughtered much of their livestock before Samhain rather than trying to feed the animals on the foliage through the long winters. In southern Germany, ritualized hunts were held in the weeks before Samhain to gather food. They gave homage to the Horned God as Master of the Hunt, and rode in wild frenzies as they chased their prey.

Pigs were a traditional part of the feast in many pagan cultures, particularly in the Middle East where they were sacred to the goddesses of that region. It was in an effort to wipe out goddess worship that the Jews (and later the Muslims) banned the consumption of pork.

Potatoes, harvested from August to October, were also a part of the feast in Ireland where they were made into a Samhain dish known as colcannon. Colcannon is a mashed potato, cabbage, and onion dish still served in Ireland on All Saint's Day. It was an old Irish tradition to hide in it a ring for a bride, a button for a bachelor, a thimble for a spinster, and a coin for wealth, or any other item which local custom decreed in keeping with the idea of the New Year as a time for divination. If you make colcannon with these little objects inside, please exercise caution against choking.

Colcannon
(Serves eight)

    4 cups mashed potatoes
 2½ cups cabbage, cooked and chopped fine
   ½ cup butter (avoid corn oil margarines as they will not add the needed body and flavor)
   ½ cup evaporated milk or cream
   ¾ cup onion, chopped very fine and sautéed
   ¼ teaspoon salt
   ⅛ teaspoon white pepper

Sauté onions (traditionalists sauté in lard or grease, but butter is acceptable). Boil the potatoes and mash them (do not use artificial potato flakes). In a large pan place all of the ingredients except the cabbage and cook over low heat while blending them together. Turn the heat to medium and add the chopped cabbage. The mixture will take on a pale green cast. Keep stirring occasionally until the mixture is warm enough to eat. Lastly drop in the thimble, button, ring, and coin. Stir well and serve.

⇥ ⇤

Since Samhain marks the end of the third and final harvest, Celtic custom decreed that all crops must be gathered by sundown on October 30. To dare to harvest anything after this night was risking the worst luck since the *phookas* (nasty-tempered hobgoblins) claimed for themselves whatever remained uncut in the fields.

Other cultures had similar taboos about unharvested grains. In Asia, cutting the last remaining stalk was thought to impair male virility, and in Native America, it was believed to kill the revered Corn Grandmother. In Scotland, cutting the remaining grain would bring down the wrath of the Cailleac Bhuer, the Cold Hag or Blue Hag of the Highlands, who brought death in winter. In Saxony, the last stalks could be cut completely, but they had to be harvested by a young woman dressed as a bride.

All manner of faeries, mostly baneful, were believed to roam the earth on the night of October 31. The pagan Scots were known for giving obligatory libations to their faery folk during their Samhain rituals. A libation of milk poured on a stone for them was called the Leac na Gruagaich (roughly translated as "Milk to the Hairy Ones") and was an obligatory task. To forget this ritual was to risk finding your prized sheepdog or your entire herd dead and rotted in the morning.

In Ireland, it was believed that sidhe mounds, or faery burghs, were dangerously opened to the world of humans on Samhain Eve, and if one was careless, he or she risked falling under a faery spell, never to be returned to the human realm.

Fortunately most faeries are friendly and would not mind your joining in their revelry, but, as with people, there are a few who have other agendas. If you seek out faeries on Samhain, carry with you a piece of iron which will give you power over almost any faery you meet.

The Norse invaders probably brought the idea of blood sacrifice into the Celtic Samhain observances, a custom not unfamiliar to the Celts because of similar Druidic practices. Blood sacrifice was a logical addition to this Sabbat since this is when the pagan God dies, his sacrifice enabling the Goddess to start the year anew by giving him rebirth at Yule. Blood sacrifice not only symbolized the God's demise, but sought to offer a substitute for him in death so that he could be more quickly reborn. Fortunately the Pagan Rede of "harm none" also applies to animals, and we have happily evolved out of our need to make a blood sacrifice of any kind to our deities. Today wine, ritually poured onto Mother Earth, usually suffices as a sacrifice in both the Norse and Celtic traditions.

With October comes the last of the apple harvest, and the idea of wassailing the apple trees was a Samhain ritual which was later moved to Yule, and then to Christmas through Roman and Nordic influence. The word "wassail" is an English contraction of the Anglo-Saxon words "wes hal," which mean "good health." To wassail people, or the apple trees, meant to drink to their health and well-being.

Wassailing was usually done by a group of "rowdies" who had imbibed too much Samhain ale. They gathered weapons, stones, and cider and went out to find the largest apple tree around. They fired their weapons or stones into its branches to frighten away evil faeries, and drank to the tree's health and sustenance. Today wassailing has come to mean the drinking to the health of anyone with a spiced punch prepared especially for the holiday.

Wassail is served warm, usually in a punch bowl. There are numerous recipes for this concoction. This one is from the Galway region of Ireland.

Wassail
(Makes one large punch bowl)

1½ cups water
½   cup heavy cream
6   baked apples, cut into small pieces
5   egg whites
1¼ cups granulated sugar
½   teaspoon nutmeg
2   teaspoons allspice
1   teaspoon cinnamon
½   teaspoon ginger
8   whole cloves
1   quart ale
1   cup cooking sherry
1   cup Irish whiskey

Bring the water and cream to a slow boil and remove from heat. Beat the egg whites well. Thoroughly mix in all the remaining ingredients except the alcohol. Allow this mixture to cool slightly—enough so that the heat from it will not crack your punch bowl. If you have a non-glass container for your wassail, you can skip the cooling process. Blend in the alcohol just before serving, and be sure to offer the traditional toast to the old apple tree before drinking.

⇥ ⇤

Apples found their way into other Samhain lore. In Ireland, it is traditional in the weeks before the Sabbat to take an apple, carve it in half, pour your illnesses or bad habits into it, put it back together, and bury it in the ground. This custom has been handed down as today's New Year's resolutions. In Teutonic traditions, apples were seen as signs of life, the very life force that animated the deities. Apples were buried at this time as a sacrifice to the deities to ensure the continuance of earthly life. In Rome, Samhain coincided with the Festival of Pamona, the Apple Goddess.

Bobbing for apples, a common Halloween party game, evolved from the idea of capturing the spirit of the dormant goddess who will grieve for her consort until Yule. To capture the fruit sacred to her was to ensure her continued presence and good will even though she was to be in mourning for the next six weeks.

In the Welsh tradition, apples represent the human soul as is evidenced by the name they use for the Land of the Dead, Avalon, which means "apple land." In Wales, apples were often ritually buried at Samhain to feed the dead souls in the underworld who were waiting rebirth in the coming year.

In the English tradition, Samhain altars featured apples which is the food offered to the visiting spirits. A spirit who ate an apple was thought to be reinfused with life energy and would soon reincarnate. In England, this Sabbat is sometimes referred to as both the Feast of Apples and the Feast of the Dead.

Divination Network Devices

Samhain has always been considered the best time for divinations and other psychic work which may have helped give rise to the anti-witch hysteria surrounding the Sabbat. Divination is the art of seeing into the future, or discovering information about a person or situation by means of connecting with the universal collective unconscious, a vast storehouse of psychic knowledge.

Several Samhain divinations concerned apples. If you pare an apple all in one piece on Samhain night and allow it to fall to the ground unaided, it will spell out the initials of your future mate. Hang an apple from a string with a coin pushed deep inside and try to bite out the coin without using your hands. Succeed, and your pockets will be full throughout the coming year. If you walk backward into a dark room while looking into a mirror and eating an apple at the same time, you will see your future mate's face in the mirror's reflection.

From the Druids, we get hazelnut divination. Hazelnuts were sacred objects to the Druids who would first toss them into divination patterns and then bury them to honor the old gods. Druids also ate the nuts to induce mystic wisdom while barring their use by the common folk.

To divine with hazelnuts, draw a small circle about one foot in diameter on the ground in front of you. Take thirteen nuts and shake them around in your cupped hands while concentrating on your question. Gently toss the nuts in front of you. Those that land directly in the circle have the most bearing on you. If more land in the circle than out of it, you have a right to be concerned about the question you asked. Study the nuts for patterns which you can interpret. For example, if the nuts are all pointing in one direction this could be an indication of a direction you need to take your problem. If they appear in the form of a familiar object, use that information to apply to your question. Occasionally they might fall to appear as letters of the alphabet which you can relate to your question. A letter "n" might mean "no" and a "y," "yes." Or they might be the initials of someone you know.

Popular divinatory devices used in modern paganism are tarot cards, palmistry, the runes, and the controversial Ouija™ board. Unlike other divinatory devices, the Ouija™ board does not use the collective unconscious as the source for answers, but relies instead on asking unknown spirits to take over the device. Opening such a portal without having any control over who or what comes has its risks, but you will have to decide for yourself if they are worth it or not. With the possible exception of the Ouija™ board, these divinatory methods all take some time to learn to use properly. Your local occult shop or mail-order catalog can direct you to these items and to books which explain in detail their use.

There are two other methods of divination which require little in the way of equipment, and can be learned by anyone with a little patience. These are scrying and using a pendulum.

Scrying is the art of gazing into an object while focusing your mind on one particular question or issue. The objects used usually have reflective surfaces, such as mirrors, water, or crystals. To scry, focus your mind on one issue or question and soften your focus and gaze—but do not stare—into the surface of the object. After some time, visions should form. These may come either as entire scenarios played out with all the detail of a high-tech movie, or they may be only symbols that you will have to interpret for yourself.

Many pagans like to set aside one special object for scrying, which they dedicate to their work like any other magickal tool. The objects usually chosen are a small round mirror, available at craft or drug stores; a small bowl with the bottom painted black which can be filled with water; or a crystal

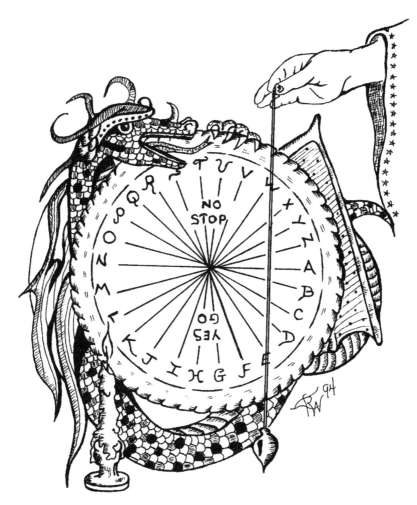

The face of a typical pendulum board, a divinatory tool associated with Samhain.

ball which can be costly, but many feel it is worth the expense. The choice is yours. Use what you feel best suits your needs.

The pendulum is another divinatory tool associated with Samhain which is easy to make and use. A pendulum is a heavy object on the end of a long chain whose movements provide answers. Almost anything can be made into a pendulum. In medieval Germany, women used their wedding rings tied with a strand of their own hair. Today, pendulums are for sale in most occult shops and by mail order. Usually they consist of a quartz crystal on a silver chain.

With a question formed firmly in your mind, hold the pendulum steadily over the center of the board. Allow the point to go where it chooses. Have pencil and paper ready to write down your answers. Record your findings in your Book of Shadows for later reference and to chart your progress and successes.

You can make a special answer board for your pendulum by cutting a round piece of white posterboard about the size of a dinner plate, and marking the alphabet around the perimeter. You can also add numbers, or use the letters to represent numbers such as A=1, B=2, C=3, etc. You can also have arrows pointing clockwise for YES, GO, and FUTURE, and counterclockwise for NO, STOP, and PAST. These are the traditional directions which have been used by pendulum users for centuries.

Because one's psychic powers and powers of concentration are greatly enhanced on Samhain, it is a good time to meditate. Western meditation is the art of altering your consciousness by concentrating solely on one thing or object to the exclusion of all else. In the Eastern traditions, meditation goes a step further and seeks to have you completely empty your mind.

Acquiring an altered state of consciousness has taken on an unnecessary aura of mystery in our modern world, yet we all do it everyday. Since the day you were born, you have changed your focus of consciousness every night when you go to sleep. If you were attached to an EEG (brain scanner) machine as you read this page, the cycles per second read-out would show that you are in an alpha state, a light hypnotic trance just below the level of normal wakefulness. When you concentrate your efforts and energy on a spell, you have also shifted your consciousness. When you prepare for a ritual, your deep mind, often conditioned by your preparations, will automatically slip into a slower cycle per second. At that relaxed level, your subconscious is more in tune with your conscious mind, and the two are able to act in harmony to help you focus on your magickal goal.

With practice in meditation and sustained concentration, your altered states can become longer and deeper, and at these deeper states (the theta and delta levels) you can do more advanced work, such as astral projection and regression. These are very natural states. The only difference is that you are seeking to gain conscious control of them. The key to these techniques is in learning to concentrate for increasing periods of time on one idea only.

Because the veil between the realms of the living and dead is at its thinnest on Samhain, it is also a prime time to attempt spirit contact. These contacts are not the creepy affairs portrayed in B-rated horror films, but beautiful and meaningful communications with departed loved ones.

Scrying and meditation are popular methods of contacting the dead, as are using a Ouija™ board or conducting a seance.

Seances have gotten a bad reputation in the late twentieth century due to two influences. One is the entertainment industry, which has repeatedly profaned them, and the other was the religious movement known as Spiritism or Spiritualism which flourished in England and America from World War I to the Great Depression. This movement began back in 1848 when a young American girl named Margaret Fox was exploited as a medium by her fame-seeking father. Margaret admitted in later life to the parlor tricks her father used in her seances. In the late nineteenth century, when hypnosis was in its infancy as a medical tool, it too was exploited as a means for spirit contact with all sorts of sensational claims made on its behalf.

In the early twentieth century, fueled by the many deaths of the war, families on both sides of the Atlantic sought to say their final farewells to their loved ones through mediums who were reported to have successfully contacted the dead. While some of these mediums may have been legitimate, the craze brought out the scoundrels and con artists who set up elaborate hoaxes in order to bilk grieving families out of their life savings.

Eventually the United States Congress was asked to step in to investigate and, if necessary, regulate the fortunetelling industry under which Spiritualism fell at that time. The issue was one of the most volatile of the 1920s with serious Constitutional issues at stake, such as the rights of free enterprise, free speech, and freedom of religion.

Fortunately the hysteria died out with the coming of the Great Depression and, as with any movement, only the truly interested and serious hung on. Today Spiritualist churches are still active, with over 400 congregations in the United States alone. Those interested in their doctrines and ideas can contact the General Assembly of Spiritualists in Norfolk, Virginia, or the Chesterfield Camp near Anderson, Indiana, for more information. They will be glad to teach you the proper way to conduct a seance and to help you understand the walls of consciousness which separate our worlds.

If you wish to contact the spirit of a deceased relative on Samhain and are not sure how to proceed, it is suggested that you simply cast a circle, sit in it alone and begin to focus your mind on the one whom you wish to contact. If you like, you may have some object with you to help you project or focus your energy, such as a crystal, a wand, or an amulet of protection. Also have with you one solitary candle, a light to guide your loved one's way.

Align yourself so that you are facing the direction of the Land of the Dead according to your tradition. Usually this is either the west or the north. If you have no such preconceptions, you can face the direction from which you feel your relative will most easily come to you.

Close your eyes and allow your mind to slow down. Enter a meditative state while still concentrating on the face and form of your loved one. After some time has passed, visualize a beam of white-gold light streaming down in front of you just outside your circle. See this as the light reflected from the opening of the veil between your world and theirs. Shortly after this you should feel a distinct presence in the room with you. You may open your eyes if you like, or keep them closed. But don't be surprised if you cannot actually see your relative or hear them speak. It is rare that someone is psychically gifted enough to hear or see someone from another realm of existence on the physical plane when first learning this art.

When you feel your relative is present you may speak to him or her either out loud or in your mind. Tell him or her they are missed and loved. Then sit quietly for a moment and try to feel a response.

Spirit energy never remains long on the earthly plane, and soon you will feel the presence fading. Allow it to go unhindered. When you are sure it is gone, visualize the white-gold shaft of light disappearing, thereby shutting down a portal that could drag in other unwanted entities later. Close your circle and place the candle near a window to guide your relative, and other spirits, along their way.

Other pagans have made spirit contact as they are about to drift off to sleep during the dark nights from Samhain to Yule. If you are one of those who distinctly hears a familiar voice speak your name as you drift off to sleep, this could be a deceased loved one trying to contact you. Train yourself not to be startled awake by the voice, but instead mentally allow yourself to answer. After a few attempts you should be able to make some sort of contact. Though this sounds very simple, it is effective. My grandmother had this experience after the death of my grandfather. When she finally allowed herself to respond to his voice, she and he were able to say the farewells that they were denied on the earth plane. She always said it was a beautiful meeting, and she mourned him much less intensely afterward.

If you have a another method of spirit contact that you like, you can aid its efficacy by burning an incense of lavender and cinnamon. This is an old Middle Eastern formula for helping to manifest spirits. Also, mandrake tied to a personal belonging of a dead person will help him or her to contact you. On the other hand, if you fear ghosts and are not ready for a Samhain visitation, carry the herb larkspur which is said to repel ghosts.

Samhain is also the best night to conduct a past-life regression—a trip into the collective unconsciousness for a glimpse at a previous incarnation.

Some of the clearest regressions I have witnessed were done at this Sabbat. I still have transcripts of many of these and they are fascinating to reread. In one case a young man's voice perceptibly aged with him through a long nineteenth century life, a phenomenon that stunned everyone present.

Common methods for achieving past-life regression are meditation and guided meditation, along with focused and concentrated relaxation and herbal aids. You can take yourself back through time by getting into a meditative state and focusing your mind on seeing a past life. Or you can have someone else talk you through the process. If you are interested in practicing this and need a guide, check the Bibliography and the Appendix IV: Resources and Merchants Guide for the names of books and sources of audio and video tapes which will lead you through the process.

Oils or teas which are known to help open the psychic centers can help to facilitate past-life visions. One of the most popular is the essential oil of lilac placed on the temples, palms, third eye (just above and between the eyes), between the breasts, on the solar plexus, just below the navel, and on the soles of the feet. These roughly correspond to the chakra points, or centers of energy, used in Indian and Hindu rituals, and might have come to western Europe across the continent from India with the ancient Celts.

To make herbal teas, place a half-teaspoon of each herb in a tea cup of boiled water and let it steep for about five minutes. Use any of these herbs alone or blended to taste: valerian, catnip, mugwort, sage, lemongrass, lemon balm, comfrey, jasmine, goldenseal, white oak bark, or orris root. As with any new substance, check first for allergic reaction before using by scratching yourself with a small portion of it and waiting to see if a hive develops.

Astral projection is another ancient art which is associated with Samhain. It has been defined as the art of sending out one's consciousness at will to a location away from his or her physical body. Some people believe you have a subtle, or astral, body which actually leaves your physical being during this practice. But this is not logical. It is your deep mind which projects its consciousness into other places or realms, very much as it does when you are dreaming. In fact, "lucid dreaming" is one of the best synonyms available to describe astral projection. But don't be confused by the word "dream." Projections are real. Don't think that because they take place only in your mind that they are not. After all, it is within your mind where magick takes place.

Herbs can be crushed and stored for magickal and medicinal purposes.

Not everyone is as adept at consciously controlled astral projection as they would like to be. It takes much effort, more than most people are willing to give. But again, certain herbal potions can aid this process. Pagans once used dangerous herbal concoctions mixed in lard to induce projection states. These odious mixtures were called flying ointments and were a guarded secret for those who had discovered them. The Druids were said to be skilled in the art of "becoming invisible," which is another way of saying they could astrally project with ease. Their method was said to include a dead raven, a crossroads, and baneful herbs.

Today flying ointments are still made by pagans to facilitate this state, but without the baneful ingredients. One witch I know burns jasmine incense to promote astral travel and has had good success. If you wish to make an ointment, you can mix equal portions of mugwort, lavender, and sage in a base of unscented lotion. Or you can forgo the ointment and drink a tea of valerian, catnip, and mugwort instead.

There are many methods of astral projection, and everyone has to find the one that works best for him or her. Perhaps the easiest way to experiment is to meditate for an extended period while concentrating on moving your consciousness out from yourself. After a while your mind will become bored with the exercise and go elsewhere looking for more lively entertainment.

Before or after Samhain is a good time to crush and store the Midsummer herbs which have been drying in your home. Take a white cloth and untie the herbs from their hanging place, and place them on the cloth. This will protect their energies. (For instructions on how to gather and tie them, see the chapter on Midsummer.) With your mortar and pestle or other heavy tool, grind the dried herbs one at a time into fine pieces. Place them in separate storage containers, well-marked, and store them for later use in your magick cabinet or another dark place.

At a recent gathering at Circle Sanctuary, a pagan spirituality center in southeastern Wisconsin, a poll showed that nearly a third of those pagans responding to a questionnaire picked Samhain as their favorite holy time. Samhain/Halloween parties are part of our popular culture and there is no reason why pagans should leave themselves out of this fun. Some pagans express offense at such parties, but if the party does not buy into the negative stereotypes of the season, then there is no reason why anyone should feel this way. After all, our traditions have had the Lord of Misrule longer than the new religions have had their traditions of solemnity.

Hosting a Samhain Party

You can host Samhain parties whether you have pagan friends or not, and even if no one knows of your religious preferences. My best friend and I once hosted annual Samhain parties for our eclectic friends who were both pagans and non-pagans. Many present knew of our religious preferences, and many others did not. But the parties were always a rousing success, a combination of the best old and new traditions. Later that night, those of us who were pagan were able to steal off into the backyard circle for some silliness and ritual after everyone else had left.

If you choose to host a Samhain party, avoid featuring creepy seances, evil hags, and other negative decorations and images that only damage pagans rather than promote the truth about us. Games should also be carefully chosen for fun and a bit of fright, without falling into that trap.

Divinations are excellent pastimes for Samhain parties, and people enjoy these even if they indulge only for the fun of it rather than with any serious intent. Have someone skilled in tarot, runes, or palmistry give readings for your guests, but avoid the controversial Ouija™ board if possible.

Another idea that combines divination and game playing is an old trick called Chinese Numbers. Take eight or ten small sticks or dowels cut about eight inches long. Tell your guests that these are Chinese divination sticks, and that before you can successfully divine with these sticks anyone you are reading for must first learn how to read Chinese Numbers from zero to ten. Sit on the floor cross-legged, and arrange the sticks in front of you in any pattern you like. Tell your guests that the ancient rules state that you are not allowed to help them learn the secret of the numbers. In your lap, hold your hand unobtrusively, but in sight, and hold the number of fingers the numbers should represent. Allow everyone to take a guess, then arrange the sticks. The game is that the sticks mean nothing at all. Only your fingers indicate the arbitrary number. People will eventually catch on to the gag, but in the meantime they will be counting spokes, stacks, and everything else imaginable.

Try a twist on the tired old costume party by having a "Come As Your Ancestor Party." Ask all your guests to come dressed as an ancestor and, if it was one they knew, to adopt their demeanor. At one such party a friend came as a stuffy Victorian aunt she barely knew. She remained in character all night, feigning shock at every turn, and she was the best court jester ever to grace any party to which I've been. Ask everyone present to tell about their ancestor (all dubious family legends and apocryphal embellishments are most welcome), and hand out a prize for the best tale told.

Another fresh idea for a Samhain party is to have one with a Mexican theme. Tie in the Day of the Dead festival with the traditional meaning of Samhain, play mariachi or Tejano music, serve Mexican food and the chocolate drink recipe given in this chapter. An easy, serve-yourself, Mexican buffet can be made with seasoned meat (made with commercial packages or with a can of added salsa), grated cheese, lettuce, tomatoes, and hard and soft tortillas.

You can add a special twist on the trick-or-treat theme to your Mexican party by making or buying a piñata to fill with candy. Piñatas are hollow papier-mâché objects or animals filled with confections. These are usually featured at Mexican Christmas and birthday celebrations. To open them, each guest takes a turn. Blindfolded and stick in hand, each should bat at the piñata which will be hanging from a tree or ceiling. When the piñata bursts open, everyone grabs for as much of the booty as they can hold. Give a prize for the person who collects the most, and give the uneaten candy to a local charity for kids who might otherwise have no Halloween fun.

If you cannot find a piñata for sale in your area, you can make one with papier-mâché. Form the body of your object (usually a burro or star, but pagans can try jack-o'-lanterns) around a large, blow-up balloon. Be sure to leave a small opening to put in your candy. When you have formed

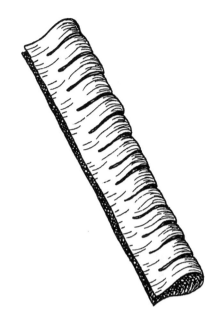

Folding a crepe paper strip in half the long way and making cuts in the folded side is the traditional way to decorate a piñata. Attach these to the piñata with glue.

the piñata the way you want it, allow the piece to dry overnight. To decorate it, cut crepe paper in long strips, fold them over, and cut into it to make a ruffle.

Glue the strips onto the piece to give it a full and colorful appearance. This is the traditional Mexican way to finish the piñata.

You might also consider sponsoring a trick-or-treat circle in your neighborhood for safety. To make this event even safer, you might encourage families to give non-edible treats such as pencils, neon shoestrings, notebooks with popular teen idols on them, or trading cards. Ask these families to post a sign in their yard specifying that they are giving away safe, nonedible treats. If you prefer to give candy, please make sure it is securely wrapped in its original packaging.

One idea to paganize your treats is to get round suckers and place a white tissue over them (leave the original wrap on underneath). Tie them under the "neck" and, with a pen, draw eyes on the "head." The result is a bunch of cute little ghosts.

You can use this same idea to make a decorative Ghost Tree for your yard. Use polystyrene balls and white cloth instead of suckers and tissues. Hang the ghosts by a string around their necks in a tree or bush. To make them less forbidding, you can glue on goofy eyes purchased at craft shops.

For any party, or just to greet trick-or-treaters, have mood music on in the background. Celtic music serves this purpose well. If you wish to opt for something a little spookier, use "Danse Macabre," "Night on Bald Mountain," or buy one of the haunted house sound effects records available in almost any store throughout October.

With the death of the God, the Wheel of the Year turns again, bringing us to Yule and his rebirth. In paganism, death has never been seen as an end, but as a transition. We, like our God, will be born anew as the Wheel of the Year turns on and on.

⇥ 3 ⇤

Yule:
The Winter Solstice
December 22

Yule is a time of mixed emotions for pagans. All around us we see evidence of the Christmas celebration, a religious holiday not a part of our traditions, but one which we know takes its form and meaning from ancient pagan practices. Virgin births, decorated trees, festive lights, feasting, wreaths, bells, and fragrant fires, were—and still are—at the heart of pagan Midwinter observances.

When the Wheel of the Year brings us to Yule, the God (who died at Samhain) is reborn of the Virgin Goddess. The God is represented by the sun which "returns" after this darkest night of the year to again bring warmth and fertility to the land. The profusion of lights on houses and trees at Christmas is a modern version of the pagan custom of lighting candles and fires as acts of sympathetic magick to lure back the waning sun. Today it is still a custom in Ireland and Norway to leave lights burning all through the house on Yule night to not only lure back the sun, but also to honor the Virgin Goddess who gives him birth.

Interestingly enough, the word "virgin" is one which was mistranslated and misrepresented by the early Church, enough to make even people today forget that the term had absolutely nothing to do with the hymen. The term "virgin" was first applied to priestesses in Mediterranean temples, particularly during Rome's pagan period. The term identified a woman who was a complete entity unto herself, who was not bound by secular law, had no husband, and was free to take all the lovers she chose. She needed nothing else and no one else for completeness. In other words she was said to be "intact"—a virgin. Paganism remembers the old meaning of the word, when the Goddess, a complete and whole being unto herself, gives birth to her son, who will be her lover at the spring Sabbats and also the father of his next Yule incarnation.

Yule has been the most widely celebrated of all the Sabbats because its customs and lore have so deeply invaded popular cultures and the mainstream religions, and virtually every culture in the northern hemisphere in some way once acknowledged the return of the sun at its weakest point. Some anthropologists, such as E. W. Budge, believe Yule was first celebrated as a religious festival 12,000 years ago, and some claim it dates many millennia earlier.

Yule's importance was obvious to early human civilizations. As the nights grew darker and longer, and the days colder and shorter, it was imperative that the sun be lured "back" to the earth. Though most cultures understood astronomy long before we give them credit, and knew the sun was where it had always been, they still felt moved to celebrate the old rites which were symbolic rather than factual to them. The festival was important because it kept them in tune with the cycle of the seasons, marked the New Year, allowed them a time to gather with friends and family, and to worship their deities in joy and thanksgiving.

Yule was a Sabbat of primary importance in the Norse and Roman traditions, and it is from these cultures that many of our modern Yule customs originate. For both of these civilizations, this was the time of the New Year, when the Goddess turned the Wheel of the Year to its beginning point once again. In fact, Yule is an Old Norse word which literally means "wheel," and the Sabbat was often referred to as Hweolor-tid, the "turning time."

In the Norse tradition, Yule is a twelve-night-long celebration, a concept which probably came from the pagan Near East where it eventually became incorporated into the Christian myths. The first Eve of Yule (the night before the Solstice) is called Mother Night, and is a night when Norse pagans sit up and await the rising and rebirth of their Sun Goddess, Freya. It is also a night for spirit contact and celebration with one's ancestors in much the same manner as the Celts observe Samhain. The Norse Goddess, Holde, guardian of the spirit world, opens her doors at Yule to all sincere seekers. The final night of observance, called "Twelfth Night," became for a while a sort of ninth Sabbat on the Norse pagan calendar.

The popular winter song "The Twelve Days of Christmas" no doubt has its roots in the blending of Norse and Celtic Yule customs. A very old and lengthy Scottish nursery rhyme is called "The Thirteen Yule Days." The poem tells us what a wealthy Scottish king once sent his lady love on each of the celebratory days. Within the ballad, the number three, a number sacred to the Celts, is prominently featured:

DAY 1: A PAPINGOE
DAY 2: THREE PARTRIDGES
DAY 3: THREE PLOVERS [A GAME BIRD]
DAY 4: A GREY GOOSE
DAY 5: THREE STARLINGS
DAY 6: THREE GOLDSPINKS
DAY 7: A BROWN BULL
DAY 8: THREE MERRY DUCKS A-LAYING
DAY 9: THREE SWANS A-MERRY SWIMMING
DAY 10: AN ARABIAN BABOON
DAY 11: THREE HINDS [HOUNDS] MERRY HUNTING
DAY 12: THREE MAIDS MERRY DANCING
DAY 13: THREE STALKS OF CORN

In ancient Eygpt, the Winter Solstice was not only a time to celebrate the rebirth of their Sun God, Ra, but to commemorate the creation of the universe as well. In Eygptian mythology it is taught that in the beginning there was nothing but Nun, the primordial black sea of chaos often likened to the womb of the Mother Goddess. From this ocean of unrest Ra was born, and he in turn gave birth to the other deities. After this great exertion he cried the dark tears given to him by Nun, and each tear became the many men and women of Egypt. In sun-parched north Africa, December marked the beginning of the short rainy season. If it rained on the eve of the solstice, it was considered to be a special blessing from Ra whose tears were once again bringing new life to Egypt on the night of his rebirth.

Wreaths and the Cycle of Life

The Wheel of the Year is often symbolized by the wreath. There is ample archaeological evidence to support the fact that wreaths have been used in this symbolic way for more than 4,000 years. Its circle has no beginning and no end, thus illustrating that the Wheel of the Year is also like this, with everything in its time coming back to its point of origin and traveling onward, over and over again. Wreaths came to be used at Christmas through the influence of Scandinavian pagans who hung them at Yule (their New Year's Eve) to commemorate a new beginning of the ever-moving cycle of life. The profusion of this decoration at this time of year is a direct result of the pagan practice of creating these wreaths out of natural materials to decorate homes and altars for the New Year's celebration.

In Sweden, it is still customary to have a young woman wear a lighted wreath to the ritual space. The Swedish folk song "Jeanette Isabella" comes from this custom which was adopted for Christmas, a custom now largely observed by pagans at Imbolg.

Wreaths can be made of materials easily found in nature, or can be bought ready-made in craft stores and other places that sell seasonal decorations. Or you can make your own unique Yule wreath out of wire, pine cones, and artificial fruit. Pine cones are frequently seen as decorations at Yule because they are representative of male fertility. Most fruits—especially apples—are symbols of the Goddess. Creating a wreath out of them makes a complete symbol of the union of deity—the God (the pine cones) fertilizing the Goddess (the fruit) on the Wheel of the Year (the wreath).

To make this wreath you will need to gather as many unbroken pine cones as you can find. You may even want to begin gathering them at Midsummer when they are plentiful in most of North America. Estimate how big a wreath you can construct with what you have gathered. Four dozen average-sized cones will make a wreath about eighteen inches in diameter. Then go to a craft store and purchase a sturdy wire wreath frame in the size you need, and also some wire twist ties or florist's wire, and the artificial fruit. You may also want to get velvet ribbons and bows to add an extra splash of color to your wreath.

Give yourself a large work space, such as a kitchen table, and set all your materials in front of you. Beginning with the largest of your pine cones, tie them onto the wire frame by using the twist ties or florist's wire. You can attach the wire to either the center of the pine cone or wrap it tightly around one individual prong.

Keep adding the largest cones until you have filled in most of the wreath, then go back and fill in any gaps and thin spots with the smaller cones.

The natural look of the wreath is attractive, but because pine cones are organic, they will not last forever unless some effort is made to preserve them. When you are satisfied with the way the pine cones are tied onto your wreath,

Wreaths symbolize the Wheel of the Year. This one is decorated for the Yule Sabbat.

you can either paint or spray on shellac or varnish to preserve your wreath and give it a smooth finish. When it has dried, you can add your artificial fruit, ribbons, or any other seasonal decorations.

Because the symbolism of the wheel was so important to this Sabbat, it became a day sacred to Goddesses of the spinning wheel. In this instance, the spinning wheel is a metaphor for the great Wheel of the Year over which the Goddesses have always been thought to control. The idea of spinning to create things anew has come into modern paganism in the context of casting spells. Often, when we are making magick, we say we are spinning a spell or spinning a charm.

In Germany, the Goddess demoted to witchy-woman, Frau Holde, was believed to ride on the wind in a sleigh on Yule Eve and give gifts of gold to her faithful followers. She especially awarded fine spinners of cloth. On this night, no rotary action of any kind was permitted. People had to walk or travel by sleigh; they could not spin, run their mills or mortars, or use any watches or clocks containing round mechanisms. All use of any wheel was reserved for Frau Holde.

Even today in parts of rural Germany, the symbol of the wheel is not forgotten. The rolling of a giant wreath, known now as the St. Catherine's Wheel, recalls another old pagan custom which involved sympathetic magick to lure the sun's return to the earth. A giant four-spoked wheel is created and an effigy of a human being is bound spread-eagled to the spokes. The wheel is then set on fire and rolled down a high hill. While the symbols of the fire, wreath, and the four-spoked wheel are still potent pagan symbols, the use of the human figure is more elusive and may have descended from a time when human sacrifices were made in plea to the sun. If you wish to copy this custom, you can make the giant wreath out of woven twigs or straw, or try to find an old wagon wheel at an antique store. For making a human effigy, you can use straw-stuffed clothing, like an old scarecrow, or merely purchase an inexpensive doll. If you want to set fire to the wheel, please make sure that you will not endanger any people or property when it goes rolling downhill.

In some traditions, Yule was once a more important holiday for honoring the Sun God than was Midsummer. Winter was a time of death and stagnation in the eyes of early humans. Mother Earth was barren and unproductive, shelter was drafty, disease was common, and food was scarce. In retrospect, it is easy to see why the sun came to be viewed as the Father God who fertilized Mother Earth and made her fruitful and full of life once again. This observance and its meaning were so deeply part of the human experience that the early Church was forced to move its Christmas celebration from August to December in order for it to be accepted. (By the Julian calendar used in ancient Rome, the solstice fell on December 25, now Christmas Day.) From there was born the holiday we know today as Christmas, a date which celebrates another God born of a virgin mother.

Yule Customs Preserved

One of the most persistently venerated of all the reborn sun gods was Mithras, whose cult spread far beyond his native Rome and into Greece, Persia, Egypt, and Asia Minor. His festival day, the Solstice, was dubbed Natalis Solis Invicti, or the "Birthday of the Invincible Sun." Some scholars go so far as to argue that, but for a few quirks of history and politics, the pagan cults who worshiped Mithras might have been as widespread and accepted today as Christianity. It is no accident that some of the myths surrounding him are similar to the Judeo-Christian ones which surround Jesus.

Mithras was born in a barn to a virgin mother, was the sun (son) personified, was the child of the God of all Gods, and his followers continually pray for his return which will herald new life and life eternal for all humankind.

For pagans, this usurping of Yule has one great advantage—it has preserved for us many ancient Yule customs which might otherwise have been lost. Look in any book on Christmas customs around the globe and you will find a plethora of pagan traditions.

The tradition of Yuletide gift giving comes from Roman pagans who called Yule by the name Saturnalia, a festival to honor the God Saturn. It was also a New Year's festival where gifts were given in honor of loved ones who had died during the previous year. Early Roman explorers and conquerors carried this tradition throughout Europe, where it remained part of the Yule celebration.

The Norse used bells to herald the dawn after the long, dark night. This custom is still observed in Lappland. The jingle bells we see today on sleighs, carriages, doors, etc., also came from the Norse who used them ritually to frighten away the powers of darkness that reach their peak at Yule.

In Sweden, painted wooden roosters, long a symbol of the Sun Gods of Europe, are used as centerpieces at the Christmas table. In their pagan past, the largest roosters were brought into the house on Yule Eve and given a place of honor throughout the next twelve days. The rooster ate with his host family, slept with them, and was treated like a little prince because he represented the Sun God whose blessing they hoped to invoke. He was also fattened up during this time, then killed and eaten on Twelfth Night.

The Romans bathed with gold coins on this Sabbat to absorb their energies so that they might have a prosperous New Year. Gold was sacred to their Sun God, Sol. This practice is at the root of the Jewish custom of giving gold coins as gifts on Hannukah, their Festival of Light, which also falls near Yule.

From another Roman sun deity (one shared with their Greek neighbors), Apollo, we get the custom of hanging bay around our homes at Yule. Bay was sacred to this God, and since it was he who drove the chariot in which the sun rode, it was imperative to honor him in order to persuade him to steer his course back to earth. In nearly all of the Romance languages, we can still see the vestiges of old Rome as they often refer to bay as "Laurel of Apollo." This custom of hanging bay was adopted by the Celts to bring the blessings of strength and health in the new year. Bayberry-scented candles are still popular today, their scent rarely failing to revive memories of the season.

The Native Americans of the Southwest called Yule "Soyalanwul," which means "to bring new life to the world." They aided the Sun's birth with a birthing ritual which consisted of having one person, masked as the Sun God, crawling between the legs of the tribe's women.

Kwanza, a modern holiday celebrated by many cultures of West Africa, is also connected with Yule. It is a festival of fire and light which once honored the Sun Gods of central Africa. It resembles the Jewish Hannukah in that the celebration involves the lighting of candles, an additional one for each night of the observance.

Other pagan cultures also used fire as a symbol for the return of the sun. Many of them tended perpetual flames throughout the year which were allowed to burn out on Yule Eve and then were rekindled the following morning to celebrate the triumph of the sun over darkness. Some modern covens still follow this custom by placing a large, single, white candle inside an iron cauldron which is carefully watched throughout the year so it is not allowed to die. During their Yule rituals, the candle is extinguished and then relit with joyous ceremony and thanksgiving.

The Yule customs of the Celts are the ones most well-known to Westerners today. The Celts drew their Yule practices both from the Norse invaders and from the Druids, the priestly class of their society. The Druids venerated evergreen trees as manifestations of deity and as symbols of the universe. To the Celts, these trees were sacred because they did not "die" from year to year as did deciduous trees, therefore they represented the eternal aspect of the Goddess who also never dies. Their lush greenery was symbolic of the hope for the sun's return to green the earth once again, and their massive height associated them with eternity. Their intricate root systems which reflected this height associated them with the old magickal adage, "As Above, So Below." This means that what is the macrocosm, or the world outside our own, is also in the microcosm, or our world, and can be made manifest by us as tools of the deities.

It was from these beliefs that the custom of decorating Yule trees (now popularly known as Christmas trees) evolved. The Celtic Druids decorated evergreen trees at Yule with all the images of the things they wished the waxing year to hold for them. Images of items to be used at future Sabbats, fruits for a successful harvest, love charms for happiness, nuts for fertility, and coins for wealth adorned the trees. Even on today's Christmas tree many of these images remain intact, though their original meaning is long forgotten. Other decorations were candles, the forerunner of today's electric tree lights.

The symbolic evergreen tree prevails even today in pagan and non-pagan Yule and Christmas celebrations.

In the Scandinavian traditions Yule trees and other greenery were brought inside, not only for the reasons previously mentioned, but also because they had wanted to provide a warm and festive winter's resting place for the tree elementals who inhabited their woodlands. This was also a good way to coax the native faery folk to participate in the Solstice rituals.

Some pagans argue that the Yule tree came to us not from the Druids or Scandinavia but from southern German pagans, since the idea of the Christmas tree did not catch on in Great Britain until the Victorian era, when the Queen's German Prince Consort, Albert, brought the custom from his native country. The Saxons, a Germanic pagan tribe for whom the principality of Saxony is named, also revered trees. Some believe they were the first to actually place lights, in the form of candles, in the tree itself.

Christian legends tell us that it was the German Protestant leader, Martin Luther, who, in the early sixteenth century, began this modern Christmas tree custom after walking in the woods one Christmas morning and seeing a lovely fir tree with the golden morning sun shining delicately on its ice-encrusted boughs. He thought it so beautiful that he cut one down, took it home, and placed candles on it so that his family could see just how beautiful and inspiring it was. It is more likely, however, that Martin Luther was out walking on Yule and that he came across a group of Saxon pagans holding their Solstice rites in the woods around a pine tree upon which they had placed candles.

Wherever it originated, the delightful concept of the Yule tree spread rapidly throughout Europe and was heartily adopted by many other pagan traditions. Thus, the majestic evergreen tree as a symbol of Yule prevails, and even today in modern Germany, it is customary for children to dance sunwise around the tree while singing and making wishes.

The influence of the Druids on modern paganism is also seen on Yule altars with their holly, pine, and mistletoe coverings, all plants sacred to various deities of the Yule seasons. Mistletoe, dubbed the "golden bough" by the Druids, still features prominently in Yule observances. Kissing under the herb was, and still is, the most common way it was used. But originally, it was an important part of handfasting. Because of mistletoe's significance, all legal matters were sealed beneath its boughs. Hence, a couple who kissed beneath it was announcing their intent to be married. They would kiss beneath the herb again after the official ceremony to further seal their vows.

Feasting was also a part of the Celtic festivities, but only after a day of fasting and prayer. In some Celtic covens it is still tradition to fast during Yule, with feasting and celebration to begin on the following day when the sun was on its way back to the earth.

The use of fragrant herbs to scent the season is a custom which comes from a blending of Celtic and Nordic traditions. The Yule hearth fire was the scene of many wish-making rituals, and aromatic herbs were thrown onto it to create an incense in which wishes could be carried to the world of spirits.

The Fight for Supremacy

From the Celtic tradition we get two sets of ancient pagan images who fight for supremacy at Yule. One duo is the Holly King and the Oak King, and the other battlers are the birds, Wren and Robin.

The Holly King and the Oak King are probably constructs of the Druids to whom these two trees were highly sacred. The Oak King (king of the waxing year) kills the Holly King (king of the waning year) at Yule. The Oak King then reigns supreme until Midsummer when the two battle again, this time with the Holly King as victor. Vestiges of the Holly King's image can be seen in our modern Santa Claus. He wears red, dons a sprig of holly in his hat, and drives a team of eight (total number of solar Sabbats) deer, an animal sacred to the Celtic Gods. Holly and mistletoe came into modern Christmas celebrations through commemoration of this battle. The holly was hung in honor of the Holly King and mistletoe in honor of the Oak King.

The Oak King and Holly King are mortal enemies at Yule and Midsummer, but they are two sides of a whole, and neither could exist without the other.

The other battle image is probably a much older one, one which was observed as soon as people became aware of which animals were prevalent through which seasons. At Yule the Robin, the bird symbolic of the waxing year, kills the Wren, the bird symbolic of the waning year. At one time it is a certainty that at least one wren per family or community was slain in an act of sympathetic magick on Midwinter Eve.

Irish witches Janet and Stewart Farrar, in *Eight Sabbats for Witches*, tell that in County Mayo, "Wren Boys" still go door to door carrying a representation of a dead wren on a bed of holly while soliciting coins for its burial. In terms of sympathetic magick, to "bury the wren" would mean to bury winter.

The old English nursery rhyme about Jenny Wren was created to hide the pagan meaning of this bird battle from the witch hunters. It clearly points out that the two birds are two halves of a whole, even though they must slay a part of themselves twice a year. The "merry time" mentioned is the Sabbat itself, and the cake and wine refers to the Ceremony of Cakes and Ale which is always observed at the Esbats (Full Moons):

> JENNY WREN FELL SICK
> UPON A MERRY TIME,
> ALONG CAME ROBIN REDBREAST,
> AND FED HER CAKES AND WINE.

There is another lesser-known Scottish nursery rhyme in which Robin laments never being able to dwell in the same place as Wren, for being dual aspects of one entity they can but fleetingly pass each other as the seasons change:

THE ROBIN CAME TO THE WREN'S NEST,
AND KEEKIT IN, AND KEEKIT IN,
"OH WOE IS ME ON YOUR OLD POW,
WOULD YOU BE IN, WOULD YOU BE IN?
FOR YOU SHALL NEVER LIE WITHOUT,
AND ME WITHIN, AND ME WITHIN,
AS LONG AS I HAVE AN OLD CLOUT,
TO ROW YOU IN, TO ROW YOU IN."

The Ceremony of Cakes and Ale is also observed at Yule in many traditions. The cake or bread, symbolic of Mother Earth, and the ale (often a juice or wine), a symbol of water and the moon, is blessed and ritually consumed. Some of the cake and ale is left for the birds, and some is poured onto the ground as an offering to the Goddess. Thus, earth and water, the two feminine elements of the four quarters, are used in this ritual.

The Ceremony of Cakes and Ale is always observed while inside the circle after the ritual is completed. There are various ways to bless the food before it is eaten, and even more ways of honoring the Goddess, as mother of the newborn God, with them. This Esbat observance may have been moved to Yule as a way of restoring some feminine balance to this Sabbat where the male principle is sometimes over-emphasized.

The following is a brief Cakes and Ale ritual adapted for Yule use. It is written for a group, but can easily be altered to reflect solitary practice:

(The Acting High Priest/ess takes a piece of the cake in the left hand and holds it upward.)

Acting High Priest/ess:

> *Blessed Lady Goddess, mother of our newborn King, we thank you for the bounty of your earthly body . . . our home. This bit of life-giving grain of your earth we give back to you now in humble thanksgiving. You are in and of this cake, young mother. Allow us to use it to fill ourselves with your boundless presence.*

(The Acting High Priest/ess passes the cake clockwise around the circle so that everyone may take a piece. As the covenors do this, they should honor the Goddess in their own way. Part of the cake should be sacrificed to her by being crumbled onto the ground or, if you are indoors, by placing a portion on a plate which will be taken outside later and emptied onto the earth. A portion may also be eaten if the covenor chooses to do so. Next, the Acting High Priest/ess takes the ale and holds it upward.)

Acting High Priest/ess:

> *Blessed Lady Goddess, great womb from whom all life*
> *flows, we thank you for your gift of our newborn King.*
> *The water of your earth, as necessary for life as blood of*
> *your womb, we give back to you now in humble thanks.*
> *You are in and of this ale, young mother. Allow us to use*
> *it to fill ourselves with your boundless presence.*

(The chalice is also passed clockwise around the circle. Each covenor should honor the Goddess as they see fit. Some will offer a toast either aloud or silently, others will simply pour a libation onto the ground. All offerings are correct and good. Covenors may also drink a portion if they choose, but this should never be required. Some persons cannot handle even small amounts of alcohol either because of medication they are taking, or for reasons related to allergies or alcoholism. When the chalice returns to the High Priest/ess, s/he holds it in his/her left hand and a piece of the cake in the other.)

Acting High Priest/ess:

> *Behold, the Triple Goddess is one!*

(S/he places a piece of the cake in the chalice onto the remaining ale, allowing it to soak for a moment or two. Then it is placed on the ground as a sacrifice to her or, if you are indoors, left in the chalice to be taken outdoors later.)

Covenors:

> *Behold, the Triple Goddess is one!*

Acting High Priest/ess:

> *Blessed be the eternal Lady!*

Covenors:

> *Blessed be the newborn God!*

(The rest of the ritual consists of eating the cake and ale while visiting with your friends. All uneaten cake is to be left out as an offering to the Wren and the Robin.)

The concept that what one consumes will be made manifest is another pagan belief with roots in history. Ancient warriors used to consume parts

An eclectic collection of cookie cutters for all seasons.

of their dead so that they could be reborn into the clan. Native Americans would eat the heart of a brave animal they killed to take on its characteristics and to keep it propagating. And in the Irish myth cycles we see the faery queen Etain consumed by Etar and reappearing as a mortal child.

Another "you are what you eat" idea is the custom of baking and exchanging Christmas cookies. This practice comes from the pagan Germanic practice of wanting to wish everyone a sweet and prosperous New Year. The following is a simple recipe for cookies which can be cut into various shapes and then decorated as you desire. This recipe has been used for baking holiday cookies in our family for three generations, and they make excellent cakes for the Ceremony of Cakes and Ale.

All-Purpose Holiday Cookies
(Makes about 2½ dozen cookies)

 2 cups all-purpose flour
 ¼ teaspoon ground nutmeg
 ⅛ teaspoon ground allspice
 1¼ teaspoons baking powder
 ¼ teaspoon salt
 1½ teaspoons vanilla
 1 egg, beaten
 ⅓ cup vegetable oil
 ¼ cup milk

Preheat oven to 400° F. Mix the dry ingredients and the oil together in a large mixing bowl. Beat remaining ingredients until light and fluffy. Add to the mixing bowl with the mixture and stir together. Allow the mixture to chill for at least two hours—overnight is better. Divide the mixture into four sections for easier handling. Roll the dough out on a generously floured cutting board until it is about ⅛th of an inch thick. Cut with cookie cutters and place the cut-outs onto an ungreased cookie sheet. Bake for 7 to 8 minutes, until cookies are stiff and a light golden color. Do not bake until brown or cookies will become hard and brittle.

⇥ ⇤

You can find cookie cutters designed for Yule and many holidays. Hallmark stores usually carry them, as do specialty shops and baking supply stores. Look for trees and bells for Yule, roosters and stars for Midsummer, eggs for Ostara, flowers for Bealtaine, and turkeys and apples for autumn festivals.

Another cookie popular at Yule is the Gingerbread Man. Ginger was an herb sacred to both Apollo and Sol, Sun Gods from the Greco-Roman pantheon. Even though these ginger cookies are thought of as German confections, they probably have their roots in ancient Rome.

Gingerbread Men (and Women!)
(Makes about 3 dozen medium-sized cookies)

1 cup brown sugar, packed
1 cup dark molasses
¾ cup shortening
¼ cup butter or margarine
4 cups flour
2 eggs, slightly beaten
2 teaspoons cinnamon
¾ teaspoon powdered cloves
⅛ teaspoon allspice
4 teaspoons ginger
1½ teaspoons baking soda

Preheat oven to 350° F. Mix all ingredients except the flour. Add the flour slowly, mixing each addition thoroughly. The dough should be slightly stiff. If the mixture seems too dry, add a teaspoon or two of water; if too wet, add more flour. Roll out the dough on a floured cutting board to about a ¼-inch thickness. Use cookie cutters shaped like little dough people to make the shapes. Place these on a lightly greased cookie sheet and bake for 10 minutes (time is only approximate). Transfer the cookies to wax paper to cool. Give your gingerbread people features by using colored frosting from a pastry tube.

The Yule log, another ancient symbol of the season, came to us from the Celts. The log, a phallic symbol, is usually cut from the God-related oak tree and carved into a small section which can be easily brought into a dwelling to be placed on a table or altar. Originally these logs, made of oak, were brought into homes with much dancing and ceremony before being lit in fireplaces. Later they became smaller altar relics sporting three holes, one each to represent the Triple Goddess. These holes were bored into the top, and the log was "impregnated" with three candles. Sometimes the candles were all virgin white, or God red. Most often they were the Goddess' triple-aspect colors of white, red, and black. The entire log was then decoratively covered with holly, mistletoe, and evergreens to represent the intertwining of the God and Goddess who are reunited on this Sabbat.

There are two reasons these smaller, stylized Yule logs have remained popular today. First of all, fewer and fewer homes sport fireplaces in these modern times. Second, by the late medieval period, the idea of a single Yule candle, usually in white or red, had taken the place of a log in many parts of England and the Celtic world. The latter reason may have been partly in response to fear of persecution, or simply because it made the Yule log ritual easier to observe.

Hopes for good fortune were invested in the Yule log image, and it was given a central place in the Celtic Yule rituals. This ancient doggerel of unknown origin reflects the importance of the Yule log on the Sabbat:

> MAY THE LOG BURN,
> MAY THE WHEEL TURN,
> MAY EVIL SPURN,
> MAY THE SUN RETURN.

In Slavic traditions the Yule log often has only one candle and is usually colored orange or gold, also god colors. To the Slavs, the Yule log is a symbol of health and fertility as well as a tool of sympathetic magick for the sun's return. They keep the ashes of burned logs tied up in a cloth for the entire year to serve as a charm of protection, fertility, strength, and health.

Many types of Yule logs are available commercially in December, or they can be commissioned from your local crafts people. If you are ambitious and have the right tools, you can make your own, one which can be used over again each year.

To make a Yule log, you will need a round log at least thirteen inches long and five inches thick. With a saw (preferably power), flatten the bottom of it slightly by trimming off an inch or two so that the log will sit without wobbling. Next, determine where the three candle holes should be drilled by marking them along the top of the log, evenly spaced from one another. The size of the hole will depend on the size of the candles you wish to use. Drill the holes down one-half to three-quarters of an inch to accommodate the base of the candles.

The log will need to be painted or sprayed with shellac or varnish to preserve it and keep it from drying out.

When the varnish has dried, you can put your candles in and decorate it with holly, evergreens, and mistletoe—all symbols of the season.

In December it is not difficult to find bakeries and confectionery shops selling edible Yule logs made of cake and decorative frosting. Many of the recipes for these are highly complex, especially where the decorations are concerned, but here is a simplified version you can try.

Easy Yule Log Cake

1 package commercial cake mix, preferably chocolate
2 cans (24 oz.) pre-made frosting in a dark brown color
   Several tubes of cake decoration frosting in green, red, and white
   Several toothpicks

Preheat oven to 300° F. Grease and line a jelly roll pan with waxed paper. Mix the cake according to package instructions and pour a thin layer—no more than ¼-inch thick—into the prepared jelly roll pan. Bake the cake until just underdone. If you can't tell by looking, then use the knife test. When the knife emerges not quite clean from the center of the cake, and when a light touch does not bounce back easily, it needs to come out. Check the cake at 7 minutes, and then every 2 minutes after that. Do NOT over-bake or the dough will be dry and hard to work with. Remove the cake from the oven and let it cool slightly. Then remove the cake from the pan by lifting out the wax paper. With the dark frosting, coat the top of the cake. Carefully lift one end of the cake and begin gently rolling it up as if you were rolling up a map. When you are done, anchor the cake with toothpicks and let it cook for about 5 more minutes. Cool the cake for 30 minutes, then frost it with the the dark brown icing. Next, take the tubes of colored cake decorating frosting and make holly and mistletoe over the top. You can also use artificial greenery until it is time to eat the cake. To finish, take a toothpick and etch lines into the frosting to resemble tree bark.

⇥ ⇤

A Yule log.

Balefires were not a part of the Yule customs in either Teutonic or Celtic traditions. The reasons for this may have been twofold. First of all, it was just too cold to hold Midwinter rites outdoors, and second, the small controlled fires of the Yule log or the hearth better represented the condition of the newborn sun. One notable exception to this was in northwest Africa, where balefires were used extensively at Midwinter.

With the coldest days of winter still ahead, Yule is a good time for pagans to plan their indoor projects. Needle arts are excellent winter pastimes, and many of these old arts have pagan meanings.

The Art of Cross-stitch

The products of cross-stitch, a needle craft which has gained great popularity over the past several years, originally served two basic functions. One was as a teacher, which can be seen in the alphabet and Bible verse samplers popular in the seventeenth and eighteenth centuries, and the other function was magickal.

It is no accident that little crosses were chosen to work these designs rather than straight stitches or some other geometric form. When the cross stitch was first used in needle craft designs beginning in the mid-sixteenth century, pagans were in hiding, plying their crafts in secret and veiling their lore in hidden ways. The Church in Rome was the supreme and unchallenged authority in Europe. So while the Christians claimed to be making their own cross while working these little designs, the fact remains that the cross-stitch cross is in the shape of the Sun Wheel, or equilateral cross, which represents the two solstices and two equinoxes, and is also a symbol of protection. Many pagan needleworkers did their sewing with a focused purpose in mind—usually protection—as they made their samplers.

Pagans who wish to learn this art can find the basic elements presented here along with two patterns. One is a Yule Wreath Decoration, and the other, a Sabbat Sampler. See Appendix VIII: Cross-Stitch Guide for the patterns for these designs. More intricate patterns can be obtained at craft shops where pattern books are available. These shops also sell books which teach cross-stitch and usually offer classes in this and other needle arts.

There are many cross-stitch patterns currently on the market that can be used and appreciated by pagans, including flowers, trees, faeries, wizards, angels, and castles, as well as a host of seasonal themes. Some of these patterns are very complex, having been designed by true artists, while many others are quite simple. If you do not live near an area with a craft shop that sells cross-stitch supplies, check Appendix IV: Resources and Merchants Guide for the addresses of periodicals that carry these items.

In counted cross-stitch, the pattern is transferred onto fabric by means of counting the squares in evenly-woven fabric rather than by following a preprinted design. Even-weave fabrics made for cross-stitch are readily available in sewing shops.

For the Wreath design, use 18 count fabric. This means that there are eighteen squares across the fabric for each inch of space. For the Sampler you can use either 14 or 18 count, depending on which you feel most comfortable with. You will also need a small tapestry needle, an embroidery hoop large enough to hold the finished design (3 inches across for the Wreath and 8 to 12 inches for the Sampler, depending on which cloth count you choose), and DMC embroidery floss in the numbered colors listed in Appendix VIII.

In order to transfer the pattern to the fabric you have to look at each square in the pattern as representing one square on the fabric. You may start at any point in the design you wish. Colors and/or symbols are used in each square to tell you what color to use. Compare these to the list of DMC colors to find the right one.

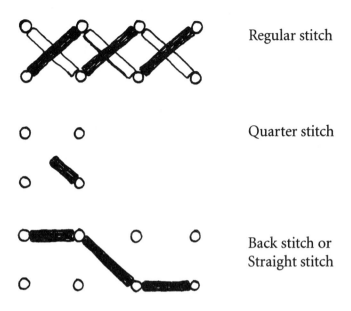

Regular stitch

Quarter stitch

Back stitch or
Straight stitch

Basic Cross Stitches

Cut off a piece of floss about two feet long. This is a good length for easy handling. All crosses are made with two strands of floss which you will need to separate from this. The crosses must flow in the same direction in order to have a polished look when finished. In other words, make all your crosses all flowing the same direction, either right over left, or left over right.

On the Sabbat Sampler, you will notice that there are some squares which contain only half a marking. These are called quarter stitches and are made by forming only a quarter of the cross—from a corner to the center only. They are used where a rounded edge is needed. Do not worry about topping it; that part will be formed by backstitching.

Backstitching, or straight stitching, is used to outline and define a design, to write words, or add embellishments and definition to a piece. Instructions will be given in each pattern as to how many strands of floss to use. Usually it is one around a design area, and two or more when making words or designs independent of sections of cross-stitch.

Be sure to recheck the color you need against the symbol every time you work a new pattern, as there are no standard symbols and they will vary with each piece you do.

The Wreath design should be worked inside a three-inch hoop, where it can remain as a decoration.

The Sabbat Sampler will need to be custom framed if you do it as is. You can adapt this design for personal preference by making changes such as using hearts in all four corners, pentagrams in all four corners, or by using no corner design. You may make the design all together in one long line, or in two rows of four, or on individual pieces of fabric so they can later be made into small hanging decorations. You can even make your own designs if the ones used here for any Sabbat don't please you. To make your own designs, get some graph paper and draw a 30 by 30 square, place the name of the Sabbat above the design area so that you know how much room it will take up, and begin doodling.

Hanging decorations can be made from the individual designs by first pinning them to a small piece of plain white or off-white cotton fabric. Place the design facing inward. Take two five-inch lengths of thin ribbon and set them in the top, to be used later as ties to hang your decoration. Machine stitch around the design area, making sure to both sew the ribbons firmly into the seam and to leave a small unsewn space to allow you to turn the design inside out. Turn it, and stuff the interior with fiberfill batting available at fabric stores. Stitch the opening shut with a needle and thread. Tie the ribbon together at the top to make a loop to hang it by. You can put them up seasonally, or all together on your Yule tree.

Storytelling and Pathworking

Another winter pastime indigenous to paganism is the ancient art of storytelling. In many cultures the travelling storyteller was a greatly honored guest in rural homes.

In later Irish history, a curious custom grew around Yule for telling stories of the heroic giant and God of Irish mythology, Finn MacCool. Finn was the giant who protected the island from invaders and who initially drove the invading Firbolgs back into the sea. It was he who created Lough Neagh in northern Ireland by scooping it out with his large hands. When he tossed it into the Irish Sea it became the Isle of Man, his gift to the Sea God, Manann. Even Scottish pagans sometimes refer to Yule as Finn's Eve and tell similar tales of the exploits of the Scottish version of Finn MacCool. Finn's tales can be found in most books on Irish mythology, several of which are listed in the Bibliography.

To add a different flavor to your Yule observance, you might want to try setting aside some time to honor either old Finn or the heroes and heroines of your particular tradition. You can also tell fairy tales with pagan lore hidden in them, and even make a game out of seeing how much of this occult lore you can uncover. Create a new tradition for yourself by beginning your stories in the old Scottish manner, with the words, "Once upon a time, when all lies were true ...."

Storytelling can be an exciting way to pass the winter nights, one much more intimate than television. Have children use their imaginations to come up with their own endings to your old stories or by creating their own.

Another type of storytelling often used by pagans is called guided meditation, a combination story and meditation trance which seeks to lead the journeyor on an inner-plane adventure that uses symbolic images and archetypes to affect a lasting change on the psyche.

Pathworking, as guided meditations are sometimes called, is a term which comes to us through Ceremonial Magick. In that tradition the designation is used to describe astrally traversing the paths on the Hebrew Tree of Life as taught in the Kaballah, the Jewish mystical teachings. Pagans have adopted the term and use it to refer to any guided meditation or any form of guided astral travel with the purpose of facilitating positive change in the life of the pathworker. This practice is as old as the art of storytelling itself, and many individuals have been transported by ancient myths into the astral realms and back again without ever knowing such an adventure occurred.

Conscious pathworking is an attempt to take one's self into the realm of the archetypal, also often thought of as synonymous with the astral world, a place outside of normal consciousness wherein all things are possible and all knowledge can be attained. From these experiences we hope to gain lasting and profound changes in the concrete, everyday waking world and in our spiritual lives. These exercises usually involve meetings with powerful beings or deities who give the pathworker verbal or symbolic messages.

Pathworking allows us to stretch our personal power to the limit. The paths gently massage our deep minds to stimulate creativity, astral projection, past-life recall, spell work, divination, and many other endeavors of importance not only to pagans, but to seekers on any spiritual path. Anyone seeking to enhance his or her mental and spiritual growth by tapping into the delights and wisdom of the unseen worlds which surround us will greatly benefit from these journeys.

Some of these guided meditations can be obtained from books on paganism, or they can be written for yourself by either rewriting fairy tales into a first or second person form (depending on whether just you or a group of you are doing this), or by having someone with some knowledge of pagan symbolism and archetypes write them from scratch. Archetypes are the deeply symbolic prototypes which work on the minds of all human beings regardless of their background. The way they act or interact with other symbols in a pathworking determines much of their meaning and effect. Look to the writings of psychologists such as Carl Jung for more detailed information on archetypes, or look into tarot decks which also use this type of symbolism.

To get you started, I have listed a few of the most common archetypal symbols. As you study the chart you will get the idea of what these are and how they have been used.

Symbol	Meaning
Apple	Hidden desire
Baby	Potential, Innocence
Bells	Wish fulfillment
Book, closed	Untapped potential
Book, open	Knowledge, Information
Bridge	Transition
Cats	Mystery, Magick
Cave	Womb, Motherhood
Cloak	Hiding
Cross	Protection, The Center
Crutch	Fear, Immobility
Dog	Loyalty, Warning
Fire	Energy, Transformation
Grain	Fertility, Abundance
Green	Fertility, Potential
Ice	Binding, Rigidity
Egg	Life
Elderly	Great Wisdom
Flower	Rebirth, Spring
Knives	Distrust
Lantern	Enlightenment, Hope

Moon	Mystery, The Goddess
Mountain	Obstacles
Owl	Wisdom, Night, Mystery, Illness
Pentacle	Creation
Pumpkin	Autumn, Transition
Pyramid	Stability, Ancient Wisdom
Rainbow	Bridge between Worlds, Promises kept
Red	Anger, Lust
Shield	Protection, Security, Guardedness
Sickle	Change, The Harvest
Silver	The Moon, The Goddess
Snake	Eternity, Rebirth
Snow	Winter, Death, Purity, Sleep
Sun	Newness, The God, Summer, Energy
Sword	Phallus, War, Protection
Tree	The Universe
Tunnel	The birth canal
Wand	Creativity, Magick, Spring
Water	Birth, Change, That which is hidden
Wheel	Cycles, Eternity, Reincarnation
White	Purity, Innocence, Higher Self, Astral
Well	The birth canal, Path to underworld
Wolf	Fearlessness, Loyalty, Family

Begin your working by gathering your group in a darkened and quiet room with one storyteller or guide. Everyone else (referred to as journeyors, pathworkers, or travelers) should get comfortable and close their eyes. Start by giving them some relaxation exercises or suggestions, and then begin the body of the working.

The following is the complete text of a short pathworking which takes us to the realm of the Goddess and her infant son/God. It is written in plural form for group working, but you can tape-record it for yourself with the language changed into the singular.

Text for Guided Meditation or Pathworking

It is early on Yule Eve as we find ourselves drawn to the winter windswept valley. The once verdant trees stand bare and black against the blue-gray sky. A light dusting of snow crunches pleasantly under our feet. It is cold, but our joy in seeing each other warms us considerably.

Behind us looms a vast mountain range, as rugged and forbidding as it is beautiful. Overhead we hear the cry of a winter bird, and we look up to see a fat wren flying swiftly towards the mountain tops. Suddenly a warm, balmy, spring-like wind sweeps down out of the mountains and briefly envelops us like a soft, familiar coat.

We turn to look up from where the welcome wind blew, and we see a spectacular silver crescent moon rising above the jagged peaks. It rests on its bottom as if floating on an astral sea, its peaks pointed straight into the darkening sky like the horns of a mighty bull. We gasp in awe as it rises slowly, pulsating with a light which seems to come deep from within itself.

The silver crescent seems to stop directly over the largest and darkest of the mountain peaks, and it throbs gently as if it is a sentient being answering an ageless question.

It is now night—the longest one of the year, and the stars twinkle brightly in the dark sky, a fitting altar for the exquisite moon.

We all notice now that the temperature has dropped considerably, and we start to shiver and look around futilely for a source of much-needed warmth. The only warmth seems to be radiating from the crescent moon which almost seems to be beckoning us to follow.

As one, we all begin moving toward the rugged mountains, as if being summoned by the gentle crescent up above. We trust in that beaming crescent, and we joyfully heed her call.

As we move into the mountains, the terrain becomes more difficult. The snow is deeper, and the night colder and blacker. It is hard, and even frustrating, to navigate through the craggy twists and turns. But whenever we grow discouraged, a thin shimmer of silver light from above bathes the path before us in a soothing glow which leads us onward.

We begin to ascend the side of the rugged mountain face, a steep and even treacherous climb. But still we push onward, chasing the moon as did our pagan ancestors many centuries ago. As we make our way up, someone begins singing an ancient pagan carol. We know not from where the words and music come, but as if all of one mind, we sing the song together.

[Pause briefly so the journeyors can hear and commune with the mystical music. Compare notes later to see how many of you heard a similar melody.]

When our song peaks, the moon seems to glow brighter as if conveying her approval of our offering of joy.

As we climb over one last small outcropping and pull ourselves up onto a large plateau, we are stunned to discover before us a spring-like oasis. New growth touches the few trees, and blades of new green grass create a soft carpet under our feet. Around the edge of the plateau, as if forming a sacred circle, are majestic evergreen trees decorated with the bounty of the Yule season. But even in the midst of all this wonder, the air around us is still bone-chilling cold, and very uncomfortable.

The moon, surprisingly close to us now, rises a bit higher above and, in doing so, illuminates a well-worn path ahead. Without a word, we all follow.

The path leads to the massive rock face of the uppermost part of the mountain. It looks to us like a dead end, and we all feel a great disappointment. But then, as if appearing by magick, the face of the rock silently opens, revealing a small cave whose opening is shaped like the moon above.

Cautiously we step inside.

The air here is perceptibly warmer, and we discard some of the gloves and hats we needed during our climb. Far off in the distance is the sound of running water, like a gentle mountain brook.

We begin moving toward the inviting sound of the water. Walking back through a long, thin cavern, we wonder at first if the opening will remain large enough for us to continue to pass through until we get to the source of the water sounds. We are forced to move slowly in the preternatural darkness which envelops us like a deep, warm ocean.

Just when we think the path can grow no narrower or become any darker, we see far ahead a glimmer of light.

We move more rapidly now through the narrow cavern towards the light, thankful that the pervasive darkness is finally broken.

One by one, we step out into a large round cave room. The walls are black like obsidian, and smooth, like the inside of an egg. No usual cave fixtures are present. The light we saw in the tunnel comes from a profusion of red candles that are collected together around a young woman who sits at the far end of the room on a simple wooden chair as regally as a queen would sit a throne. On the floor around her is an array of winter foliage—holly, evergreen, and mistletoe. Before her runs the creek we heard babbling in the distance. The water is a clear blue in color, and though the stream is narrow, it looks to be fathomlessly deep.

The young woman's robes are a very pale blue, almost white in color, and they appear luminescent, like the moon which led us to her, and her long flowing hair is pale blonde, like that of spun silver. Around her head is a band of white. In the center of her forehead is an ancient symbol of the moon—a circle with two crescents on each end pointing outward. They too are of silver, their phosphorescent glow radiating warmth and peace.

Near her side sits a spinning wheel unlike any we have ever seen before. It is made of a substance we cannot identify, and the wheel on it spins continuously in a clockwise motion of its own accord, untouched by any hands we can see.

The woman looks to be barely out of her teens, but her eyes are wide and knowing, as if the wisdom of the ages resides within her. She smiles warmly in greeting.

Instinctively we all move toward her, and sit at her feet in a semicircle, separated from her only by the deep blue creek.

"Welcome, Seekers," she says, and her voice is rich and full-bodied as fresh honey, and as melodious as the songs of the faeries.

Without any of us saying a word, she knows why we have each come, and she seeks to answer our questions. As we listen to her we each hear a message intended especially for us.

[Pause so that each journeyor can hear this message. They can all be compared and discussed later. Frequently in group working you will find that they all bear a remarkable similarity.]

When the woman finishes speaking we realize that we are in the presence of the Virgin Goddess. She smiles shyly as she realizes she has been recognized. Without another word she rises and stands before us. Her palms are upraised as if she is giving us her blessing, and we feel a potent warmth surge through us.

"Tonight is Yule, a night on which the eternal turning of my Wheel of the Year is acknowledged. From my past comes my future, and from my future the past. From age, I am young again. From mourning comes my joy. So it must always be. All things turning, returning, coming to and from and back again in a never-ending cycle."

We watch in awe as the Goddess glows with splendor, appearing now as a silver and gold light that spins and pops, electrifying the air around us. She rises like a phoenix into the center of the room, where she becomes a sphere of pure life energy.

From her core, a bright golden light, like the brightness of sunshine, pulsates as if it is her very heart. The energy fills the room and us to overflowing.

Just when we think we can absorb no more, the golden light energy from her core separates from her and takes its place next to her.

We stand in stunned silence as we look up at the two glowing orbs, one a luminescent silver, and the other a vibrant gold.

A voice, resonant and masterful, one which is neither male nor female, seems to come from the direction of the orbs.

"Blessed be, my children. Go in peace."

The vibrant voice echoes briefly off the smooth cave walls, and with that, the orbs fade from view, and we are left feeling both relieved and saddened at their parting.

We each entertain our own private thoughts about the miraculous events we just witnessed and we make our way silently back out of the cave, across the plateau, and back down the rugged mountain face. The descent somehow seems easier, and we notice that the air is warmer.

When we reach the bottom of the mountain we see that the moon is gone, and in its place is the bright sunlight of the new day. The winter sky is an azure blue, and the lean dusting of snow glistens under it like millions of tiny diamonds.

Overhead we hear the call of another bird. As we look up we can almost swear we see a plump red-breasted robin swooping down towards us from the center of the blazing sun.

Laughing and crying, we race to the center of the valley where we began our trip.

It seems as if the sun is shimmering and dancing, celebrating with us, and we are reluctant to leave this magickal place. But slowly we all take our leave of one another, and we come home.

Allow your journeyors to come up slowly, giving them a few moments of silence to reacclimate themselves to the physical world. It is a good idea to serve salty food or make some sharp noises since both of these things have a side benefit of helping to ground people in the here and now.

Foods of Yule

Foods, especially ones traditional to the Yule Sabbat, were of central importance at this holiday. This is seen in the way food is still important to Christmas, and is a carry-over from the old days when Yule was the start of a lengthy cold period when food could become scarce. Yule became a time to anticipate, one in which to celebrate abundance and forget desire.

Beans are traditionally eaten for luck on New Year's Day in Canada and the United States. This practice is from an old Norse custom which traveled to northern Scotland and Ireland before coming to the New World with Celtic immigrants, and is especially popular in the American South where they eat black-eyed peas (another type of bean) on New Year's Day. Beans are often used as fertility amulets, and eating them may have once been viewed as an act of sympathetic magick to reawaken the sleeping earth.

An easy way to make hearty and tasty baked beans is to place canned pork and beans in a crock pot with catsup, brown sugar, water, and Worcestershire sauce to taste, and let simmer all day or overnight.

Roasting chestnuts at Christmas was a pagan Germanic custom which traveled to England where it is still popular today. In England, chestnuts roasting on Yule hearth fires were used to divine information about the New Year. Depending on which region of England you lived in, you would know a fixed set of rules about the way to interpret how your chestnuts popped and danced. While these rules could vary greatly, in general it can be said that lots of movement and noise was fortuitous, while nuts that were still or quiet were not.

The Germans featured sour pickles at their feast, and pickles still figure prominently in their Christmas customs. One sour pickle was hidden somewhere in the home for the children to try to find. The child who found it received an extra gift or an extra portion of the feast. The pickle was symbolic of any sourness that was waiting to infect the New Year. To head off this trouble, it was discovered in its symbolic form, and found and eaten as an act of sympathetic magick to ward off malevolence.

The Vikings featured roast pork at their Yule feast with an obligatory portion being sacrificed to dead heroes. At their gathering they retold their battle stories and reveled in their triumphs. This was similar to the telling of Finn Tales in Ireland. The Norse also made toasts to Braggi, god of poetry and song, from whom we get the verb "to brag."

The Norse also used apples as Yule decorations and food in the same way the Celts used them at Samhain. The Norse thought apples to be the sacred fruits which held the life energy that kept the deities eternal.

As late as 500 B.C.E., the Celts entwined their hair with holly and made festival robes of brindle cow hides that were worn only to their Sabbat feast. Their feasts featured venison.

The Saxons kept sacred fires burning in a banquet hall several days before and after Yule. At the door to their banquet hall were two tables—one to take food, the other to leave alms for the poor. This was meant to symbolize the unity of all human lives, and to remind the Saxons that what one gave was returned three times over. Even today it is a Christmas custom to give food to the needy, and for this act of kindness we can thank the pagan Saxons.

The Saxon feast featured fowl and a round-bottomed tankard of ale that could not be set down. When it was filled it had to be emptied all at once. This drunken giddiness was thought to be the same excitement and euphoria the deities felt at the beginning of the New Year when they were again in their youthful glory.

The Germans made and ate festival cakes called *pfeffer kuchen* which evolved into today's German Christmas cakes. They were once baked with various trinkets hidden in them (see the colcannon recipe in Chapter Two for further clarification). The trinkets provided divinatory answers about the coming New Year.

In England, unwed girls used to make dumb cakes on Yule eve as a divination to discover the identity of their future mates. The cakes had to be baked after the rest of the household went to bed and the girls were alone and in complete silence. The cake was placed into the oven just before midnight. At midnight the future mate was supposed to come and turn the cake, or carve his initials in the top for the young woman to read.

In Sweden, red cabbage was eaten on Yule because its roundness and fiery color symbolized the sun, and a slaw made of this vegetable still graces Swedish Christmas tables.

Another traditional food of the Yule season is the potato pancake, known popularly as a latke. These originated in the Middle East, and are still made by Jews for Hannukah. Today latkes are also used in American, Canadian, Irish, and Scandinavian Christmas-Yule celebrations. Mixes for them (which save your hands from the terrors of the grater) can be purchased in the ethnic foods section of groceries after Thanksgiving, or any time of the year in kosher food stores or delis.

Jewish Potato Latkes

6 medium raw potatoes
2 eggs, beaten
½ teaspoon salt
⅛ scant teaspoon pepper
¼ cup dried onions
¼ teaspoon baking powder

Grate the potatoes into small strips resembling hash browns. Place the gratings in a large colander and let them sit for 5 minutes under cool running water to remove excess starch. In a large mixing bowl, mix together all the remaining ingredients. Meanwhile, in a skillet, heat a small portion of corn oil—about ¹⁄₁₆-inch deep—to about 400 degrees. Form the mixture into patties about the size of small hamburgers. Fry on each side until they are golden brown. Serve latkes the Jewish way, fresh and hot with cream cheese. (Hints: If you would like a short cut—one which spares your knuckles—buy unflavored, refrigerated hash browns from your grocery. Some food processors have grating attachments which can also be useful.)

One need not stretch the imagination to find creative Yule celebrations pagans can enjoy. People expect celebration at this time of year, and seasonal customs are all so similar, that even non-pagans have little trouble accepting your slight differences in interpretation and approach.

If you wish to host a gathering, you might start with a party featuring creative Yule decorations. Tree decoration parties can be a lot of fun, and are infinitely more pagan than they are mainstream. Have your tree erected but bare, and place the decorations in boxes around the room so that you won't crowd everyone into one space. For variety, have on hand decorations that not only reflect different pagan cultures, but also the winter festivals of many traditions. You can also have needles, thread, cranberries, and popcorn available to string together. These became popular during the Victorian period and are still used today.

Make sure your home is redolent with the full-bodied aromas of the season. Serve a hot cinnamon cider made with warmed cider, cinnamon sticks, and a pinch of allspice and nutmeg. Burn fragrant herbs in a fireplace or in a censer. Orange rinds and bay add a particularly nice holiday scent to the air. Have a profusion of red candles to symbolize the young Sun God, preferably ones scented with cinnamon.

Fresh baked breads and cakes also have an irresistible scent. Decorate one of these as a birthday cake to the Sun God, if you like. Color it gold or red to correspond to the season.

Gift exchanges are part of the holiday, and can be included in any Yule gathering. You can further paganize the gift-giving process by asking everyone to include a card with their gifts telling the recipient who the gifts are in memory of, and why they were important to you. This is a beautiful way to give gifts because you share with others the most precious gift you have— your memories of a life. From now on someone else will also carry on the memory of your loved one in his or her heart.

At Saturnalia, the Romans further honored their dead by placing sprigs of protective mistletoe on their graves. If you live in a climate where you can comfortably venture out on Yule, this is a lovely way to remember your passed-over relatives and friends at this festive time of year.

If you live where it snows in December, but doesn't get bitterly cold, hold part of your party outdoors. Sleigh rides, sledding, snowman building, and snowball fights are winter pleasures in which no one is ever too old to indulge. You can even paganize your snowman by making him into a representation of a deity of the season.

Music for Yule

Music is another important part of Yule, and Christmas carols are yet another idea taken from paganism. Many common Christmas carols contain pagan images that are not so subtle. "Carols" are from an Old French word meaning "joyous songs," and were also the name of round dances celebrating the rebirth of the Frankish pagan gods.

In ancient pagan Russia it was customary to sing *kolyadas*, or ancient carols, that featured pagan deities. Many of these still survive, though most have been christianized. In Native America, it was required by the Sun God that he be sung back to earth throughout the long, dark night.

The English Christmas Carol "Deck the Halls with Boughs of Holly" contains not one Christian religious image. In this carol, we sing of decorating with holly, singing Yuletide carols, dancing ("merry measure"), and the telling of pagan myths ("Yuletide treasure"). Another example of such a song is the Old French carol "I Saw Three Ships Come Sailing In." The third verse contains the line, "Three pretty girls were in them in …." which clearly is a reference to the return of the Triple Goddess after her croneage and period of mourning. Look into other Christmas songs for hints on how to adapt them to your Yule rituals. You will find you need make very few changes.

When Yule rolls around you should feel free to have a lighted tree in your home, hang a wreath on your door, ring the jingle bells, and give gifts in memory of loved ones. Remember that this is a Sabbat, a pagan festival, a time that marks the return of the Sun God both to his Goddess Bride and to his joyous people.

⫷ 4 ⫸

Imbolg
February 2

I mbolg (Em-bowl/g) was not originally a Sabbat as we think of one today, but a special day set aside to honor the Goddess who was slowly turning the Wheel of the Year back to spring. Winter was a harsh season for our pagan ancestors, one during which many died of disease and malnutrition. Therefore, it is not surprising that most of the customs surrounding this Sabbat are designed as acts of sympathetic magick to lure back the sun, and speed up the coming of the balmy warmth of spring.

In Ireland, where much of our Imbolg lore originates, this was a holy day for honoring the Great Mother Goddess, Brigid, in her guise as the waiting bride of the youthful Sun God who was now returning to her. Among her many sacred interests were fertility, creative inspiration, metalsmithing, and medicine, and she was also a protectress, healer, and a guardian of children. Her festival was so ingrained in the Irish culture that the Church was forced to rename the holiday "St. Bridget's Day" in honor of a saint who is, in reality, the Goddess. In the not-too-distant past it was customary in Irish villages for young women—and sometimes young men—to dress up as Brigid/St. Bridget in old, worn clothing, or to carry her image through town with them. The girls would go begging from door to door asking for alms for "poor Biddy," a nickname for Brigid. Giving to her was thought to bring good fortune in the harvest to come.

In France, Imbolg is a day to honor yet another saint. The Feast Day of St. Blaize, a thinly disguised version of Brigid, is a saint of winter protection and healing who was once widely worshipped and revered by the Celtic

Bretons. In keeping with the theme of this fire festival, Blaize's name is associated with the English word "blaze," as in a fire.

Two other names commonly used for this Sabbat are Imbolc and Oimelc, both meaning "ewe's milk." In Europe, this was the time when pregnant ewes began lactating, and the event was celebrated as another sign that winter was ending. In Cornwall they honored this event by making a ritual drink from cider, mashed apples, honey, and the milk of pregnant ewes.

The Romans dedicated this Sabbat to Venus, and the Greeks named it the Festival of Diana, both Goddesses of Love. That ubiquitous first flower of spring, the crocus, was sacred to both these deities, and the flowers were picked and used to lavishly adorn homes, altars, and people—especially young women who represented the virgin goddesses at the Sabbat rituals.

Though the Roman version of the Imbolg Sabbat was dedicated to Venus, the month of February was dedicated to the Goddess Februa and the God Februus for whom the month is named. Februa is the Goddess of Fresh Starts, and her month was often euphemistically referred to as "the cleansing time."

The Romans also had a board game they played each year at Imbolg which is mentioned briefly in the eighth-century Irish manuscript, *The Book of Lismore*. The board featured a crone and a dragon at one end, and a maiden and a lamb at the other. The object was to have the lamb conquer the dragon, making the Crone Goddess into the Virgin Goddess once again, and thereby turning the Wheel of the Year to spring.

In the Nordic tradition, Imbolg was known as Disting-tid, and was a day to ritually prepare the earth for future planting by strewing it with salt, ashes, and sacred herbs. This was done even if the land was still covered in snow and ice.

Candle Customs

Imbolg is also known as Candlemas, a name which was derived from the practice of ritually lighting fires to lure back the slowly waxing sun. In Anglo-Celtic cultures, one of the most popular of these candle lighting customs was to have a young woman, representing the Virgin Goddess, enter the ritual area carrying a circle of lit candles. This was, in essence, a lighted Sun Wheel, a symbol of the Wheel of the Year being warmed and lighted again by the returning sun. Later they adopted the custom of wearing the candles as a chaplet on the head. This idea came from one of the Norse invader's Yule customs, and many modern covens and solitaries still practice this ritual at Imbolg.

The Swedish folk song "Jeanette Isabella" commemorates the carrying in of the Candle Wheel upon the head of a young woman dressed in virgin white (the music for this tune appears in the Ritual section of this book). In modern Sweden, this custom remains intact, though the crown is usually made up of woven wortleberry twigs or, less commonly, of evergreen boughs, and is used with the celebration of St. Lucia's Day, which falls near Yule. Lucia's original incarnation was that of Lucina, the Roman Goddess of Light, whose Latin root word "lux" literally means "light." Lucina's Sabbat became a tradition through a belief that any work done on her day would be found undone the next morning, and all the household candles would be broken.

To Make a Candle Wheel

To make a Candle Wheel to carry or wear, you will need heavy cardboard, wooden candleholders, eight white candles no more than four inches long and sized to fit in your holders, a super-strength glue, a package of aluminum foil, scissors, a pencil, a ruler, and artificial green vines.

First decide how large you want your circle to be. Remember that it will need to be big enough to comfortably hold eight candles. A good size is an outer circle eleven inches wide and an inner-circle nine inches wide. This will be more than large enough for table-top use, and will also fit most heads if it will be worn.

Use a ruler to evenly space the candles, and then mark their places with a pencil. With super-strength glue, affix the candleholders to the cardboard. When you are satisfied that they are evenly spaced, place something heavy, such as a book, on top of them to help them stay tightly together. Let the wheel dry overnight.

The next day, wrap and mold the aluminum foil around the cardboard. This is done both to slightly round its form, and to further lock the candleholders in place. The foil will also help make the cardboard sturdy enough to hold the weight of the candles.

Next, take your greenery (you can use the real thing if it is available in your area, but artificial works well, destroys no living thing, and can be used year after year), and drape it around the foil to finish decorating the wreath. You can fasten it in place with either glue or florist's wire, available at craft stores.

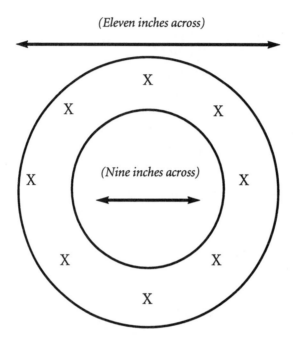

(Eleven inches across)

(Nine inches across)

Candle Wheel Form

The next step is to place the candles in the holders and light them. *Note: If you choose to wear rather than carry your candle wheel into your circle, be careful that you do not burn yourself, set fire to your clothes or surroundings, or get hot wax in your hair or on your scalp.*

Another way to carry fire to a ritual site is to give participants torches or candles of their own to carry. See the Sabbat Group Ritual for Yule in Section II: Rituals to find out how to make simple candle wax drip catchers.

Candles are extremely important to this Sabbat as they are often used instead of balefires. This is probably because the gentler fire of a candle better represents the sun at this time of year, just as the roaring balefire of Midsummer better represents that season's sun. Many pagans make their own candles through the winter so they will be ready for this and other Sabbats. By making the candles yourself, you can ensure that they will be colored and scented for your specific ritual or magickal needs.

Many books are on the market about this art, and many craft stores offer candle-making supplies and classes. If you have never tried candle-making before, please use extreme caution. *Hot wax can be hazardous.*

A completed candle wheel.

To make your own candles you will need petroleum wax (do not use paraffin as it tends to melt unevenly), wire-core wicks (for even burning), a large double boiler, scented oils, scissors, wood dowels, clip clothespins (to hold wicks in place), a candy thermometer, and something to use as a mold. Milk cartons, ice trays, tin cans, or purchased commercial molds are all usable.

Treat the mold with an additive that will allow the hardened candle to be easily removed. Ask in craft shops for one of these products, or ask for mottling oil which also works. The stores will have other additives that will help candles harden and will also seal any cracks that may develop during solidifying.

Wrap the ends of your wick around sections of dowel and clip them into place with a clothespin. Set the dowel across the top of your mold with the wick hanging into the center, making sure it reaches to the bottom.

Next, begin melting the wax over a double boiler, *making sure it does NOT come into contact with a flame. Wax is extremely flammable!* Also, never heat the wax above 280 degrees. Use your candy thermometer periodically to check the temperature of the mixture. *If the wax does catch fire, do NOT throw water on it.* Like hot grease, it will splatter, spreading the fire and possibly burning you and anyone around you. Try instead to smother the flames with baking soda, a heavy towel, or a pot lid.

Stir the wax constantly and gently with a wooden spoon—one you do not wish to keep. Add crayons or food coloring as needed to obtain the desired color. You can also purchase wax coloring at craft shops and stores that specialize in candle-making supplies. These provide the richest colors.

Just before the candle is ready to be poured, add the scent. Do not add this sooner, as the constant heat will dissipate or alter it. The scent may be obtained from a perfume, an essential oil, or a blend of your own choosing. The more you add, the stronger the scent will be when the candle burns.

When the wax is ready, turn off the burners and carefully pour the melted wax into the mold, leaving at least one to two inches of wick at the top. This can be trimmed down later to a manageable size of about a quarter-inch. Allow the candle to cool several days before removing the mold.

The Grain Dolly

Guessing how long it will be until spring shows itself is as common a February pastime today as it was centuries ago, and it's one which absorbs much space in the annals of ancient folklore. In America, Groundhog Day, on February 2, is a weather divination ritual which tries to predict when the warmth of spring will break through. We are told that the groundhog, named Punxsutawney Phil, will pop his head out of his burrow on this day to have a peek at things for himself. If he sees his shadow, he will be frightened back into his hole where he will stay for another six weeks of winter. If he does not see his shadow, he will emerge from his underground home and spring will soon follow.

In Celtic lands it was considered a sign of an early spring if one heard a lark singing on Imbolg. Larks are sacred to the God, and this belief may have stemmed from a conviction that the God was coming early, in a hurry to find his Goddess bride.

Another pervasive symbol of the Imbolg season is the Grain Dolly, often called the Bride. The Dollies are sheaves of grain (straw, corn, wheat, or barley) woven into either human or symbolic form, and were probably once part of crop fertility magick. The Dolly, made at Imbolg with dried grains kept from the last harvest, are dressed throughout the year to symbolize the goddess of each Sabbat. She is shown pregnant at Midsummer and Lughnasadh, and as a crone at Mabon and Samhain. At Imbolg she is dressed as a bride. Her form is then laid in a Bride's Bed, usually a small corn crib, but today's pagans usually buy or make wooden doll beds. Here she awaits her husband/sun/son. Sometimes male fertility symbols such as nuts are tossed in the cradle with her. Traditionally the old Dolly is buried at Yule, but today she is most often stored between Sabbats in a place of honor in your home.

To make a Grain Dolly, all you need are stalks of wheat, corn, etc., that you have kept from your last harvest. In many places during autumn, dried corn shocks are sold as seasonal decorations and make excellent Dollies. You will also need string and scissors to tie off your creation, and glue to hold it in place while you're making it.

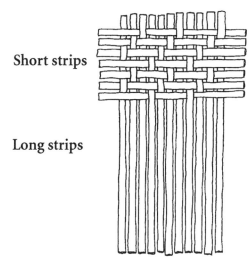

Short strips

Long strips

Weaving a mat-style Grain Dolly.

The Dolly does not have to take a human form, and many people are uncomfortable making a human-shaped Grain Dolly. You might want to consider weaving a mat to be rolled up, dressed, and honored.

The mat Dolly is easy. Just count out about a dozen grain leaves approximately eighteen inches long, and about two dozen that are half that size. Lay the longer ones side by side in a row. Taking a strip of the shorter ones, weave over the first sheaf and under the second, and so on until you have woven the strip in and out of the entire layout of grain. The next short length will be started by going under the first grain and then over the next one. Continue this way until the next leaf has been woven in. Push it up against the first one you wove in, and it should be exactly opposite in form—where the first one goes under, the second should go over, and vice-versa.

The mat-style Grain Dolly is rolled up and tied off with three strings to represent the Triple Goddess.

When you have woven all the grain sheaves in, loosely roll up the Dolly. With your string, tie the top and bottom of the mat loosely so that it will not unroll. You

This Grain Dolly is made by tying sheaves over a small ball.

might want to add a third string in the center for extra strength and to represent the Triple Goddess.

The mat-style Dolly can be dressed as easily as a human-shaped one, perhaps more so because it is sturdier. But if you wish to try a more realistic Dolly, wrap a few of the grain leaves around quilt batting or a polystyrene ball available at craft stores. Leave the loose ends free to represent the body.

If you wish to go a step further, you can take more grain sheaves and tie them around the center of the Dolly to look like arms.

To dress your grain Dolly as an Imbolg Bride, swaddle it in lengths of white, natural fabric, or purchase commercially-made doll clothes. If you are good with a needle, you can make a dress yourself.

In feminist traditions, Imbolg is a night for the rededication of one's spirituality. The members of these covens tend to the Bride's Bed throughout the night, symbolic of a royal court preparing a princess for her wedding. They believe this was once done by the women of Wales, that it was once a sacred act, a women's mystery which was deeply respected, and may have been the source of the old Welsh folk song, "All Through the Night:"

> SLEEP, MY CHILD, AND PEACE ATTEND THEE,
> ALL THROUGH THE NIGHT.
> GUARDIAN ANGELS GOD WILL SEND THEE,
> ALL THROUGH THE NIGHT.
> SOFT THE LONELY HOURS ARE CREEPING,
> HILL AND DALE IN SLUMBER SLEEPING.
> I, MY LONELY VIGIL KEEPING,
> ALL THROUGH THE NIGHT.

Sun Wheels

Sun Wheels, also known in some traditions as Brigid's Crosses, are also symbols of this Sabbat, and wheels made of vines are often woven at this time for the entire year's use. Sun Wheels are equilateral crosses encased in a circle that represents the Wheel of the Year. They are used especially at Midsummer and Lughnasadh when the sun is at its peak, and smaller ones can be made to hang on Yule trees.

To make your own Sun Wheel, purchase several yards—about six to eight—of unbroken, dried grapevine. Place the vine in a tub of warm water for several hours until the vine becomes pliable. Aim to make your Sun Wheel about six to eight inches in diameter. Cut two or three yards of vine into strips about ten to twelve inches long. Make two such lengths, and lay them crosswise to form a cross. You can weave them in and out of each other or set them one atop the other.

About six to eight inches from the center of the design, anchor one end of the rest of the unbroken vine. While trying to keep the vine going in a perfect circle, take the vine around to the next crossbar and intertwine one strand of the crosspiece in the vine to hold it. Move on to the next crosspiece and repeat.

Keep moving around the perimeter of the Sun Wheel, weaving the vine in and out so that it holds. You may find that you need to cut it off in places and start over to get a true woven effect. Weave a strand of each of the long crosspieces into the circle each time you pass it.

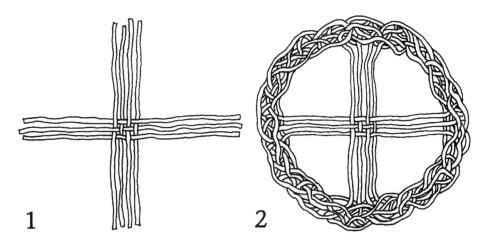

1   **2**

1) Weaving the crossbars for the Sun Wheel;
2) A finished vine-woven Sun Wheel

A short cut in creating a vine Sun Wheel would be to take a grapevine wreath already assembled and simply add the crossbars.

Crossroads also figure prominently in this Sabbat because of their association with the Sun Wheel. Imbolg is a night that spirits of the dead are said to walk among the living in both the Norse and Irish traditions, and for centuries, it has been said that these people have seen spirits seeking the safety of a crossroads. The Irish often went on the eve of this Sabbat to bury negativity at a crossroad so it couldn't escape, much in the same way a Latin cross on a coffin was designed to keep vampires contained. The Norse would move their ritual site to the center of a crossroad, and build enough roaring fires around it to warm the bitter winter night. The pattern of the fires around the crossroad resembled a Sun Wheel with a center point.

In England, Cornwall, and Ireland, Imbolg is a Sabbat when magickal wells are visited. In the Goddess' name, people throw coins into them in hopes of making wishes come true. The well is symbolic of the birth canal of the Goddess, from which all things are birthed. Many of these ancient magickal wells were usurped by Church authorities and either covered over or encased within church walls, but a few of them can still be found.

If you are in the rural British Isles, ask the locals about them. Most will be delighted to tell you all about the folklore.

You can mimic this custom with any well or body of deep water. Go to it when you can be alone, and throw in three coins while stating and concentrating on your wish for the coming year. Before you leave, ask the guardian spirits of the well to look after the energies you have left behind and to bless them until they manifest.

The traditional foods of Imbolg come to us from the Celts, the French, and the Swedes. Many of them are round in shape, or contain the traditional foods of the spring Sabbats such as honey and milk. No doubt this was another form of sympathetic magick to wish back warmer weather.

Pancakes or waffles, usually round and made with rich cream, are still a Swedish tradition for Imbolg, especially on farms and in the Lappland where sheep, goats, and deer (the latter two sacred to their gods) form the basis of the economy.

The Honey Cake is a French Imbolg dessert with Middle East origins. Both recipes follow.

Swedish Waffles
(Serves four)

1 teaspoon granulated sugar
1 cup evaporated milk or cream
3 eggs
¼ cup melted butter (not margarine)
1½+ cup flour
2 teaspoons baking powder
¼ teaspoon salt

Prepare and preheat waffle iron. Mix all ingredients until the mixture takes on a slightly fluffy appearance. Pour the batter into a hot waffle iron and bake until done (about 3 minutes). In Sweden it is traditional to use preserves or honey to top the waffles.

Honey Cake

2½ cups flour	4 eggs, beaten
½ teaspoon baking soda	1¼ cup granulated sugar
2½ teaspoons baking powder	½ safflower oil
1 heaping teaspoon allspice	1 cup raw honey
¾ teaspoon ground cinnamon	*1¼ cups unsweetened orange juice
⅛ teaspoon nutmeg	*1 tablespoon milk
1 teaspoon ground ginger	*2 cups confectioners' sugar

Preheat oven to 350° F. Grease and flour a 9 x 13 baking pan. Combine all ingredients well, pour into the pan, and bake for 45 minutes. This cake is traditionally served unfrosted, but you can make a frosting with the confectioners' sugar, milk, and orange juice.

Because of the Sabbat's association with ewe's lactation, milk is also a featured item at the feast. And since the weather is still cold in most places at this time of year, serve it hot with a bit of chocolate and honey flavoring.

The Norse tradition dictated that pork be eaten on Imbolg, and that the bones be saved as talismans of strength and virility until planting time. In Celtic lands, poultry and lamb doused in dill are still traditional Imbolg dishes.

The Roman holiday of Lupercalia also occurs near Imbolg. Lupercalia celebrated the beginning of the wolves' mating season, and was the originator of our St. Valentine's Day. Wolves mate for life and their union was seen not only as a sign of spring, but of the eternal union of the Goddess and her Sun God. To honor this occasion, make the All-Purpose Holiday Cookie recipe from Chapter Three and cut the dough into heart shapes, or indulge yourself in a box of Valentine chocolates found in every corner store.

Symbols of Imbolg

Because the heart has always been thought of as the organ of love (from a pagan Aryan concept associated with the attributes of the chakra system), it was adopted as a February/Imbolg symbol. These associations were transferred to Lupercalia and later to St. Valentine's Day, and they are still with us today. Both antique and modern Valentine's cards feature bright red hearts and hopeful young women (as in the young Goddess) waiting for their affections to be returned from distant lovers.

Another reason the heart came to symbolize Imbolg was due to an ancient Druidic divinatory practice that once regularly took place on this Sabbat. At their center on the Isle of Anglesey in the south of Britain they would gather to remove the heart from a living white bull in much the same way that the Aztecs of old Mexico removed the beating human heart from their sacrificial victims, and then would examine its final convulsions and appearance for clues about the future.

Imbolg was also the traditional time to collect stones for new magick circles and for general magickal use. Stones have always been seen by pagans as containing within them the vital energies of the Earth Mother from whom they are born. Stones were used to create the megaliths of Europe such as Stonehenge. Granite or red rock outcroppings were sacred to the Native Americans, and burial cairns in Celtic lands were constructed of native stones. Today, stones often mark off ritual circle space, and stone spells for protection and strength are known worldwide.

Below are listed some commonly found or easily obtained stones, along with some of their meanings:

Stone	Meaning/Uses
Agate	New beginnings
Amethyst	Spirituality
Aquamarine	Stress reducer, Water-related spells
Bloodstone	Protects during childbirth
Carnelian	Dispenser of Justice, Used to help locate the guilty, Increases energy
Coral	Increase psychic awareness, Protection on the sea, As currency
Diamond	Eternity, Strength, Prosperity
Emerald	Love, Peace, A natural tranquilizer, Aids neurological diseases
Flint	Protection from faeries
Fluorite	Increases mental powers
Fossils	Past-life work, Magick for animals
Garnet	Healing blood diseases
Geodes	Fertility, Earth magick, Meditation
Granite	Protection, Fidelity
Hematite	Grounding
Holey Stones	Fertility
Jade	Prosperity, Fertility, Balances female hormones
Lapis Lazuli	Promotes courage, Psychicism, Healing, Protection, Helps sore throats heal
Lodestone	Fidelity, Binding spells, Retrieving lost objects, Attraction, Job hunting
Meteorite	Astral projection, Teaches psychometry
Moonstone	Sacred to Moon Goddess and Mother Goddesses, Psychicism, Fertility
Obsidian	Symbol of the Crone, Stone of mourning to Native Americans, Scrying stone

Opal	Boost immune system, Protection, Psychicism, Promotes youthful appearance
Quartz	Crystal Healing, Grounding, Centering, Focusing energy, Connecting with other intelligences
Pearl	Sacred to most ocean deities, Moon magick, Water spells
Red Sandstone	A dwelling place of spirits as in Arizona
Rose Quartz	Used to facilitate love spells, Bring peace, Help end violence, Promote longevity, Romans believed it prevented wrinkles
Ruby	God energy
Sapphire	Psychicism, Healing, Used to energize the psychic center known as the Third Eye
Tiger's Eye	Balances male hormones, Protection
Tourmaline	Protection, Helps anemia
Yellow Topaz	Protection, Defense, Strength in battle, Promote vitality, Healing, in Egypt was sacred to the Sun God Ra

Collect stones on or before Imbolg and look up their ancient meanings, or use them as decorations to mark off your ritual space. If these stones can be left at a permanent circle site, the individual rocks are often painted with the colors and symbols of paganism. Doing this can be a fun and rewarding project for an entire coven, or a solitary.

To begin collecting ideas for the stones, look through books on magic and witchcraft and find designs and symbols that appeal to you. Also study color lore to decide what colors you would like certain rocks to be. For example, those in the west might be painted in varying shades of blue to symbolize water. Don't limit yourself, especially if you are a solitary—you don't have to justify your choices to anyone. Feel free to create your own decorative stones to signify items and/or events meaningful to only you.

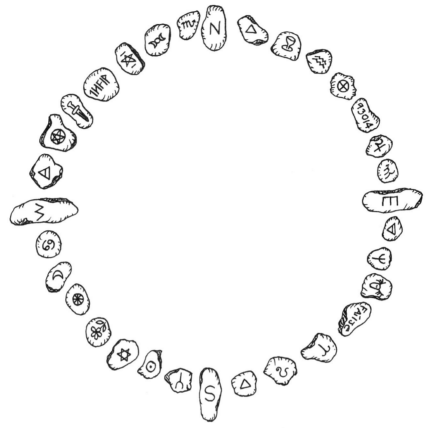

A personalized stone circle.

Light Energy

Imbolg is a time of hope and looking forward, but it is still bitterly cold in much of Europe and North America at the time of this celebration—a time to be near home and hearthside. Therefore, it is not surprising that fireplace lore is a large part of this Sabbat.

Before we had central heat, fireplaces were the only sources of warmth, and still are in most of the world. They were in the center of every cottage, and in every room of larger homes. Families used to gather near the fireplace at night not just for warmth, but to share stories, songs, and games. Besoms usually stood near the hearth to protect it, and protective herbs were often thrown in the blazing fires. In Scotland on Imbolg night, it was a tradition for each member of the family to throw protective salt in the fire and divine their immediate futures by the pops and lights it made.

Divining to determine how much longer it would be until spring was another use of the Imbolg fireplace. In Brittany, grain sheaves not used to

make the Grain Dolly were thrown onto the fire. If they were quickly consumed it meant that spring was at hand; if they took a long time to burn,
the winter would be a long one. If they broke in half and burned in two distinct pieces, there would be a brief respite from the cold, with more winter
to come.

Seeing Auras

If you wish to put the frustratingly long nights of February to good use, why
not learn to see auras, or, if you are already adept, teaching this art to others?

The aura is a ring of light energy which surrounds the bodies of living
things, humans included. The light energy has been photographed by using
specially formulated film, and psychics adept at seeing them have been able
to accurately diagnose from it numerous physical and mental disorders.

While you may never learn to see patterns and other symbols in the
aura, anybody can train themselves to see the predominant color or colors
of an aura and to accurately interpret their general meanings.

To practice reading auras, you will need a partner and a single, neutral
colored background to stand against. White, beige, or black are the best.
Have your partner dress in neutral clothing or go nude, and stand against
this background facing you. Use subdued lighting and soften your focus.
Look either at the person's third eye (just above and between the eyes), at the
throat, or across the right shoulder. Don't look directly at the place you
expect to see the aura as this will cause its image to fade. You have to rely on
peripheral vision instead. By doing this you should quickly see the misty outline of the aura, and soon a color, or the impression of a color, should appear.

If you don't succeed at first, switch places with your friend and let
him/her try reading you, then you can try again. If you still have no luck,
burn mugwort or jasmine incense, or drink valerian tea. These help to open
the psychic centers.

Once you are able to see each other's auras, it is time to practice outside
of your own homes. Three of the best places to see auras are in classrooms
where teachers are standing against blackboards, at concerts where players
are usually in black and set against neutral backgrounds, and in non-fast
food restaurants that sport neutral decors and subdued lighting. When I
was an undergraduate, my best friend and I used to frequently practice
reading auras at a late-night coffee shop near our campus. We found it
worked very well, though more than a few people were put off by our blank

stares. You can double-check your accuracy by working together. By looking at the same person, see if you both come up with the same color. People who have no working partners can also practice these out-of-home readings with success.

Below is a list of auric colors and what they generally mean.

Color   Meaning

Red   Often seen in athletes and in young children. Denotes an inner vitality and is usually indicative of good health. These people enjoy lots of social interaction and have a very strong sex drive. Deep reds can indicate touchy tempers, and paler reds have more in common with pink. Professional dancers are usually surrounded by red auras.

Orange   Individuals with orange auras are very outgoing, but often have knee-jerk reactions to stimuli, both positive and negative. These people are generally healthy, but orange can indicate a need to reduce stress. Darker orange indicates someone living under extreme pressure, an overly aggressive personality, or too much time in the public eye. Politicians are usually surrounded by dark orange.

Yellow   Yellow is the color of the intellect and is often seen around teachers and serious students. The deeper the yellow, the deeper the intellect. Paler yellow indicates less creativity, and deeper yellow indicates more. Yellow auras frequently surround writers and journalists. Deep yellow bordering on orange indicates someone who uses his or her intellect to hurt and cheat others.

Green   Green indicates a loving and trusting nature. It is the color of people who prefer their home life to any other, and is often seen around happy parents. Green is also seen around artists. Lighter greens can indicate an over-inflated ego, and deeper greens can indicate the deceitful nature of a good con-artist. Not surprisingly, nature lovers also have lots of green in their auras.

Blue   Blue is the color of the natural healer and is often seen around herbalists and the better doctors. People with blue auras are usually extremely concerned for the welfare of others and are often found in jobs and activities that aid other people. Paler blues are indicative of deeply spiritual persons or ones who are musically gifted. Deeper blues indicate individuals with psychic gifts or those deeply into natural magick. Blue shafts of light are often seen rising from the heads of creative personalities.

Indigo   Indigo is the color of the highly clairvoyant. Those with indigo are usually gifted in magick and are often very spiritual, though they must guard against becoming too self-absorbed. This color lower on the body indicates a need to change one's outlook on life.

Violet   Violet is a color rarely seen in an aura, and is indicative of the sort of person we would all like to be. These people have a profound understanding of spiritual matters, are deeply empathic, and have well-integrated personalities—combining the best of all worlds and states of being. Some New Age thinkers believe those with violet auras are not on earth to work out their own karmic agenda, but to aid the rest of us in achieving their advanced state of mind-spirit.

White   Be careful when you see a white aura that you are not merely seeing the misty shadow of the auric field itself. White is a rare color in an aura, and is similar to violet in its properties. Persons with white auras are also very idealistic and often seem dreamy and disconnected to the everyday world.

Pink   A pink aura indicates a very romantic nature—people who are generally at peace with themselves and enjoy their lives. Pinks have a strong sense of justice and are grossly offended by violence and bigotry. They should be cautioned about giving too much of themselves to others as they tend to allow themselves to be martyrs for those they care about. This color is often seen around the heart centers of young lovers.

Olive   This color is indicative of a person who is encased by his or her own negative emotions. This person often displays the petulant behavior of a child, and is someone who is usually searching for the pot of gold at the end of the rainbow while ignoring the joys and pleasures at hand.

Aquamarine   This color surrounds sedentary people—not necessarily people who are bad—just a little lazy. These people need daily exercise which will usually turn their auras to a blue or green. This color can also indicate individuals who spend too much time in meditation and metaphysical pursuits at the expense of their physical life.

Peach Peach is another rare color, one which indicates a person with lots of compassion, understanding, and ability to sacrifice for the needs of others, but not in a martyr-like way.

Lavender Lavender auras are usually found around those who lead a double life. They live one way while wanting to live another, or they are dishonest in their dealings with their family and friends. Lavenders are usually not malicious, but are nearly always unfocused and may have an underlying problem such as alcoholism.

Blue-Green This color indicates a dreamy person, someone very emotional—a thinker rather than a doer. This color can also mean that the person combines traits of both blue and green auras.

Turquoise This is a less common shade of blue. It indicates someone with a deeply analytical mind. Turquoise is insightful and these people make good counselors. They communicate well and are often gifted in one or more fields of study. Brilliant music composers and innovative inventors and scientists often have turquoise in their aura.

Red-Violet People with this aura are usually highly driven toward their personal goals which are often in conflict with their ethics. This fragmentation causes them frustration and, in large amounts, can indicate the presence of stress-related illnesses.

Beige Beige indicates mediocrity and a slow intellect. This does not mean that beiges are bad people. They are usually placid and pretty happy, just not overly bright or active.

Green-Brown This aura surrounds a person who is tied to convention, has no aptitude for critical thought, and is often fearful of the world and new ideas and things. They can be obsessive and dangerous, and become a threat to others. They usually have vigilante mentalities and are usually quite cowardly despite their blow and bluster.

Brown   Brown can indicate an obsessive-compulsive personality, or it can surround someone who is currently in a miserable or frightening situation. It usually means the person has given up trying to fight their problem and has slipped dangerously into a depression that requires medical intervention. Large brown auras are usually temporary. In small patches it can mean the beginning of an illness affecting that region of the body.

Silver   Silver indicates a person interested in spiritual attainment, though they often only get it in superficial doses. It is also the color of wisdom, and, when it is seen at all, is often around elderly persons.

Gold   Gold is extremely rare, but when seen, it is usually mixed with white, blue or violet. It indicates a very strong and vibrant personality, one to which others are highly attracted. Gold persons are closest to the highest ideals of violet, blue and white in their make-up, only more strongly felt. Some New Age thinkers say that a gold aura surrounds those who are not native to this plane of existence.

Gray   Gray is a very negative color in an aura. If the color is localized it indicates a serious illness in that part of the body, otherwise it means a negative personality, one who is violent, dangerous, and best avoided.

Black   This is another rarely seen aura, and that is good for all of us. Black indicates just what one would think it does—an evil, sick personality devoid of human warmth. This color is often seen in sociopathic personalities, or locally around regions of the body where life-threatening illnesses are centered.

Bonding with Winter Wildlife

In much of the northern hemisphere Imbolg comes in the dead of winter with freezing temperatures and deep snows. In such places looking for signs of the new life of spring can feel like a futile effort. But people who are blessed with snow in February (yes, I said blessed) have a unique opportunity to bond with winter wildlife.

Remember that, though you may be mentally turning your thoughts to the coming spring, the birds and animals around you are still thinking only of surviving through the winter until vegetation and game again become plentiful and the threat of falling into traps set to snatch their warm winter coats from them are removed. Whether you live in the middle of a busy city or out in the country, you should not forget to continue feeding your animal friends until well into spring. Drug, grocery, and feed stores carry a variety of inexpensive bird seed and small animal food which can be placed in special feeders, scattered on the ground, or placed in a window box. Watching the birds and animals come to feed is not only relaxing and satisfying, but an excellent way to bond with the nature we pagans cherish. And if you have a dog or cat, a window-view of these feeding critters is better to them than television!

If you have the opportunity to get out where small animals live you can learn to recognize and identify their footprints in the snow. I never had any interest in learning about animal tracks until I lived in a house that was set against a small woods. As the area around it was fairly urbanized it did not occur to me that there could be an abundance of wildlife there waiting to make itself known to me. As I began to notice a variety of small footprints in the snow I decided it was time to learn just what sort of creatures made them. It became a rewarding pastime.

Imbolg is a holiday that needs some celebration outside of the ritual circle to brighten up the days. You might have a Groundhog Day party. Build a bonfire and take everyone outside to roast food over the open flames and to drink hot drinks while waiting for the groundhog to pop his head out of the ground and tell us if we are going to have six more weeks of winter. You may even want someone to dress up as old Punxsutawney Phil and have him put in an appearance to answer prophetic questions for your guests.

Host a Lupercalia party, one with all the trappings of a modern Valentine's gathering. Serve food with festive names such as "Wolf Burgers," "Wolf Milk Cheese," or "Wolf Meat Casserole" (all made of everyday ingredients, of course) to complement the Lupercalia theme. Play games like Spin the Bottle, or ones in which mates have to guess what each others' responses to various questions will be, questions such as: "Who picked the color scheme for your bedroom?" "What is your mate's favorite relative of yours?" "What was the name of the person your mate dated just prior to you?" The answers and the uproar they cause can be riotous fun.

The Chinese New Year also takes place in February, and this is a good time to have a party featuring a Chinese pagan theme. Dragons, prominently displayed at this time, are symbols of the sun, and in the Chinese tradition it is a large dragon who turns the Wheel of the Year. As with any new year's celebration, divinations should be a big part of the observance. Use Chinese fortune cookies to fulfill this role. They are readily found in most supermarkets or ethnic food stores and gourmet shops. Fortune cookies can also be brought into your ritual circle to divine what spring will hold for each of your fellow covenors. For pagan gatherings, consider entering your ritual space dressed as one long dragon turning the Wheel of the Year.

Imbolg is a season of hope, filled with new possibilities for the future, and a time to look forward to the warmth, joy, and lustiness of the spring Sabbats.

⋙ 5 ⋘

Ostara:
The Spring Equinox
March 22

Ostara (Oh-star-ah) was the name of the Virgin Goddess of Spring in ancient Germany. It is for her that this Sabbat is named. Ostara was a Sabbat of great importance in Greece, Rome, and in Nordic and Germanic lands, and it is from these traditions that the vast majority of our current Ostara customs come. Many of the equinox myths from these cultures concern trips by deities into the underworld, and their struggle to return from the Land of the Dead to earth. When they eventually do return to the world of the living, they have a new life, both literally and figuratively, and this idea of life renewed plays heavily in the symbolism of the holiday. Some of these resurrected deities include Odin, Attis, Osiris, Dagda, Mithras, Orpheus, Hera, and Persephone.

In keeping with the early Church's practice of grafting saintly feast days onto any pagan festival they could not eradicate, it assigned St. Patrick his feast day near the time of the equinox. After being repeatedly driven out of Ireland, Patrick's reformed procession was said to have arrived at Tara, the seat of government, to present his new faith to the High King on Easter Sunday. Easter itself falls near Ostara, and celebrates yet another resurrected deity.

At Ostara, the Teutons honored their Goddess of Spring, Eostre—for whom the Christian holiday of Easter is named—with feasting and ritual. The Norse also honored their Virgin Goddess and celebrated her mating with the young God, an event most pagan circles have moved to Bealtaine.

Sexual relations were almost obligatory on Ostara Eve, as was a communal meal featuring foods associated with fertility such as cake, honey, and eggs.

The Greco-Roman tradition would celebrate Ceres, their Grain Goddess, from Ostara until first harvest. She was believed to go from field to field at the equinox, blessing the newly-sown crops. Ostara rituals in these traditions seek to urge her special blessing on their freshly-tilled lands.

The lily, appropriated as a Christian symbol of death, was a symbol of life in pagan Greece and Rome, where it adorned Ostara altars and temples. Young men, playing the role of the lusty young God, would present them to the young women they were courting. Accepting the lily meant much the same thing as accepting a diamond ring does now.

In Celtic lands the Ostara Sabbat was virtually overlooked until the Norse invaders brought it into prominence and it became another cherished festival. In Celtic Cornwall and Wales, Ostara was renamed "Lady Day," and was the time of the official return of the young Goddess after her winter hibernation. On this day of balance, they believed she was able to meet her youthful God on equal terms, mate with him, and become impregnated with not only the God who will be reborn at Yule, but with the autumn harvest as well. It was also the customary day for farms to change hands even if the purchase had been made months before.

In England the youthful deities are honored as the Lord of the Greenwood, a version of the Horned God, and the Green Goddess, a fertile young virgin/mother.

Other celebrations of pagan deities that took place at or near Ostara were the Feast of Isis (Egypt), the Feast of Cybele (Italy), Aphrodite Day (Greece), the Festival of Astarte (Greece/Rome/Persia), the Festival of Athena (Greece), and Hilaria (Rome). All these deities are still worshipped by pagans today; their holidays and customs are well-incorporated into the modern Ostara celebration.

In Slavic pagan traditions this was believed to be a day when death had no power over the living. In their tradition, a personification of Death is symbolically killed by throwing him into moving water to drown. Flowers, symbols of life renewed, are tossed in after him and he is sung to as he floats down river. People who died on Ostara were thought to be favored by the deities, and would be accorded princely treatment until the time they reincarnated. After Death's drowning, brightly-painted red eggs were passed around during a procession to the ritual site, where the new life of spring was celebrated with food, dance, and strong drink.

The idea of wearing new clothes at Easter and other spring festivals also came from an earlier Teutonic pagan tradition. It was considered the worst of luck to wear one's spring clothing before Ostara, and the Teutons would work through the winter in secret to prepare elegant finery for the Sabbat celebration. The entire community would gather together at Ostara for games, feasting, and religious rituals while showing off their new clothes.

The lamb is another symbol of Ostara, and was sacred to virtually all the virgin goddesses of Europe, the Middle East, and north Africa. This symbol was so ingrained in the mindset of the people of that region that it was carried over into the spring religious rituals of the Jewish Passover and Christian Easter.

The Egg as New Life

The most pervasive symbol of Ostara is, without a doubt, the egg. Since antiquity, eggs, the universal archetype of new life, have been held in reverence as sacred objects of eternal life, carried as fertility amulets, decorated to honor the deities, placed on spring altars, and given as cherished spring gifts.

The modern belief that these eggs are delivered by a rabbit known as the Easter Bunny, comes from the legend of the Goddess Eostre. So much did a lowly rabbit wish to please this Goddess that he laid the sacred eggs in her honor, gaily decorated them, and then humbly presented them to her. So pleased was she that she wished all humankind to share in her joy. In honoring her wishes, the rabbit went through all the world and distributed these little decorated gifts of life.

Many pagans like to use natural dyes that come from flowers and herbs for the eggs, rather than relying on the commercially-packaged kits. To get the natural dyes, boil a large handful of an herb or flower until the water is well colored. Place the water in a heat-resistant glass cup, mug, or other non-metal container. Stir in a teaspoon of vinegar and a pinch of salt, then place a hard boiled egg gently into the mixture. Getting the color to "take" requires a good bit longer than with the commercial dye kits, but most pagans feel it is worth the effort to have this connection with the old ways. However, the dyes do tend to be less stable, so protect the eggs from being scratched.

Below is a list of the most commonly used natural dyes, but feel free to experiment and find your own combinations with any non-toxic herb, vegetable, or flower.

Desired Color	Herbs
Yellow	Carrots, Turmeric, Fenugreek, White grape juice
Orange	Onion skins, Paprika
Red	Red onion skins, Madder root, Cayenne
Red-Violet	Purple grape juice, Red raspberries
Green	Carrot tops, Bracken
Blue	Blueberries, Red cabbage, Black raspberries
Blue-Violet	Blackberries, Beet juice, Mulberries
Pink	Heather

Eggs can also be painted with brushes and non-toxic watercolor paints. With this method you can express your creativity and design eggs to personally represent yourself, loved ones, the Sabbat, and/or your favorite God/dess aspects. With a few trinkets and school glue, you can add even more dimensions to the eggs. Use sequins, feathers, synthetic hair, glitter, or commercially-made doll accessories to add a humorous touch or to make a statement.

Making a *Cascarone*

In Mexico and the American southwest, there is a beautiful Easter custom, also pagan in origin, revolving around *cascarones*. *Cascarones* (cahs-cah-roe-nays) are eggshells that have been carefully hollowed out, painted, filled, and then resealed with tape. Traditional fillings for them include perfume, confetti, lavender and sage—all pagan symbols of spring. The *cascarones* are taken out on Easter morning, when the object is to catch your loved ones by surprise and hit them over the head with an egg. As the insides rain around you, you are blessed with the love, luck, and new life of the season.

To make your own *cascarones*, you will need a dozen eggs, acrylic craft paints and brushes, clear carton sealing tape, and items such as those mentioned above to stuff the eggs with, and a use for the one dozen egg innards you will have on your hands when you are finished.

To empty the eggs you will need to make a small hole in both ends without cracking the rest of the egg. Do this by gently tapping on the ends of the egg with the round side of a spoon. Holding the egg over a bowl, gently blow on the larger end of the egg and push out the yolk and whites. Rinse out the eggs in a small stream of cool tap water, and replace them in the carton to dry overnight. They can then be carefully painted and decorated.

Tape up the bottom holes with the clear sealing tape and replace the eggshells in the egg carton. Carefully stuff the shells with any herbs, confetti, etc. you wish to use. A small kitchen funnel is helpful. When they are full, seal the top hole. Use the minimum amount of tape needed to cover the holes or your eggshells will resist cracking open.

Hanging Plastic Eostre Eggs

Eggs do not have to be real to function as symbols and decorations of the season. Make an Eostre egg tree with the plastic eggs available at supermarkets and drug stores each spring. These colorful eggs usually come with a divider in the middle so that they can be taken apart and filled with candy and other trinkets. To prepare them to hang, pull them apart, and on the small end, drill a tiny hole directly in the top. Use a drill bit no bigger than one-sixteenth inch, and keep the drill on a low speed so you don't melt the plastic.

Next, take embroidery floss or a very thin section of ribbon about fifteen inches long, loop them together, and tie the ends with a large knot. Thread the floss through the hole in the egg so that the knot will hold up the egg from the inside. Replace the bottom half of the egg and it is ready to hang on trees or bushes around your home.

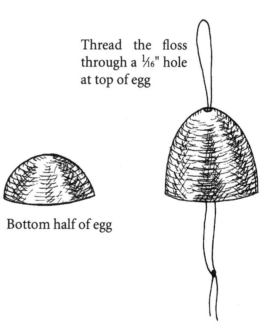

Thread the floss through a $\frac{1}{16}$" hole at top of egg

Bottom half of egg

Put an anchor knot at the end of the floss

Painted wooden eggs can also be made from egg-shaped blocks from craft stores. The wooden eggs come in various sizes, never rot, won't break, and can be reused year after year as altar decorations or part of your seasonal home decor. Paint them with pagan symbols or intricate designs that will further identify them with the Ostara season. As they are not fragile like real eggs you have a lot of flexibility with their adornment.

Wooden Eostre's eggs painted with spring colors and pagan symbols adorn this festive tree.

Significance of Colors on Eggs

The colors you choose to paint your eggs can also have significance. Below is a list of colors and their general pagan meanings.

Color	Pagan Meaning
Red	New life, Vitality, Lust, Sexuality, Color of the root chakra (energy center), Color of the Mother Goddess, Strength, War, Heat, One of the traditional colors of May Pole ribbons
Orange	Color of the God, Attraction, Color of the navel chakra, Summer

Yellow	Creativity, Knowledge, Intellect, Color of the solar plexus chakra
Green	Color of the Earth Mother, Fertility, Prosperity, Color of the heart chakra, Earth
Blue	Healing, Peace, Meditation, Astral projection, Color of the throat chakra, Cold, Air, Robin's Egg, Spring, The Virgin Goddess, New life, The waxing year
Indigo	Past lives, Healing, Clairvoyance, Color of the forehead chakra (third eye)
Violet	Healing, Tranquility, Ending quarrels, Color of the crown chakra, Ability to contact other intelligences
White	Purification, Barrier against negativity, Color of the Virgin Goddess, Good fortune, Color of death and mourning (in Eastern traditions), One of the traditional colors of May Pole ribbons
Black	Mystery, Absorption, Color of the Crone Goddess, Winter, Color of death and mourning (in Western traditions)
Silver	The moon, Triple Goddess, Psychicism, Spirituality, Water
Gold	The sun, The God, Activity, Money, Fire
Brown	Autumn, Animals, The waning year, Earth
Pink	Romantic love, Peace, Color used for both Ostara and Bealtaine
Turquoise	Spiritual knowledge
Red-Violet	Hidden knowledge, Color of the Medieval occultists
Pale Green	A traditional color of Ostara
Pastels	Traditional Ostara colors since the Middle Ages

Easter Egg hunts have become popular spring events, thanks to President Abraham Lincoln. In 1862, when the United States was deep into the second year of the Civil War, he invited the children of Washington, D.C., to hunt for eggs on the White House lawn. It has been an annual Washington event since, one mimicked in many communities. But this custom is much older than President Lincoln. Spring egg hunts have origins in pagan India and China, where the belief in karma is strong. Karma is the conviction that what one does in a past life will return threefold in his or her next life. The practice of hunting for eggs is symbolic of the belief that we are fully responsible for ourselves, and we must each find our own path to new life.

Eggs were buried by the Teutons at Ostara in much the same way as apples were buried by the Celts at Samhain. The idea was to infuse the earth with the life-giving properties of these objects. Eggs were planted in fertile fields, in window boxes, in flower beds, in animal barns, and were eaten by people who also hoped to reap their life-giving benefits.

Eggs feature prominently in this Sabbat feast. Eat them as omelettes, scrambled, poached, deviled, and hard-boiled. Or make them into a creamy egg nog. The word "nog" is Old English and means a "strong ale." While this drink has become a feature of Christmas through Nordic pagan practice, you should not hesitate to make it at Ostara and even at Bealtaine. The alcohol in the following recipe should always be thought of as optional, and you should keep in mind the needs and safety of your guests when mixing it.

Egg Nog
(Makes approx. 1 gallon)

12 eggs, separated
1 lb. confectioner's sugar
1½ cups whiskey, ale, or dark rum
2 quarts whipping cream
¾ teaspoon ground nutmeg
¼ teaspoon salt
1 teaspoon vanilla
1 cup tap water
1 cup milk

Mix the egg yolks, sugar, alcohol, and salt and let stand in the refrigerator overnight. The next day, beat the egg whites until just stiff, and mix them and the rest of the ingredients together. Serve chilled.

⇥ ⇤

Other traditional foods of Ostara are fish (Pisces rules the heavens at Ostara), cakes, biscuits, cheeses, honey, and ham. Most of these are also Bealtaine foods and are often seen at both Sabbats.

The Sun Wheel, a symbol of perfect balance at the equinox, was the inspiration for the traditional spring roll known as the Hot Cross Bun. These buns were pagan traditions long before they were adopted into the Christian Easter and are sold everywhere around this time. There are many versions of this bread, and every good cook has his or her favorite.

Hot Cross Buns
(Makes approx. 1½ dozen)

3 cups flour
¾ cup sugar
1 cup evaporated milk
¼ cup melted butter or margarine
¼ teaspoon salt
1 package (1 oz.) dry yeast
1 large egg, well-beaten
1 teaspoon cinnamon
⅛ teaspoon allspice
¾ cup raisins (optional)
2 cups confectioners' sugar
1 tablespoon milk
2 cups orange juice

Combine all ingredients except yeast and eggs and mix well. Dissolve the yeast in ¼ cup hot water. Add yeast and eggs to the rest and mix well. Cover with a cloth and allow the dough to rise in a warm spot until it has nearly doubled. This will take about an hour.

Preheat oven to 400° F. Shape the dough into round balls about 3 inches across and place them on a lightly greased cookie sheet or jelly roll pan. After 5 minutes, remove buns and cut into the dough about ¾ of an inch down, slicing equilateral crosses into the tops. Return to oven. Allow to bake for another 15 to 20 minutes. Remove the buns from the oven and drizzle on the Honey Cake frosting mentioned on Page 97.

⊰ ⊱

Pashka, a Russian Easter cake, was also once a pagan delicacy. Cakes have always been symbols of fertility and of the Mother Earth. Regional variations on this recipe abound. This is one from the region once known as the Pale of Settlement.

Pashka

2½ pounds small curd cottage cheese
1¼ cups sugar
¾ cup chopped almonds or pecans
¾ cup chopped peaches
½ cup maraschino cherries or dried cherries
1¼ teaspoons vanilla
2 sticks butter, melted
¼ teaspoon salt
2 cups evaporated milk or cream
2 eggs

Mix all ingredients except the cottage cheese in a large pan over low heat until it thickens to the consistency of pudding. Remove from heat and allow to cool completely. Mix in the cottage cheese and beat well for about 3 minutes. Place in a cake pan and chill over night. Decorate the cake with candied eggs, flowers, chocolates, or other spring delicacies. Keep refrigerated.

Honey is a universal pagan symbol of the spring Sabbats, and many cultures have found it also works well as a medicinal tonic and restorative. One of the best known of these is a concoction called Honegar, a blend of raw honey and apple cider vinegar. Together they react in the human body much as garlic or onions do. They thin the blood, improve circulation, lower blood pressure, and act beneficially on the heart muscles. Often Honegar is made at the Esbats, but it is also associated with Ostara because of its associations with balance. Its origins are obscure, but some attribute it to an old Teutonic recipe. Take the Honegar on a daily basis to reap its benefits. Four to six tablespoons in a large glass of water is the recommended dosage.

Honegar

(Serves two people, 30-day supply)

6 cups each, raw honey and apple cider vinegar

Heat equal parts (no more than 2 cups of each at a time) of the honey and vinegar in a large non-metal saucepan over medium heat. Stir occasionally with a wooden spoon. The honey will melt into the vinegar in a few minutes, making the mixture easier to stir. Keep stirring until you no longer feel heaviness or see any areas of thickness on the spoon (about 15 minutes).

Remove from heat and let cool for 30 minutes. Pour into canning jars and cap tightly. Store in the refrigerator.

Planting an Herb Garden

Ostara is a good time to consider planting an herb garden, both for medicinal and magickal purposes. If you don't have a yard, you can plant herbs in flower pots, window boxes, or even in a sandbox filled with soil.

A list of common herbs and their magickal and medicinal uses appears in Chapter Seven. You will need to decide which herbs you wish to grow, and find out which ones thrive best in your climate. A multitude of books on herbology are available in bookstores or your local library. Many communities have gardening societies which specialize in the cultivation of medicinal herbs. Look in the special events section of your newspaper, or check with a librarian to learn if your town has such an organization.

There are several ways you can "paganize" your herb garden. In either an inside or outside garden you can place pagan symbols among the plants. Use statuettes, Sun Wheels, or precious stones. In an outside garden or sandbox you can mark off the area with stones and then further divide each herb into its own section, as shown on Page 120.

Herb garden layouts

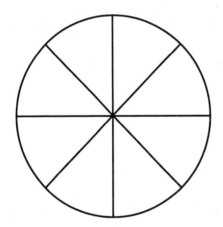

These are ideas for laying out herb gardens in a sandbox or outdoors that utilize pagan symbolism.

Mark these spaces off with stones for high visibility.

You can also write a ritual to purify and dedicate the ground and its bounty for positive purposes. Do this under the full moon nearest to Ostara. Take your ritual tools with you and walk the perimeter of the garden. You can also place a pouch of protective herbs or an egg into the ground so that their energies can fuse with the newly-planted herbs. You can also dedicate the garden to a particular deity by naming him/her in your ritual.

With so many modern religious festivals occuring at Ostara, pagans often forget that this season and its symbols are theirs too, and that they have every right to celebrate them. One celebration idea for parents comes from the feminist tradition that uses this Sabbat to celebrate First Blood or Coming of Age of their daughters. If you are the mother of a girl who began menstruating during the previous year, use Ostara to treat her in a special way. Take her out to lunch, buy her some new clothes, or give her her own ritual tools. This idea can also be used for a boy who has come of age, usually at age thirteen.

You can also host an egg-dying party. Children love this idea, but don't overlook doing this as a coven, or even with your own family. It is a beautiful way to connect with the season and share quality time with those you care about.

Or have a "Welcome Spring" party for everyone you know. With the profusion of spring holidays and their blended traditions and symbolism, no one ever need know (unless you wish them to) that you are honoring a pagan holy day.

Ostara is not only a time of balance, but one where light becomes triumphant over darkness as the Wheel of the Year carries us forward to the lusty month of May and to Bealtaine.

⇛ 6 ⇚

Bealtaine
May 1

Bealtaine (Beel-teen or Bell-tayn)—called Beltane in England and Wales, and Bheallttainn in Scotland—falls opposite Samhain on the Wheel of the Year. These were the two most important Sabbats on the Celtic calendar, marking the beginning and end of the two recognized seasons.

Even though this is a fertility Sabbat, one that celebrates life above all, some scholars believe the holiday takes its name from the Irish death god, Beltene. Another possible derivative of the name might be from the Welsh god Beli, but he appears to be more of a sun deity like Lugh, who would be honored at Midsummer or Lughnasadh rather than in the spring. Other intriguing possibilities of the origin of the name are from a little-known Celtic fire god from Gaul called Belanos or Belios, or from the Phoenician vegetation god Baal, a deity demonized by the new religion.

Still another explanation—and probably the one most popular with pagans—is that the Sabbat's name is derived from a word meaning "balefire." Even today, balefires are lit all over Britain and Ireland on May Eve, just as they were in the past. In the times of the High Kings of Ireland, it was illegal to light a balefire until the king had lit the one atop Tara, the seat of government. Many other cultures also sought out high spots for their ritual fires, including the people of the Alps and of Germany. The Royal Family of Britain still burns their Bealtaine balefire each May Eve in order to keep the family line going.

The Russian tradition requires that everyone wait until moonrise to light balefires rather than lighting them at sundown on April 30. They toss holly sprigs into the fire, perhaps in deference to the soon-to-return Holly King. They also toss aromatic herbs onto the coals to make a ritual incense for the occasion.

An old Swedish custom states that the balefire has to be lit by two people striking two flints together. This is symbolic of the sexual union of the Goddess and God.

In Norway the balefires are called Balder's Fires in honor of their own Sun God. Old brooms were often thrown upon these fires and new ones, made during winter, were brought out and dedicated to their proposed purpose.

Germanic and Dianic covens celebrate Bealtaine as a Night of the Dead, and ancestors are asked to join them at the warmth of the fire in much the same way the Celts do at Samhain.

In Slavic countries, young men travel from house to house just before sundown to collect items to fuel the balefire. In this tradition, wreaths are tossed into the flames by individuals who wish for healing.

In Scotland, the balefires were required to be lit from another fire known as the *tein-eigin*, or "need-fire," which had to be created by using the friction of a wheel. This fire was termed a "need" because it was used solely to cook with, and it was the only non-ritual fire permitted to burn on this day. Starting the need-fire from a wheel was symbolic on two levels. First of all, it was the symbolic association with the ever-spinning Wheel of the Year on this first day of the Celtic summer. Secondly, it is traced to a minor god of Celtic Gaul called Taranis, the God of the Wheel, who was also honored in early May.

It is traditional to take home a smoldering piece of the Bealtaine balefire to bring summer blessings into your home. The first cookfires of the summer season were once lit with part of this fire. But note that the custom asks you to take part of the balefire home, and not ask it as a gift. There was a strong taboo in Ireland and Scotland against giving away any portion of the Bealtaine fire. It was a basic belief of most Europeans that faeries could not start their own fires, but must obtain them from human sources. The Celts respected faeries, active at this Sabbat, and were sure that these Little People would come to the celebration disguised as humans to ask for a part of the fire which, when freely given, would give the faeries some measure of power over the giver.

The Faeries of Midsummer

Bealtaine is next only to Midsummer in the pervasiveness of faery lore. Daisy chains woven just prior to the Sabbat were placed around children's necks for protection, and livestock was fed fresh dill weed. Fresh butter was at particular risk, and it was customary to toss a hot coal into the churn to protect it from marauding faeries. In the Arthurian myths, Queen Guinevere rides out on May Day to collect white hawthorn for protection.

Perhaps the best protection against faeries is the ringing of bells. Bells in any form are supposed to hurt the Wee Folks' ears and make them flee. Therefore, it is not surprising that bells figure heavily in the Bealtaine festivities. Most pagan altars sport bells, and bells are often used to ring in the rising May Day sun in the Norse tradition. But the most prominent display of bells is on the heels of Morris Dancers. Morris Dances are old fertility dances traditionally performed around a Maypole. The dances from English and Celtic lands still survive, and on May 1, one need not look long or far to find a group of these dancers with bells tied to their heels.

You can make your own bells for Bealtaine dancing by getting two three-foot lengths of white or red ribbon and several jingle bells. Lace the bells through the ribbons until they are in the center. Wrap one ribbon around each of your ankles and tie it in a bow.

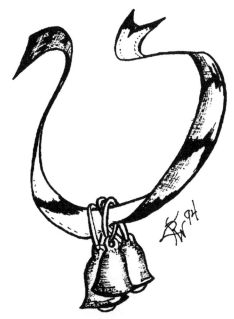

Morris Dance bells made from jingle bells and white ribbon.
Wrap them around your feet and ankles to hold them in place.

Other bells once used for protection are still in everyday use, though their original meaning has been largely forgotten. These are the folk art items we call wind chimes and door harps, both once set out to frighten faeries and other baneful spirits away from open windows and doors.

The primrose flower was also believed to repel Bealtaine faeries, even though most faery lore tells us that this is a flower they like and to which they are attracted. It is still a popular custom in rural Ireland to strew primrose blossoms over the front porches of homes on May Eve to prevent mischievous faeries from entering.

The Norse believed you had to sleep at home on Bealtaine Eve and keep a strong hearth fire blazing until dawn. Today's Easter fires are derived from this Norwegian practice.

In China a group of men used to wander through the villages reminding people to put out their old fires at the end of April so that all communal fires could be rekindled anew on May 1. Cold food was eaten for a night to ensure that there was no fire in the house.

In Ireland all home fires had to be relit with part of the balefire. To use old fire was thought to bring bad luck—perhaps even bringing the winter season back to stay.

In Wales the balefires were kept burning from the first to the third day of May, three being a sacred number to the Celts, and warriors and warrioresses took turns tending the fire throughout the night.

In many other lands, this Sabbat was not a Sabbat as we know it today, but a day to honor special deities. The best known of these holidays were from ancient Rome: the Floralia, to honor Flora, the Goddess of Flowers; and the Bacchanalia, to honor the God of Wine and Frolic. The Romans also honored Lares, a Roman household god whose original Etruscan name means "Lord."

High in the Tyrolian Alps of Italy, spring comes late, with May marking the first new blooms of the season. There Floralia is celebrated as it has been for thousands of years with community festivals that feature dancing, singing, and the drinking of delicately flavored—but very potent—wines made from the flowers and plants picked on the first of May the previous year. All the old wine must be consumed before midnight on the first, and new blooms gathered to ferment the next year's batch. Fresh flowers are featured as the primary decorations and they are used to lavishly adorn single young women. Young men who wish to publicly express their intention to court or to become betrothed to any of the women will scale the dangerous alpine slopes and collect the elusive edelweiss, a delicate white perennial

The first blooms of the season are often incorporated into Bealtaine celebrations.

herb which grows only in the alps. A man will then return to the festival and present it to the girl of his choice. If she accepts the tiny blooms in front of witnesses, the couple is as good as engaged.

If you do not have the time and money to travel to the Italian Alps but wish to catch a glimpse of this festival, rent a copy of the 1937 MGM classic film *The Bride Wore Red,* which features a fairly accurate look at the modern-day celebration.

Bealtaine was called Walpurgisnacht in Germanic lands, and takes its name from a christianized Teutonic Mother Earth Goddess named Walburga who was thought to marry the God on this night and become impregnated with her son/lover of Yule.

Other festivals that honor deities on or near Bealtaine are the Festival of Sheila-na-Gig (Ireland), Tithe Day (Germany), and the Festival of Pan

(Greece). Pan is another name for the Great Horned God of western Europe, often called Cernunnos (Ker-noon-noes) by the Celts. The Horned God is probably the most widely worshiped god-form in paganism. He is the master of the hunt and comes into his full power in late summer and early fall. In spring he is also the primal fertility God, consort to the Great Mother, and his goat-like appearance intimately associates him with the lusty sexuality of Bealtaine. Ancient paintings of him have been found on Eurasian cave walls and in Egyptian hieroglyphs, and he is probably the most persistent and common of god images throughout Western paganism.

The Great Rite, an often misunderstood pagan ritual, is enacted on this Sabbat in nearly every modern pagan circle. The Great Rite symbolizes the sexual union, or sacred marriage, of Goddess and God from whose union comes all creation. The Rite is performed by one male and one female who are representative of the male and female polarities of deity. They unite sexually in a symbolic manner by placing a knife (a phallic symbol) into a chalice (primal female image), though some traditions allow for everyone to leave the circle except the two participants, the only ones to know how the Rite is enacted.

In old Europe, whole communities would celebrate the enactment of the Great Rite and the positive effects such sympathetic magick would surely have on the crops, the animal populations, and the people.

Patriarchal religious teachers have often criticized paganism's use of the Goddess' son as her lover, a man who will again be her son. They use this imagery as "proof" of the "sinfulness and immorality" of pagan religions. Remember that these stories are symbolic, and represent the eternal existence and oneness of the deities rather than concrete familial relationships.

Concerns during Bealtaine

For most European cultures, Bealtaine marked the time of the final phase of spring planting, and their immediate concern was for the condition of the tender new shoots. Before modern farming techniques, little could be done about drought or pests, and European history is sadly riddled with miserable famines resulting from such blights. Our pagan ancestors had many crop fertility spells and charms to try to counteract the worst of Mother Nature. Besoms were ridden hobbyhorse-style over fields and through pastures by women in symbolic fertility rites. Menstruating women were especially sought after for this act, as the sacred blood of which all life is made was clearly present to saturate crop land and animal feeding grounds. A calving cow was often taken into a field to have her calf there, and ritually consecrated chalices containing a mixture of sheep's blood and milk were poured on the crops to encourage their growth.

Ashes from the Bealtaine balefire were scattered over the fields to bless and protect them, and infertile women would take these ashes and tie them in a bag around their necks. Whether this helped the women or not is not known, but as for the crops, modern science has discovered rich nitrogen in ashes which would have been beneficial for growing vegetables.

The welfare of livestock also figures prominently among the concerns of Bealtaine. Hunting of summer animals was now permitted, and the hunting of winter game such as the deer was prohibited. Special summer pastures set aside for cattle and sheep were opened for the first time each year only after May 1. Before May Eve the fields were still the province of the phookas, malevolent faeries who claimed them after Samhain. May also marked the beginning of the lambing season, and the condition and color of the first born lamb to a clan or community was indicative of how the rest of the year would go for them. Driving the animals through or over the balefire as the blaze waned was an old Bealtaine ritual of protection, healing, and purification.

You can ritually purify anything you wish over the Bealtaine balefire smoke. Pass through ritual tools, cherished possessions, heirloom jewelry, and especially newly-acquired items whose history you do not know. Or pass yourself through the smoke for your own purification prior to your Sabbat rituals.

You may also wish to purify yourself before the start of the Bealtaine festivities by anointing your body with morning dew from a Hawthorn tree. Ritual purification was—and is—an inherent part of pagan practice, but we have two sources of information which strongly suggest that cleansing was even more deeply a part of this Sabbat observance, especially for females. The first of these sources can be found in the Arthurian legends that tell us that Queen Guinevere rode out early on Bealtaine morning with her handmaidens to gather white hawthorn, and the second is a very old English nursery rhyme that states:

THE FAIR MAID WHO, ON THE FIRST OF MAY,
GOES TO THE FIELDS AT BREAK OF DAY,
AND BATHES IN DEW FROM THE HAWTHORN TREE,
WILL EVER STRONG AND HANDSOME BE.

The May Pole

Another custom of Bealtaine which has never died out is that of the May Pole. In many places in Britain, Ireland, and North America, children are still encouraged to grab the white and red ribbons and dance the old Morris Dances.

In the days of the old ways, the May Pole was made from the communal pine tree which had been decorated at Yule, with all but its uppermost branches now removed. The ribbons attached to its top are traditionally white and red, white for the Goddess and red for the God, or white for the Virgin Goddess and red for the Mother. The May Pole is a phallic symbol impregnating the birth canal being woven around it by the dancers. There are two thoughts on the symbology for the white and red streamers. One is that the red stands for the Sun God and the white for the Virgin Goddess. The men, holding the red streamers, and the women the white, weave the birth canal together, representing the union of Goddess and God. The other is that the white, held by the women, stands for the Virgin Goddess, and the red, held by the men, stands for the mother aspect. Together the men help the virgin aspect meld herself into motherhood on the phallic pole.

The dancers then do a Morris Dance, the Anglo name for May Day dances, which are rich with pagan symbolism. There are usually eight dancers—one for each Sabbat of the year—paired into four couples. The dances involve moving in circles and weaving under each other's interlocked, upheld arms in mock sexual unions.

It is not difficult, even in modern North America, to find such a celebration going on at May Day. My Indiana elementary school celebrated May Day every year under the label "Health Day," with festivities culminating in a May Pole dance in the school gym. While this may at first seem incongruous, it is not. Healing rituals were very much a part of the old Bealtaine observances. *Slainte*, an Irish word used to toast one's health, was a time-honored Bealtaine tradition. In Cornwall individuals would make Bealtaine pilgrimages to the standing stones known as Men-an-Tol to pass themselves through to be healed.

If you wish to wrap a May Pole of your own, you will need a tall object to act as a center pole, such as a branchless tree or a flag pole. If you have neither of these available to you, you might be able to buy a large wooden beam at a hardware store or a demolition site. In any case, the pole needs to be at least ten feet tall. (You can hang your ribbons at that height even if the pole you have is significantly higher.) You will also need long lengths of rib-

Making your own May Pole for this Sabbat is as easy as finding red and white ribbon.

bon or cloth about two to three inches wide and at least six feet longer than the length of your pole so you have room to work with them. For example, if you have a ten-foot pole, each ribbon will need to be sixteen feet long. Ask at a fabric or craft store for the type of ribbon or cloth you need. You will also need at least seven other dancers, though having more is fine, and bells for your heels. Celtic, Breton, or English folk music is the best choice, but American square dance music is a good substitute.

Hang your evenly-spaced ribbons, alternating red and white, at the ten-foot high point on your pole. You can tack them up any way you like. Use nails, glue, or tie them to a wreath which slips down over the pole. Drape them downward so they flow out at even intervals from your pole.

When you are ready to begin the dance, turn on your music and have the women take the white ribbons and the men take the red, and each stand facing their partner. The women will stand with their right sides to the pole, ribbon in their right hands, and the men will be standing with their left to the pole, the ribbon in their left hands. Begin weaving the symbolic birth canal by having everyone move forward from where they stand, moving alternately over and under the person coming toward them. It is tradition to start with the men moving their ribbon and selves under the upheld ribbon of the women. Proceed in this fashion unitl the May Pole is wrapped about eighteen inches down.

As you move to the music, make your steps a cross between a skip and a jog so that the bells on your heels hit the ground with enough force to mark off the beats of the music.

Many old folk song lyrics that proclaim the praises of this glorious Sabbat survive from remote parts of Britain. Many of them have become shrouded in arcane language over time, either deliberately or by accident, while others are remarkably straight forward. The following is an example of this music, the joyful lyrics of an old song from Cornwall. It is entitled simply, "A May Day Carol." Though the sentiments have been somewhat Christianized, they still reflect the themes of courtship, fresh flowering, honey ale and dairy foods, and making merry, for which Bealtaine is noted.

AWAKE, AWAKE, MY PRETTY PRITHY MAID,
COME OUT YOUR DROWSY DREAM,
AND STEP INTO YOUR DAIRY HOLD,
AND FETCH ME A BOWL OF CREAM.

IF NOT A BOWL OF CREAM, MY DEAR,
A CUP OF MEADE TO CHEER,
FOR THE LORD KNOWS WE SHALL MEET AGAIN,
TO GO MAYING ANOTHER YEAR.

A BRANCH OF MAY I BROUGHT YOU HERE,
WHILE AT YOUR KEEP I STAND,
'TIS BUT A SPROUT ALL BUDDED OUT,
BY THE POWER OF OUR LORD'S HAND.

MY SONG IS DONE AND I MUST BE GONE,
NO LONGER MAY I STAY,
GOD BLESS YOU ALL, THE GREAT AND SMALL,
AND SEND YOU A JOYOUS MAY.

A seventeenth century English engraving showing a Maypole. During England's Commonwealth period (1648-1660), such cherished pagan customs (including the observances of Easter and Christmas) were made illegal.

Finding the lyrics of folk music with their pagan meanings still intact is an exciting pastime for many pagan people, and a rewarding one since it is easy to do. As the established Church (either the Roman or the Anglican, depending upon location) became the ruling presence in the cities and towns of Europe, paganism was left to the countryside where often the custom-killing hand of clerical power did not reach. For many centuries the farmers and rural folk continued to live by and with the cycles of the sacred seasons, and it was they who preseved folk songs for us through their oral traditions. Much of the folk music whose origins can be traced to at least the sixteenth or seventeenth century often hints at this division of religious life. One of the most glaring examples of this is the British folk song, "The Oak and The Ash," which honors three of the sacred trees of the Celtic people, the oak, ash, and ivy. The song tells of a north country girl (most likely meaning she is from Yorkshire) who has gone to London and misses her homeland with all its attendant customs. The chorus of the song is: "... Oh, the oak and the ash and bonnie ivy tree / They flourish at home in my own country."

Bealtaine circles were once constructed with the May Pole at the center and a balefire at a distance, at one or all four of the cardinal points. The altar was lavishly decorated with fertility symbols such as holy stones, geodes, pine cones, flowers, and spring-time greenery. The rituals were erotic in nature, symbolizing the union of Goddess and God.

The Foods of Bealtaine

Goats and rabbits were sacred to the Bealtaine Sabbat both because of the goat's horns which symbolized the Horned God, and for their reputed randiness. Goats (sacred to the God) and rabbits (sacred to the Goddess) were prolific breeders who could be relied upon year after year to provide food and clothing.

The goat also provided milk, cheese, and butter, and dairy products figure heavily in the Bealtaine feast. Sweets were also an important part of the feasting. To combine the two elements, a rich dairy cream pie was baked for the celebrants.

Bealtaine Cream Pie
(Makes one nine-inch pie)

- 1 cup whole milk
- 1 cup rich cream
- ½ cup butter (not margarine)
- 3 tablespoons cornstarch
- 1½ cups sugar
- 1¼ teaspoons vanilla
  Ground nutmeg
  Prepared pie crust, baked

Melt the butter in a wide pan over medium heat. (Traditionalists will use a heavy cast-iron pan.) In a separate bowl slowly add the milk to the cornstarch, making sure it is fully dissolved and absorbed before adding more milk. When the cornstarch is fully blended, add this and all the other ingredients, except the vanilla, to the cooking pan. Stir constantly over medium heat until the mixture becomes thick. Remove from heat and stir in the vanilla. Pour the mixture into the waiting pie shell and sprinkle with nutmeg. The pie may be eaten while it is still warm, as long as it has cooled enough to set. Or the pie may be chilled and eaten later.

⇥ ⇤

Eating noodles in the spring is considered good luck in China, where pasta originated. Blend them with goat cheese, another Bealtaine food, to make this Greek favorite.

Makaronio Me Feta
(Serves six to eight)

    1   pound macaroni, cooked and drained
    ¼   cup butter, melted
    ⅓   cup olive oil
    4   tablespoons cornstarch
    ⅛   teaspoon black pepper
    2   cups milk
    1   egg, beaten
    ½   cup parmesan cheese, grated
    ¾   teaspoon nutmeg
    2   tablespoons parsley
    1   cup gorgonzola cheese, crumbled
    1½ cups feta cheese, crumbled

Preheat oven to 375° F. Mix all ingredients together and place them in a greased 9 x 13 baking pan. Bake until the top is golden brown, about 40 minutes.

⇥ ⇤

Honey is also part of this Sabbat's traditional foods, and bees are one of its many symbols. Serve honey at the feast, offering it as a libation to spring faeries, and burn beeswax candles to honey-scent the air at your ritual site.

Another way to bring honey into your celebration is by making the traditional Celtic ale known as meade. Meade is a savory honey-ale rich in tradition and folklore in the British Isles. In the Celtic tradition it is an aphrodisiac and sexual stamina builder whose recipe was once thought to be a direct gift of the Great Mother. Our modern word "honeymoon" has its roots in the Celtic custom of making and consuming meade. It was a drink shared by couples who began mating at Bealtaine with plans to marry in June (after the month of May, when the deities wed, was over). The "honey" part of the word refers to the meade itself, and the "moon" part from the approximate period of time that would lapse between the Sabbat and the time of the official handfasting.

Meade, akin to the Irish "midhe," meaning "center," represents spirit, and the drinking of this potion of the deities made one more in tune with that elusive fifth element. Connoisseurs of meade cultivate their brew as carefully as do makers of fine wine, and jealously guard their family recipes.

Making meade is not easy since, like wine, it requires a lengthy fermentation period. Here is one of the many recipes for meade.

Meade
(Makes ¾ of a gallon)

½ gallon water	⅛ teaspoon nutmeg
1½ cups raw honey	⅛ teaspoon allspice
¼ cup lemon juice	1 package brewer's yeast

Heat all ingredients together over medium heat in a large stockpot. As the honey melts, an oily crust forms on the top. Some say to leave this crust on, for it adds to the flavor of the meade; others will tell you to skim it off. I prefer to leave it on. When it is well blended, remove it from the heat, stirring occasionally as it cools. Stir in one package of brewer's yeast and pour the meade into a wooden cask or some other receptacle where it can ferment. You can drink the meade as is without the fermenting process, but it will not have alcoholic content. Like this, it will taste like a sweet honey-lemon tea. The meade needs to ferment for a period of at least 6 months. During that time the casks must be aired daily to allow any built-up gasses to escape. At least once a month it should be poured into a fresh cask. At the end of the six months you should have a drinkable meade.

⤙ ⤚

If you prefer to try a short-cut method of meade, you can stop the process just before fermentation and add a touch of grain alcohol to the mixture before bottling. You don't get the full-bodied flavor or euphoric intoxication that meade is famous for, but you still get the taste and the idea.

Another old Bealtaine drink, one decidedly less pleasant, was a mixture of cow or sheep blood mingled with their milk. This recipe from Cornwall was thought to ward off evil faeries, though it may have come from an earlier belief that what one consumes is born of them. Hopeful mothers may have drunk this mixture for fertility at this strongly symbolic fertility Sabbat.

Oat cakes were a Scottish tradition at Bealtaine, and even today some Scottish covens still use oatmeal to outline their Bealtaine circle. Oats were also eaten for luck and fertility. This dish, Farls, was a popular Bealtaine treat in both Scotland and northern Ireland.

Farls
(Serves eight)

3 cups real mashed potatoes
2 cups dry oats
2 tablespoons margarine or butter
½ teaspoon cornstarch
½ teaspoon baking powder
⅛ teaspoon salt
   Pinch pepper
   Pinch rosemary (optional)

Soak the oats in warm water for 15 to 20 minutes until soft and slightly swollen. Mix them with all other ingredients in a large mixing bowl. Knead until the mixture is like a thick dough. If it seems too thin or moist, add a teaspoon or two of flour. When it is thoroughly mixed, form small sections into round patties. Fry the patties in hot vegetable oil in a small skillet until lightly browned. Serve immediately.

⇒ ⇐

Bealtaine Calendars

Bealtaine is second only to Samhain in its popularity with modern pagans, and the anticipation can be a strain, especially on children. Counting calendars became popular holiday distractions for children in the nineteenth century, and these can be easily adapted to fit pagan lifestyles. They usually consist of buttons, or some other method of counting days, a cut-out poem, and a few seasonal decorations. Despite the lengthy instructions and the long list of supplies, these calendars are really quite easy to make and can be done in about four hours.

Following are complete instructions for making your own calendar for Bealtaine.

To make a Bealtaine Counting Calendar, you will need twenty-four one-inch buttons in white, red, or green (or a mix), all with just two needle holes in them; a piece of yellow or white felt cut to 36 x 6 inches; yarn in green, white or red; a darning needle; a quarter-inch dowel cut seven inches long; six small bells; several small pieces of felt in a contrasting color to the large piece, such as green, yellow, white, or red; a small square of light-   colored construction paper; school glue; scissors; a pen; and a piece of poster board to make templates for the border decorations.

Copy the following poem, or one of your own creation, onto the construction paper:

> HOW LONG MUST WE WAIT TO DANCE
> AROUND THE MAY POLE TALL AND HIGH?
> HOW LONG MUST WE WAIT TO KINDLE THE FIRE,
> THE FLAMES THAT CRACKLE AND FLY?
> YOU'LL BE DANCING SOON, MY LITTLE ONE,
> WITH BELLS UPON YOUR FEET.
> UNTIE A BUTTON EVERY NIGHT
> BEFORE YOU GO TO SLEEP.

Next, take the 36 x 6 inch piece of felt, and lay the cut-out poem at the the top about one inch from the top edge. Begin laying out the buttons, evenly spaced from the bottom and stopping just under the poem. With a pen, mark the spot of the two needle holes in the laid-out buttons.

Turn the felt over and, using about eight inches of yarn and the darning needle, string the buttons through and tie them with a tight square knot.

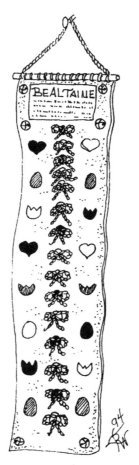

A Bealtaine counting calendar.

This will permanently hold them onto the calendar, and you will only untie loose bows made in them for practical use.

Now take the poster board and draw small symbols of the season such as hearts, balefires, flowers, or eggs, and cut them out to make a template from which to trace these symbols on contrasting pieces of felt.

Make as many of these as you like, then cut them out and glue them around the border of the calendar. Next, glue the poem at the top.

At the four corners, and under the poem, tie on the six bells with the yarn. This gives the calendar a festive look, and it will jingle when used.

The principle behind it is simple: untie a button from it every night before bedtime, starting twenty-four nights prior to Bealtaine Eve (night of April 7). These calendars are as delightful to look at as they are to use. Appendix V: Sabbat Calendars offers additional ideas for poems, and instructions for making calendars for all the Sabbats.

Celtic pagans once decorated for Bealtaine with much the same frenzy as people today decorate for Christmas. Greenery, flowers, and other symbols of spring were brought into cottages and homes and placed around doors and on hearths. Wreaths, those ever-present symbols of the Wheel of the Year, were gaily festooned with ribbons and flowers. Occasionally a flowered wreath is still seen topping a modern-day May Pole.

Chaplets and Flowers

Another form of Bealtaine wreaths were the leafy crowns woven by elders of the clan for the May King and May Queen. In an ancient Frankish tradition May was the month to celebrate womanhood, motherhood, and the Goddesses, and it is associated with the Anglo-Celtic crowning of the May Queen. This practice still flourishes in rural Anglo-Celtic areas, and the "royalty for a day" idea is still used in modern May Day celebrations. It is derived from the custom of having a young lass and lad perform the Great Rite within the Bealtaine circle. The May King and Queen were ritually crowned with these chaplets of flowers.

In today's covens, most participants wear these to the celebration. You can easily make a chaplet of your own out of artificial flowers that will last for years. At a craft or hobby shop, purchase a dozen or so small white roses with wire stems, a large spool of green florist's tape, and several yards of white ribbon.

Begin by arranging the flowers in a small circle. A diameter of about nine inches easily fits most heads. Allow the flower stems to overlap each other as much as needed. When the flowers are spaced the way you want them, begin twisting the stems one around the other so that the circle holds together. Handling it carefully, begin wrapping up the woven stems with the florist's tape. This will not only hold the stems in place, but will give the illusion of natural greenery. Tie the ribbon into a nice bow and attach it to the back side of the chaplet, letting the ends trail down your back.

Florists can make a chaplet of either real or artificial flowers for you, too. Headdresses are frequently requested for spring weddings and are easy for these professionals to quickly put together. Prices vary depending upon the type and number of flowers you choose to use. Roses are the traditional flowers chosen for Bealtaine chaplets.

In Rome, the cult of Flora, Goddess of Flowers, focused heavily on the symbolic meaning of flowers. This knowledge spread across Europe and was

*May is the month to celebrate womanhood, motherhood, and the
Goddesses. A carry-over from old pagan traditions, chaplets of flowers
are still used by pagans celebrating Bealtaine today.*

nearly lost until it was heartily revived by Victorians who were very conscious of flower symbolism. Following is a list of flower meanings. These are
not magickal or medicinal uses, but the hidden meanings assigned to them
by the cult of Flora, with a few nineteenth century modifications.

Flower	Meaning
Azaleas	Nearness
Bachelor Buttons	Work, Individuality
Buttercup	Friendship
Bluebells	Protection
Camellia	Company, Gatherings
Clematis	Security, Steadfastness
Cowslip	Secrets
Crocus	Birth, Rebirth

Flower	Meaning
Daffodills	Communication of secrets
Daisy	Simplicity
Hawthorn	Divination
Heather	Powerful woman
Heliotrope	Wellness and vitality
Honeysuckle	Fertility
Honesty	Honesty
Iris	Frail but hearty
Jasmine	Night rendezvous
Lady's Slipper	Wealth
Lily	Purity, Life
Lily of the Valley	Death, Change
Lupin	Passion
Magnolia	Unfolding events
Morning	Glory, Quickness, First
Mum	Affection
Myrtle	Remembrance
Orchid	Promises kept
Pansy	Weakness
Petunia	Gentleness, shyness
Primrose	Modesty, guardianship
Queen	Anne Lace, Gentleness, Quiet strength
Rhododendron	In waiting
Rose, Red	Love, Fidelity
Rose, Pink	Youth
Rose, Yellow	Infidelity
Rose, White	Silence
Snapdragons	Power, Man
Sunflower	Power, Strength, Watchfulness
Snowdrops	Children
Tulips	Constancy
Verbena	Motherhood
Violets, Purple	Fidelity
Violets, White	Betrayal
Water Lily	Other-worldliness, Dreams
Wintersweet	Eternity

Another Bealtaine symbol is the May Basket full of fresh flowers. Baskets are symbols of sacred marriage. On the macrocosmic level this is the union of the Goddess and God, and on the microcosmic level it is the union of female and male. Readers of Lynn Andrews' books on modern shamanism may recall in her first book, *Medicine Woman*, that her quest was to capture the elusive "marriage basket," a symbol of wholeness of being.

May is also sheep-shearing time in the northern hemisphere. All that wool has to be put to practical use, just as it was in the past. The spinning and weaving of wool were long seen as sacred acts, and are also synonymous terms with making magick. This idea came from the belief in some cultures that the Goddess spun, rather than birthed, all things into being. Numerous folk songs with pagan meanings grew up around the acts of spinning and weaving, many of them still with us. One of the best-known is a song from old England called "Sarasponda." The nonsense syllables seek to mimic the

A May basket full of fresh flowers sits upon the hearth at Bealtaine.
The May basket symbolizes sacred marriage and the union of male and female.

sound of a spinning wheel, but when you listen, you can hear the old praises sung to the life-spinning Goddess. Words like "ador-ay-o" and "boon-day" clearly reflect the modern words such as "adore," "boon," and "birthday."

The Sun Wheel also has its special meaning and use at this Sabbat, just as it does in the others. The Scottish Sword Dance, traditionally performed at Bealtaine and at weddings, was danced over two crossed swords that resemble a Sun Wheel. In this case each spoke of the wheel represents a male and a female who are sacredly united by the ritual dance. Crossroads, another Sun Wheel symbol, were often visited at Bealtaine in England, where pagans used to say you could get a glimpse of the Goddess. Evidence of this belief remains in the English nursery rhyme "Banbury Cross."

RIDE A COCKHORSE TO BANBURY CROSS,
TO SEE A FINE LADY UPON A WHITE HORSE.
WITH RINGS ON HER FINGERS AND BELLS ON HER TOES,
SHE SHALL HAVE MUSIC WHEREVER SHE GOES.

The cockhorse is the besom ridden over the fields for fertility, the bells on the toes are the bells of the Morris Dancers, the Lady is the Goddess, and the music is the praises sung to her.

Nature Provides the Answers

With the onset of spring, individuals began looking outdoors for their spiritual fulfillment, and it was a natural time to use nature for divinatory rites. In Europe these took the form of nature walks, when people would wander through natural settings with their minds focused on one issue or question and would look to nature to provide the answers.

The Native Americans held such events, called Vision Quests in their tradition, in high regard. They would ritually prepare and fast for several days before going off into the wilderness to seek visions as to the course their lives were taking. Often the answer would come to them in animal form. Called totem animals, they gave answers to the seeker based upon the charateristics they possessed.

You can also do a spring Vision Quest, either in the wild or a meditative state, and interpret the basic animal meanings for yourself. The following is a list of the most commonly seen totem animals and what they may mean.

Animal

Meaning

Animal	Meaning
Ant	Prodigious worker who may be telling you to be more industrious in order to solve your problems.
Badger	Will fight to the death to defend what is his. He may be telling you that you should fight, not run or give in.
Bear	To the Native Americans, an archetypal symbol of strength and plenty. If you see a bear while Vision Questing you may be being told to look inside yourself to tap into the many resources you already have at hand.
Cat	Night creatures who move cautiously and silently with a seeming disregard for all other creatures. Act like the cat to solve your difficulties; a little detachment never hurts.
Chameleon	A chameleon can adapt to anything. Seeing one may signify that you cannot change your problem, but must adapt yourself to its reality.
Cougar	Like a cat, only more powerful. If you see a cougar you may be being led to a course of quiet power.
Coyote	The archetypal trickster in the Native American tradition, one whose appearance is not always what it seems. These canines are clever and sly and possess a wonderful sense of humor. To solve your problem, you should adopt coyote's sense of humor and be clever and resourceful.
Dog	No animal is more loyal to its pack or to its humans than a dog. When you see a dog your key words to interpreting it is "undying loyalty."
Eagle	Sees all things from the vantage point of height. From this perspective he can make informed decisions as to his course of action in any situaton. When you see an eagle, you need to get more facts before acting.

Fox	A sly dog not unlike the coyote. But a fox knows when to retreat and hide, and live to fight another day.
Gopher	Hard to track and kill because it has so many well-planned ways to get away. One gopher colony may have as many as fifty tunnels down which to escape danger. Think of this maze of possibilities when you see a gopher.
Horse	A symbol of power and endurance. Stamina will be required in order to move forward.
Lizard	Amazing regenerative powers. When it loses a tail, it simply grows another. Like the lizard, you may have to reform in order to continue on.
Owl	Symbol of age and wisdom, but interpreting its presence is not easy. An owl may be telling you to trust in your own wisdom, or to seek out the wisdom of someone whom you trust. Only you can decide which it is to be.
Rabbit	Acutely aware of everything going on around it. Its nose is always sniffing and long ears are always alert for sounds of trouble.
Raccoon	A wonderfully agile animal. The best locks and containers cannot keep it out when he makes up his mind he wants something. You will probably need to avail yourself of this same tenacity to move out of your difficult situation.
Snake	Symbolizes new life, reincarnation, and changability because of the annual shedding of its skin. If you see a snake, think of change and newness, and of emerging from your problem as a different person from the one who went before.
Squirrel	The hoarder of the animal kingdom. All year long he stores up food in times of plenty for the times of famine he knows lie ahead. Be like the diligent squirrel—don't be wasteful, but save your resources for when they are truly needed.

Wolf
Very social animals, they look after each other and care deeply for the welfare of all the members of their pack. They pick mates when they are young whom they remain with all their lives. The keywords when you see wolves are "fidelity" and "take care of your own."

Keep in mind that this list is only a starting point. Only you can accurately interpret the many symbols that come to you. Begin with this list as a loose frame of reference, and then add to and subtract from it as you have your own experiences.

The Carefree Sabbat

Bealtaine is a joyous, lusty, carefree Sabbat. Our pagan ancestors took time out from tending their fields to celebrate the day. Parties of all kinds, whether for pagans or non-pagans, should be part of the observance.

A May Day party would probably delight your older friends for whom, chances are, such simple spring pleasures have not been experienced since childhood. They may enjoy weaving the May Pole with you and help you honor the old deities. Use paper wedding bells found in gift shops as home decorations in honor of the sacred marriage of the deities. Sing old folk songs with pagan meanings such as "Coming Through the Rye" or "La Primavera."

Whether you have a May Pole for your Morris Dances or not, Bealtaine is an excellent time to host a folk dance party to celebrate the full flowering of spring. Most people respond readily to the idea of an old-fashioned square dance. If you ask, you may be surprised to discover how many people in your acquaintance know one or more popular folk dances. For instance, the Virginia Reel is taught in many junior high school physical education classes and most people remember it fairly well. You can also rent or buy records and tapes which have the calls already on them so that all you have to do is follow the instructions. You can also go to your local library, bookstore, or video outlet and ask for books and tapes that teach simple folk dances. To give this dance a more pagan flavor, dancers can tie bells to their heels in the manner of the old Morris Dances.

You might wish to celebrate Bealtaine as the Floralia and adopt some of the lovely Tyrolian customs into your own celebrations. Whether you are with a pagan coven or just in a gathering of friends and family honoring the day, you can have a May Day party featuring delicate wines, Italian folk dances, alpine music, and lots of flowers for decorations. If you know of a couple who is about to announce their engagement, this would be the perfect time to do it. Encourage them to follow the Tyrolian custom of having flowers presented and accepted to publicly signify the agreement between them. Then crown them as May King and Queen and allow them to lead the May Pole dance.

Bealtaine is a time for feasting, rejoicing, frivolity, and celebration. No solemnity is permitted. It is a time to look outward and forward, a yearly re-enactment of the primal joy all creatures and plants of the earth feel at spring, after a long cold winter's rest.

⇚ 7 ⇛

Midsummer:
The Summer Solstice
June 22

ost cultures of the northern hemisphere acknowledge Midsummer in some ritualized manner. In pagan India, Midsummer was the principal festival of the entire year. The holiday has been called by many names, including Litha or Vestalia in ancient Rome, Gathering Day in Wales, Feill-Sheathain in Scotland, Alban Heflin in the Anglo-Saxon tradition, All Couple's Day in Greece, and the Feast of Epona in ancient Gaul. In Scandinavia it is celebrated at a later date and is called Thing-Tide, a day when communities gather in a sort of town meeting, as they have since ancient times, to conduct business before celebration and feasting.

Midsummer marks the time of the Summer Solstice, the longest day of the year, the height of the sun's power. And though the hottest days of summer still lie ahead, from this point onward we enter the waning year, and each day the sun will recede from the skies a little earlier.

At Midsummer the Goddess is heavy with pregnancy, just as the earth is pregnant with the coming harvest's bounty and the cattle in the field await calving—but the fertility rites continue. Just as a human baby can be miscarried or born blighted, our pagan ancestors knew that the same was true for their crops and animals, and Midsummer rituals focused on nurturing new life both in the ground and in human and animal wombs. But motherhood is not the sole focus of this Sabbat. For every mother there is a father,

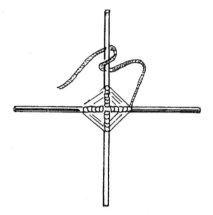

Weaving a God's Eye

and so it is in paganism. The sun is at his peak in the sky, the Sun God at the peak of his life, and we celebrate his approaching fatherhood.

Because this is a Sabbat which glorifies the sun, and the sun is a symbol of protection, many pagans choose to make protective amulets in the week before the Sabbat that are later empowered over the Midsummer balefire. Some witches choose to bury their protective amulets each Midsummer Eve and construct new ones. Rue, rowan, and basil, tied up in a gold or white cloth, is a good protective trio that can be carried in your pocket year round. A few cinnamon sticks tied over the door of your home is another good protective charm. Or you might search for a special stone that represents protection to you. It might be golden white like the sun, or in the shape of a phallus, or may look like an eye watching over you.

Another sun amulet made for protection that uses the eye symbolism is the South American God's Eye, which has its origins with the native people of that continent. These amulets are made from two sticks placed across each other to form an equilateral cross. Colored yarn is then wound around them to form the body of the Eye. By alternating the colors of yarn the finished product does look like a stylized eye, and its four points symbolize the two solstices and two equinoxes. The Native South Americans used them both for decoration and as protective talismans.

To make your own God's Eyes, you will need quarter-inch dowels available at craft and hardware stores (popsicle sticks work well, too!), a pair of scissors, and a collection of colored yarns. Cut the dowels into lengths approximately ten inches long. Holding them together at their centers so that they form a cross, begin wrapping your first yarn color around the center to stabilize the dowels.

Now begin slowly working your design outward. Wrap the yarn completely around one point of the dowel, then trail it over to the next point. Wrap the yarn around that dowel and, again, move on to the next point.

Periodically stop and push the yarn down against the center so that you have a tight weave. When you have wrapped the yarn within a half inch of the end of the dowels, stop and wrap the yarn several times tightly around

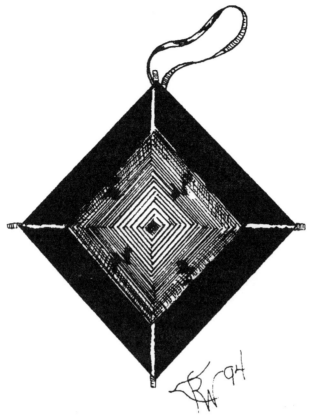

God's Eyes can be used as protective talismans or for decoration.

one point. You can then tie it off, leaving a loop from which it can hang.

God's Eyes can be made in any size, depending on how you want to use them. Larger ones can be used as blanket protection like a Native American Medicine Shield, and smaller ones in Yule colors make excellent Yule tree decorations and can symbolize the return of the sun. If they are decorative items to honor the sun, then your work is done. If they are to function as protective talismans, then you should be visualizing their purpose as you weave them and consecrate them to their purpose later on.

Another eye associated with Midsummer is the buckeye. Buckeyes, sometimes called horse chestnuts, are hard, leathery seed coverings that grow on soapberry trees in the upper Midwest and are ripe at Midsummer. Resembling eyes, these dark brown orbs, about three inches in diameter, have a single tan patch on one side. The Miami Native Americans held them sacred and used them as protective amulets. To them, these trees held the most sacred of tree spirits whose power could be harnessed to protect the tribe through the waning year from all harm. Usually they were gathered in bunches, hammered through, and strung together to make necklaces, something Midwestern children still do today. Buckeyes can also be hollowed out to make rings and other sun charms that can be charged to protect the wearer or to perform any other sun-related task such as prosperity, employment, or general good luck.

If you don't have access to real buckeyes you can make this edible version, a popular Midwestern confection, for your Sabbat festivities:

Buckeyes
(Makes about four dozen candies)

- 1 pound melted margarine
- 2½ pounds smooth peanut butter
- 3 pounds powdered sugar
- 36 ounces semi-sweet chocolate or chocolate chips
- 1 square cooking paraffin

The insides:

Mix the margarine, peanut butter, and powdered sugar together in a large mixing bowl. It will be thick and heavy. Roll the mixture into small balls about ¾-inch to an inch across.

Melt the chocolate (chocolate chips melt the best) in a double boiler with one section of paraffin. Dip the balls in the chocolate mixture three-quarters of the way so that they look like buckeyes. Lay them out on wax paper and let them set long enough to harden before eating.

The Sun Wheels you made at Imbolg should be prominently displayed at Midsummer. Hang them from your ceiling beams or place them on trees near your home. Decorate them, if you like, with gold and yellow ribbons or summer herbs.

Fire Symbolism

Though all eight of the Sabbats are in some way fire festivals, the element is most prominent at Midsummer. Fire is the most easily seen and immediately felt element of transformation. It can burn, consume, cook, shed light, or purify, and because of its heat, fire is most intimately associated with the hot Midsummer sun.

Because of the sun's obvious role at Midsummer, this was a time of fire rituals and fire magick throughout western Europe, and balefires still figure prominently at modern Midsummer rites. The Celts would light balefires all over their lands from sunset the night before Midsummer until sunset the next day. Around these flames the festivities and rituals would take place. The Old Norse word for balefire is "biiken," and is still used today in reference to the Midsummer fires.

In Scotland, the use of the cauldron, a Celtic symbol of life, death, and rebirth, is important to the Sabbat celebration that honors Cerridwen the Crone Goddess, who tends the cauldron. The cauldron is present to remind revelers that the sun is not truly dead, but will be reborn from this cauldron of rebirth from the Goddess, at Yule.

On the night after Midsummer, mock funerals were held in Greece and Rome for the now waning sun and for celebration of the start of the harvest season, another reminder that death is not final.

Processions to and from the ritual site were common at the warmer Sabbats, especially at Midsummer. The Norse especially loved lengthy processions and would gather together their animals, families, and lighted torches and parade through the countryside to the celebration site. There, their torches were placed into the ground around the sacred circle, often in lieu of balefires.

Two Christian holidays occur on or near Midsummer, both of which feature balefires, referred to as bonfires in these cases. One of these festivals is St. John's Day. This feast day was instituted at the insistence of Ireland's St. Patrick to occur just before Midsummer to draw attention away from the Sabbat celebration. Perhaps to discourage the pagan ways, patriarchal leaders in Ireland began a superstition which deemed this a very unlucky day, especially for one's animals. In a gross distortion of old folk beliefs, threats of faeries carting off prized stock and unsuspecting human revelers became an effective scare tactic to keep Midsummer festivals inside and away from the larger community. The other Christian holiday is Whitsunday.

Commonly called Whitsuntide, it is the fiftieth day after Easter. Bonfires once used to be lit to acknowledge this date, but this practice has since been replaced by candle services in nearly all British churches.

Most wild herbs are fully mature by Midsummer and this is the traditional time for gathering magickal and medicinal plants to dry and store for winter use. In Wales, Midsummer is called Gathering Day in honor of this practice. The Celtic Druids also gathered their sacred plants at Midsummer, especially their important and revered mistletoe, called "the golden bough," which they cut with a golden sickle reserved just for this event. When found on the sacred oak tree, it was especially valued, for it was believed to have been blessed by the God. Mistletoe was used in all sorts of healings, divinations, and magickal spells, and was believed to open locks, including a locked mind. But its appeal went far beyond the Celtic lands. Uses of and veneration for mistletoe are found in the folklore of Italy and France and even as far away as Japan. In Rome it was used to adorn the hearth fires of the celebration of Vestalia which signaled the rekindling of the home fires for the coming winter. Mistletoe was added to the "gris gris" (charm bags) of the Santeria and Voodoo cults, and the Swedes also gathered and displayed it on Midsummer Eve, knowing it was sacred to their Sun God, Balder, and to the Goddess Frigga.

Lavender is another Midsummer favorite, and is an aromatic herb that figures prominently in many British and Irish folk songs. Just the scent of it was once believed to be a strong catalyst to love magick. It is still burned at pagan handfastings and sought out as an aphrodisiac. Lavender in full flower was also used as a Midsummer incense to honor the deities as Parents-to-Be.

Vervain was also traditionally collected at Midsummer just before dawn, and pine cones gathered at Midsummer were considered powerful amulets for protection, fertility, and virility.

If you are gathering herbs from the wild, you will need a good book on botany to help you identify what you are harvesting. Unless you are an expert in herbalism, never ingest or burn any herb whose name, function, and side effects you are not completely familiar with. If you have planted an herb garden, you are ahead of the game since you should know exactly what the plants and their uses are.

Many pagan traditions insist that magickal herbs must be cut with a special, curved, white-handled knife commonly called a bolleen, but it is not necessary to have one to begin harvesting your magickal herbs. It is,

Dry herbs for thirty to ninety days in an undisturbed location.

however, a good idea to cut magick herbs with a knife that is only used for this purpose, but a plain kitchen knife purchased especially for your herbs works just as well. When cutting the herbs you will need a cloth to place them on, for it is essential that once cut, they not be allowed to touch the ground. The earth is a grounding force which absorbs energy, including that of your herbs. Magick herbs that touch the ground will have their power drained back into the earth. Take along a cloth of natural fabric in a neutral white or black upon which to lay the cut plants.

To put fresh herbs up to dry, you will need a space where they can hang undisturbed for several months. The best places are warm dry spots such as in your kitchen or near a fireplace. Attics are good choices too, but avoid basements which tend to be damp and cool most of the year. Bundle the herbs together in manageable groups and tie them together at their base with a piece of twine. String a long length of twine across your hearth, kitchen ceiling, or wherever else you are going to hang your herbs, and tie your bundles to this. They will be ready in thirty to ninety days, depending on your climate. The warmer and drier it is, the faster they will cure.

Seas of colorful wildflowers are in bloom all over the northern hemisphere at Midsummer, and many of these are also magickal or medical herbs. Collect them and hang them to dry in the same way you would other herbs. Or you can collect them and press them in books to dry. Later they can be identified and even framed for your enjoyment. Or you can place them on heavy paper, tape plastic wrap around them, and punch holes in the sides to bind them into loose-leaf folders that can house an entire collection of Midsummer wildflowers. You can use this as an identification guide for future finds.

Below is a list of commonly found herbs and wildflowers and their meanings and uses. Remember that when using herbs for medicinal purposes that they are not a substitute for modern medical care, but rather a support for these treatments. If you are ill, see a doctor, preferably one who is sympathetic to herbal preparations as an aid to his or her own prescriptions.

Herb	Meanings/Uses
Agrimony	Protection, Banishing evil forces
Alfalfa	Prosperity, Fertility, Strengthens cardiac muscles
Apple	Love magick, Divinations, Goddess symbol, Fertility, Helps prevents certain types of cancers
Anise	Protection, Natural cough medicine
Barley	Protection, Healing, Fertility
Basil	Protection, Used to purify circles, As a tea for female health, Kills internal parasites
Bay	Purification, Promotes vitality, Symbol of the Newborn God
Blackberry	Sacred to Goddess Brigid, Prosperity, Eaten for diseases of stomach, Take tea to treat diarrhea
Black cohosh	Helps prevent and treat prostate cancer, Lowers blood pressure, Helps relieve menstrual cramps
Bonset	Exorcism, As a tea to help heal broken bones, Helps fight off colds and flu
Catnip	Drink the tea to promote sleep, Use to attract a familiar, Love spells, Anti-spasmodic
Chamomile	Drink tea to soothe stomach, Prosperity

Cinnamon	Protection, Purification, Helps prevent infection
Clove	Protection, Pain killer, Natural antibiotic
Clover	Fidelity, Prosperity, Carry for success at any endeavor, A symbol of the Triple Goddess
Comfrey	Purification, Healing, Helps heal open wounds, Aids digestion
Dandelion	Strength, Making wishes, Past-life work, Helps prevent many types of cancer, Eases PMS symptoms
Damiana	Sexual prowess, Energy
Echinacea	Called "Heal All" by Native Americans, Boosts immune system, Purification
Garlic	Protection, Healing, Exorcism, Taken daily it promotes health and vitality, Aids blood circulation, Lowers blood pressure, Natural antibiotic
Goldenseal	Prosperity, Relief of headaches
Gorse	Protection
Hibiscus	Love spells, Lust
Holly	Protection of children, Symbol of the waning year
Honeysuckle	Prosperity, Employment
Hyssop	Protection, Drink tea as a general tonic
Irish moss	Sacred to many European Sea Gods, Prosperity, Luck, Psychicism
Lilac	Past-life work, Exorcism, Psychicism
Marigold	Protection, Psychicism
Mugwort	Induces prophetic dreams, Protects travelers, Aids astral projection, Fertility, Often used to clean magickal tools
Nuts	Fertility, Divination
Oak	Strength, Symbol of the waxing year, Fertility, Prosperity, Protection, Sacred to Horned God
Orris	Aids astral projection, Makes excellent scrying incense

Herb	Meanings/Uses
Parsley	Contains natural antihistamine, Reduces fever, Natural diuretic
Peppermint	Aids digestion, Purification
Persimmon	Exorcism, Prosperity
Pine	Money matters, Fertility, Protection
Ragwort	Seeing faeries, Astral projection
Red clover	Rich natural source of iron
Rosemary	Love, Healing, Purification, Increases mental prowess
Rue	Spiritual cleansing
Sarsaparilla	Prosperity, Healing
Thistle	Protection, Used in banishing spells
Tobacco	Purification, To honor deities in Native American traditions
Tomato	Love, Protection from faeries
Valerian	Psychicism, Astral projection, Past-life work, Protection, Tea induces sleep
Violet	Healing
Wheat	Fertility, Prosperity
White oak bark	Use as a douche to treat vaginal infections
Willow Bark	Pain killer, Anti-inflammatory, Reduces fever
Wintergreen	Healing, Protection, Stomach soother
Yucca	Protection

Another way of enjoying the lush foliage of summer is to blueprint leaves. These not only make a lovely collection, but can serve as your own field guide when out gathering herbs and other wild foliage for magick, medicine, or ritual. This is a perfect way to introduce children to the beauty of nature and to teach tree lore. My father taught this craft for thirty years at a children's summer day camp he ran, and it is one of the best remembered camp crafts by his former students.

For blueprinting you will need blueprint paper, usually found in hardware or office supply stores. Get the standard notebook-sized 8½ x 11 paper for manageability, or be prepared to cut larger sheets down to size. You will also need ammonia, a few cotton balls, a gallon-sized glass jar, a piece of stiff cardboard the same size or slightly larger than your blueprint paper, and a piece of glass or clear plastic the same size as the cardboard. You will also need a bright, sunny day and a few fresh green leaves. Make sure you pick leaves with interesting veins in them as every lovely detail of the leaf will show up on the blueprint.

Keep the blueprint paper out of the sun or other bright light or you will ruin your results.

First, prepare the glass jar where the blueprints will be developed. Take a couple of cotton balls and soak them with ammonia. They don't have to be wet, just saturated. Place them in the bottom of the gallon glass jar and snugly replace the lid.

Inside, or in the shade, set a piece of the blueprint paper down on top of the heavy cardboard, then arrange the leaves you have chosen in a pattern on top of the paper. When you are happy with the design, place the glass or clear plastic over it to hold it firmly in place.

Still holding the glass, paper, leaves, and cardboard firmly together, walk into the sunlight and let it fall on your design for a moment. Usually thirty to forty-five seconds is long enough. You will be able to see the paper yellow slightly and should be able to get a sense of when it has had enough exposure. Be careful not to let your fingers overlap the design because they, like the leaves, will leave an image on your blueprint, only it will appear as an ugly smudge on the edge of your design.

Go back into the shade or indoors and quickly and carefully remove the paper. Roll it up gently, and slip it into the glass jar, recapping it afterward. Now watch as the ammonia develops the blueprint. This only takes a few seconds. Remove the print and, if it has been done correctly, you should see every intricate detail of the leaf in the blueprint.

Identify the leaves and keep them in a loose-leaf notebook or storage box to enjoy and to help you identify other leaves. This not only makes a convenient field guide, but it is a great school or 4-H project for children.

In the rugged, mountainous lands of the Scottish Highlands, western Ireland, and Norway, Midsummer herb gatherers usually carried with them a walking stick called a staff. These often were also pagan magickal tools that served the same function as a sword, athame, or wand. Without a doubt the most well-known walking stick is the Irish *shillelagh* which is carried by Irishmen and Leprechauns alike and is traditionally made from the wood of the sacred blackthorn tree. It is interesting to note that in the English tradition blackthorn is not a sacred tree, but one which is cursed. Staves are never made from it. Those who follow the English tradition prefer ones crafted of oak or birch. This is merely a cultural difference and you should use whichever you prefer.

The Teutons ritually gathered ash sticks at Midsummer to use to make wands and staves, believing that this was the same wood that made up Yggdrasil, the Norse tree of life, which both represents and permeates the entire universe.

The easiest way to have your own walking staff is to find one lying in the woods. They need to be four to five feet long, sturdy enough to bear your weight, and thin enough for you to easily grasp. If you cannot find one, or want a more personal version, you can fashion one from a four-foot dowel. Pick a dowel one to two inches across—whichever feels comfortable in your grip—and round the ends with sandpaper. (Hint: an electric sander is just as appropriate and will save you many hours of tiring work.) You can then paint pagan symbols, zodiac colors, sigils, magickal words, etc., on it according to your own preference. Mine is stained a pale oak to represent strength. On it are painted the words of the Irish proverb, "Ni bhionn an rath ach mar a mbionn an smacht," which means, "There is no luck except where there is discipline." This is a reminder to me that one must work hard for magick and its rewards.

Another staff less commonly used is called a stang, which is a two-pronged staff. The easiest way to get one is to find one that has naturally fallen from an old tree. You can also fashion one of papier-maché with a little effort, or if you have the means, you can commission a metalsmith to make one for you.

Some English covens use a stang to mark the ritual entry and exit point of their circle, and see it as symbolizing a portal between the world of form and that of spirit. The stang's origin is in ancient Rome where it represented the two-faced God, Janus, for whom our month of January is named. Janus' two faces looked simultaneously into the past and into the future—or into the worlds of form and spirit—and is a fitting portal to any circle which is, in itself, a meeting place between two existences.

Whichever staff you prefer, it is a good idea to carry it when venturing into the woods. It not only can help you walk over difficult terrain, but it can

Walking sticks.

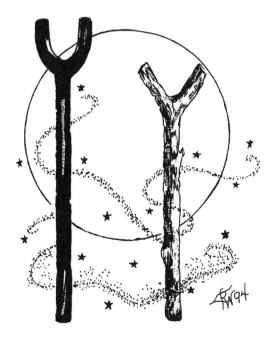

Stangs.

be an instant magickal tool if you wish to stop and do a small ritual, and it can help protect you from wild animals. You may encounter skunks, bats, squirrels, or raccoons in the woods, all of which are prone to having rabies. Keep in mind that no animal will attack a human unless it is very frightened or sick, but it is nice to have your staff along just in case.

Of all the Sabbats this is one which was most often celebrated during the daylight hours rather than at night, and our pagan ancestors took advantage of the long day by beginning their festivities early. It is not surprising that a traditional Midsummer event is to start the day by waking early enough to greet the rising sun. In western Ireland and Scotland this was commonly done by family or clan groups who would take with them a rooster, an animal long sacred to the Sun Gods of Europe. They would greet the Sun with the same joyous crows as the bird. In Lappland where the sun doesn't set at Midsummer, entire communities would climb to the top of the highest mountain to watch as the sun lowered itself, skimmed the heights of the distant hills, and rose triumphantly again.

Some traditions began looking to the coming harvest at their Midsummer rites. Eastern Woodland Indians of the United States did the Calumet Dance which asked their Gods to bless the upcoming harvest—particularly the corn crop which would be reaped at Lughnasadh, or Green Corn Day. The dance was done by two males, warriors picked for their bravery and strength. They carried feathered staves which represented male and female genitalia. In the American Southwest, the Navajo held a nine-day feast celebrating the sun's return and did a dance called Yeibichai, or the Night Chant Dance, which lasted from dusk to dawn. The purpose was to produce rain for parched desert crops.

In Korea fruit trees were blessed with a mixture of earth, cow dung, and figs in a form of sympathetic magick that would ensure their successful harvest. The idea was that, thus blessed, they would not wither with the dying of summer. Young couples drank this mixture for fertility, and it was also used to anoint the sick at Midsummer festivities.

In the United States summer squash are usually ready to eat by Midsummer, and they were a delicacy introduced to Europeans by Native Americans. These hearty vegetables sustain abuse from even the most inept gardeners and grow in abundance. Look for new and interesting ways to prepare them for the Midsummer feast—like this one.

Zucchini Casserole
(Serves six to eight)

5 zucchini
2 eggs, beaten
1 cup sour cream
1 cup sharp cheddar cheese, grated
2 cups mozzarella cheese, grated
1 teaspoon basil
½ teaspoon ground oregano
¾ teaspoon garlic powder
¼ teaspoon salt
⅛ teaspoon ground rosemary
½ teaspoon black pepper
1 cup fresh or canned mushrooms
1 small chopped tomato
½ cup bacon bits or ham cubes
2 cups prepared croutons
¼ cup parmesan cheese, grated

Preheat oven to 350° F. Mix all of the ingredients together in a large mixing bowl. Place the mixture in a lightly greased 9 x 13 baking pan and bake for 30 minutes.

Faery folk are active at Midsummer just as they are at the Bealtaine Sabbat. While more taboos exist concerning faeries at Bealtaine, many protection lores grew up around Midsummer when faeries, like the sun, were thought to be at the height of their power. Driving children and animals around or over the Midsummer balefire was thought to offer protection, especially to animals whose meat and milk might be soured by mischievous faeries. Faery rades—ritualized trooping of faeries—have been seen and reported frequently at Midsummer, and protective herbs were hung on individuals thought susceptible to being carried off by them. In England, dancing around a mulberry bush or tree was a potent faery protection both at Midsummer and at Yule, and was the source of the children's nursery rhyme, "Here We Go 'Round the Mulberry Bush."

Leaving out food for the Little People.

Faeries, like other beings, need food for sustenance and, in faery tales around the world, a common thread of nourishment is prevalent. Leaving out food for the Little People at Midsummer is as common a practice in some places as setting out bird feed in winter. Milk, water, butter, honey, wine, and bread are the most commonly sought-after foods, especially fresh, creamy milk. In Cornwall and in western Russia it is an old folk custom never to scold a child who has spilled milk, for this should be seen as a gift to the faeries and scolding would make it seem as if it were given grudgingly. This may even be the origin of the popular doggerel, "Don't cry over spilled milk."

Formal libations to faery folk can be performed in place of simply leaving out food and drink. A libation is a ritually-given portion of your food or drink, offered before you partake of it. For example, if you wish to offer your resident faeries a bit of your wine, raise the glass and say so, then pour out a portion on the ground or put some in a small bowl that will later be set out for them. Or break off part of your bread or cake and set it out in a setting where they can find it. Never toss a faery offering out haphazardly, as you might for an animal. Faeries consider this disrespectful.

Travelers on Midsummer night had to carry extra protection and stop along their way to perform prescribed protective tasks. The most common practice was to carry a stone for a few miles, then stop, and add it to an existing pile left by other travelers. This was an effort to embody all the evil that may have been following you in the stone, and then leave it behind. Today in Britain and Ireland similar stone traveling spells are still used. In Germany, one avoided traveling in the many enchanted forests at Midsummer, and numerous stories abound in German folklore of unwise persons who ventured into the woods at Midsummer, never to emerge. Even today the Black Forest, the best known enchanted wood, is still avoided by many on this day, though pagans often roam freely in it at this time.

Animal blessings were frequently conducted at Midsummer, and it became a Celtic pagan practice to take Familiars and beloved pets into the circle for a special protection blessing. Individuals whose livelihoods depend on livestock would bring in a token animal from their herds to receive the blessings. In some areas the blessings conclude with the animals being passed through or over the smoke of the balefire.

This would also be a good time to present your pet with a special talisman of his or her own to wear on its collar. If you are talented at carving wood or metal you can carve a small charm for your pet. The design is up to you—whatever signals protection and love to your own mind. You might want to put a traditional pentagram on one side. On the other you might carve a heart, a knot, or a Sun Wheel. Another idea might be to buy or borrow a wood-burning wand to make a wooden talisman. These wands have pointed tips and produce directed heat. All you have to do is draw your design and it will be burned into the wood by the wand point. Drill a small hole in the talisman and attach it to the pet's collar with an S hook available at any hardware store. And if your pet does not wear an I.D. tag, this is the time to get it one.

As a heavily-pregnant woman begins to lactate, so does the Mother Goddess, and Midsummer Sabbat rituals often substitute milk for wine or water. Magick rituals were frequently done just prior to this Sabbat in eastern Europe to ensure the continued milk production of their goat and cattle herds.

Human conception was as much of a concern to our pagan ancestors as that of animals, and Midsummer was the last Sabbat until spring when obvious fertility imagery was used. Several folk magick grimoires advise a woman to squat naked in her garden on Midsummer night if she wishes to conceive. Others suggest that menstruating women walk through fields so that fertility energy might be passed between them.

Menstruating women were pressed into service to bleed onto the fields. These customs came down from the time when the male role in conception was unknown and most people throughout the world believed that the blood was what created life without any outside help. The menstrual taboos of the patriarchal religions stem directly from this awe of the female power of procreation, a power which made Goddess worship hard to eradicate.

Pieces of unburnt balefire wood were kept as powerful talismans of light during the ever-darkening waning year. They ensured the continued presence of the Sun God as his power waned, just as capturing a bobbing apple at Samhain ensured the Goddess' presence until Yule. It was also traditional to use nine different types of wood for the Midsummer fire. Nine is the traditional number symbolizing the moon (coming into paganism from Ceremonial Magick), and this may have been another way to bring the Goddess into this god-oriented Sabbat.

Because paganism seeks to balance the male and female aspects, it was considered fortuitous if a full moon was coincident with the Sabbat. The full moon is the moon phase associated with the Mother Goddess aspect, which is also the aspect of the Goddess at Midsummer. In some traditions, when this happens, men and women will meet separately to do their Midsummer rituals, each emphasizing their own sacred gender mysteries. Couples would also want to have intercourse on this magickal night in hopes of conception.

Wedding Bells Ring

June has been a traditional month for weddings. The reason often given is that many young people wish to marry at the end of their schooling, which usually falls in June. For most ancient societies there was no formal schooling, much less ending in June. It was simply considered unlucky to marry during May because it was the month of the sacred marriage of God and Goddess at Bealtaine; it was considered a time during which no mortal should marry. In early Ireland it was common practice (one that came after women's clan groups were broken up and families became more like what we know now) to wait until a woman was pregnant to marry. Courting usually began at Yule so there were numerous conceptions by late spring. Young

June is the traditional month to wed in Europe and the United States.

men and their pregnant women then married at the first opportunity, which was June.

A children's nursery rhyme from old England echoes the beliefs of the Celts and Italians. The May and June sections of the ditty read like this:

… Marry in the month of May
Most surely you will rue the day.
Marry in June when roses grow
And happiness you'll always know.…

Ireland was not the only place such sacred marriage was honored. In the Italian province of Sardinia, where Midsummer has been supplanted by St. John's Day, it is traditional to hold mock marriages, a carry-over from the time when mass marriages were performed in June.

Many of today's marriage customs have pagan origins. The shared wedding cake, tossed rice, and flowers are all old bits of fertility magick. The white dress equates the bride with the Virgin Goddess; the wedding ring is symbolic of the magick circle; the garter is a wreath; and carrying the bride over the threshold is a piece of old sympathetic magick which hopes to bring about both fertility and prosperity.

The daisy picking chant, "S/he loves me not, S/he loves me so," was another mate divination practiced with the abundance of summer wild-flowers. Focus on your loved one and then, while plucking the petals from the flowers in a clockwise motion, say alternately, "S/he loves me not, S/he loves me so." Whichever sentence coincides with the last petal picked is your answer.

In Nordic and Germanic traditions this is a night for general divination and vision questing, a time when the power of the sun makes it easy for humans to access the unseen worlds. To this day Midsummer is a prominent Scandinavian holiday, and prophetic dreams play a large part of their folklore. The Danes used to place the toxic herb, St. John's Wort, under their pillows to induce these dreams. Mugwort is just as potent, and non-toxic, and used by Celts and the English in the same manner.

Making a Dream Pillow

To make a dream pillow to enhance your own psychic dreams, take the herbs you wish to use (usually mugwort, but lavender and lemongrass are also good), a needle, a small square of blue or purple fabric, and sew your own. Take a square piece of cotton cloth about four inches across and eight inches long, and fold it over so it is it appears equal in size all around. Sew up three sides of the pillow, leaving the fourth opened.

Then turn the pillow inside out, stuff in the herbs, and sew up the final side. Be sure to clearly visualize your goal as you do this, for it is the essence of magick. When you are finished take it to bed and place it under the top of your pillowcase where its fragrance will reach you. Scent is a powerful stimulant for the subconscious. Then, before going to sleep, fix in your mind what you wish to dream about, and recite a short verse like this:

> Mugwort cross the psychic sea,
> Prophetic dreams now come to me.

Chant this over and over until you lull yourself into a light sleep. Have a notebook and pen ready to jot down any impressions or dreams you have upon waking. Do this before you even take your morning stretch, as dreams fade as quickly after waking as smoke in the wind.

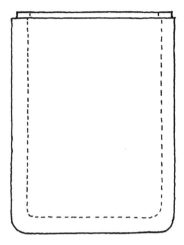

Stitch your dream pillow on three sides before turning it inside-out.

The Oak King and the Holly King who battled for supremacy at Yule fight again at Midsummer. This time it is the Oak King who is slain and the Holly King, king of the waning year, who now reigns, gaining in power and strength until Yule. The robin, symbol of the Oak King, is seen less and less, and the wren, symbol of the Holly King, is more prevalent as summer winds down.

Other cultures had similar ways to symbolize the death of the waxing year and the birth of the waning. In southern England there was an old tradition practiced until early in this century called Jack-in-the-Green. Jack-in-the-Green was a man chosen from the community to dress like a verdant, green bush and dance through the village. At the end of his merriment on Midsummer night he is symbolically killed in order to release the spirit of summer so that the waning year may begin. In eastern Europe milk was poured onto the ground to symbolize the end of the growing phase and the start of the harvesting phase of the agricultural year.

Well Dressing is another ancient Midsummer ritual activity known to the Anglo-Celtic traditions, and one still practiced in rural areas on this Sabbat. The day before Midsummer, women (usually young virgins, but sometimes young men also) would form a procession from their village or clan camp, and venture out to adorn the sacred wells. This was done to honor the spirits and deities of a well, to secure fresh and clean water for the next year, and to ensure fertility for the village, since the well is symbolic of the birth canal of the great Earth Mother Goddess. The wells were dressed with flowers, garlands, fine cloth, ribbons, and other finery.

You may want to use the time just after Midsummer to plant and bless the still-growing autumn vegetables. This is traditionally done on the first day after the Sabbat when the moon begins to wax again. Winter squash, pumpkins, and Indian corn do well in most regions and can be used as food, seasonal decoration, or in autumn Sabbat rituals.

Activities for the Midsummer Sabbat that can be pagan or include non-pagans are numerous. In honor of the Well Dressing rituals which you may be unable to do, you can have a swimming party with fire and water as the theme. Have a bonfire for roasting summer foods and gathering around, play water games, eat watermelon, and have a square dance.

Dream interpretation games can also be played without divulging your religious preference, unless you choose to do so. Dress yourself or someone else as a gypsy fortuneteller and have people tell their dreams for interpretation. This works best if you can find someone who is adept at dream work, but it is not necessary. You are celebrating a season more than anything else and it does not, and should not, have to be completely serious. You may be surprised at how insightful a novice fortuneteller may be.

Early summer brings people—all people—out in droves, and craft fairs abound. Scour flea markets, craft fairs, and out-of-the-way country stores for pagan items or items not usually used these days that would add a nice touch to your pagan life. Old kitchen utensils are especially nice finds as you can use them the same way others did in the past. Their use often requires more effort than we with our modern kitchens are used to, and therefore they are good for kitchen magick because they consume time and energy that can be focused into magickal goals.

Food for the Midsummer Sabbat or party can include any yellow or orange food—sun colors—which gives you plenty to choose from. Make the All-Purpose Holiday Cookie recipe on Page 66 and cut the dough into round circles, or in the shape of eight-pointed stars. Color the frosting yellow or orange and top them with gold sprinkles to represent the light of the sun. Or take food coloring and, with the tip of a sharp knife, trace an equilateral cross on top of the cookie to make the image of a Sun Wheel. You can also cut bell-shaped cookies to help frighten off Midsummer faeries.

Another Midsummer food that everyone likes is ice cream. Try making your own for this Sabbat. Get an old, crank-style ice cream maker and pour your energy into the end product to honor the sun. Flavoring the ice cream with mint is a good choice since it is an herb long associated with various Sun Gods.

Lemons, sacred both to the Full Moon Goddess and the Sun Gods, can be turned into a tasty pie for Midsummer. This is my mother's recipe.

Mom McCoy's Lemon Chess Pie
(Makes one nine-inch pie)

1 unbaked pie shell
2 cups granulated sugar
1 tablespoon flour
½ teaspoon cornstarch
1 tablespoon corn meal
4 eggs
¼ cup milk
¼ cup butter or margarine, softened
½ cup real lemon juice
¼ cup grated lemon peel

Preheat oven to 375° F. Place unbaked pie shell in a deep-dish pie pan.

Mix the sugar, flour, cornstarch, and cornmeal, then add the eggs, milk, butter or margarine, lemon juice, and lemon peel. Beat until smooth. Pour the mixture into the pie shell and bake for about 40 minutes, or until the top is golden brown. Top with orange slices for an added solar touch. (Note: A second crust can be used to cover the pie before baking. Pinch it to the edges of the bottom crust to make a tight seal. Make several cuts in the top crust to allow heat to escape.)

⇥ ⇤

Modern music often uses the imagery of the sun in its lyrics, and this music, either recorded or printed, is easy to obtain. For either general Midsummer parties or Sabbat pagan ritual gatherings, think about using the songs "Morning Has Broken," "Here Comes the Sun," "Sunshine on My Shoulders," "You are My Sunshine," or "You Are the Sunshine of My Life." Music has long been known to have profound effects on human moods, and any of these will help set the tone for your celebration.

Summer family reunions, regaining their popularity in America, grew out of the tribal and clan gatherings that took place at Midsummer. These ancient families came together to take strength and unity from the peak of the sun. You can paganize your gathering by emphasizing your clan or family name and its history. If you are a Scottish family, sport your tartan. If you are Norwegian build your party around a Viking theme. If you are Greek or Jewish, do the old dances of your people, many of which have pagan significance.

One of the best Midsummer activities for pagans is the International Pagan Spirit Gathering, a five day ritual and magickal event held annually at Circle Sanctuary, a large nature spirituality preserve in southwestern Wisconsin. The gathering attracts several hundred pagans each year from all traditions. While at Circle, pagans can participate in Sabbat rituals, attend workshops, exchange gifts and ideas, meet and network with other pagans, and commune with nature. They also hold life-cycle events. Make arrangements in advance as there are usually several legally ordained pagan priests/esses in attendance whose time is quickly booked. Making reservations for the PSG well in advance is a must. And if Midsummer is not a good time for you to get away, Circle sponsors gatherings at all the Sabbats and holds workshops and ritual events throughout the year. Appendix IV: Resources and Merchants Guide gives all the information you need to contact Circle.

Because of vacation schedules and weather conditions, many other pagan gatherings are held in summer. The best way to find out about them is to subscribe to one of the pagan periodicals. Again, Appendix IV can tell you how to subscribe.

The sun is now waning, and we move toward the culminating of the year—the harvests and the death of the God.

⇥ 8 ⇤

Lughnasadh
August 1 or 2

Lughnasadh (Loo-nahs-ah) is the first of the three harvest Sabbats. In Old Irish the word "Lunasa" (a variant spelling) means "August." It honors the Celtic Sun God, Lugh (Loo), but it is principally a grain festival sometimes called the Sabbat of First Fruits. Corn, wheat, and barley are ready to be picked by August, as are many other northern hemisphere grains. Native Americans celebrate early August as a grain festival in honor of the Corn Grandmother and called it the Festival of Green Corn. The ancient Romans also honored their grain goddess, Ceres, at their annual August Ceresalia. The birth of the Egyptian sun goddess, Isis, was celebrated in North Africa near the time of this Sabbat, as was a Roman festival in honor of Vulcan, god of the forge and guardian of its fire. In ancient Phoenicia this Sabbat honored the grain god, Dagon, and a substantial portion of the harvest was sacrificed to him.

Other names for this Sabbat are First Harvest, August Eve, and Lammas, an Anglo-Saxon word meaning "loaf-mass," the Sabbat's most commonly used name.

Western paganism notes that the Irish tradition is responsible for much of the practice and symbolism used by today's pagans at this first harvest. The Irish Sun God, Lugh, literally "the shining one," was a god of many skills and was even said to be able to come into human form to worship among the Druids for whom he was the primary deity. He was also the God of the Harvests, Fire, Light, and Metallurgy, and he was the protector and defender of the weak and ill. As the King of the Tuatha De Danann, a mythical race of early Celts, he was one of the consorts of Dana, the first Great Mother Goddess of Ireland. As such, much of the Celtic Lughnasadh celebration focused on him.

Though this Sabbat is named in honor of a god, the Goddess aspect figures prominently, too. The Irish Goddess Dana, as Lugh's Queen, is also venerated and her stories told round the circle. Some Irish witches enact rituals to symbolize Lugh's sacrificial death by the Dananns and his rebirth as a sheaf of grain at Lughnasadh.

Because there is much more to be grown and harvested in the coming months, Lughnasadh is not wholly void of fertility imagery. Some covens perform the Great Rite at this Sabbat, preferably in a fertile field. The Goddess is honored and thanked for bringing forth the first fruits. She is revered and treated with the respect and care shown to any new mother. Yet this Goddess is still pregnant with the future harvests of autumn and she is nurtured as such. It is no accident that most of the first fruits of summer came to be revered as fertility plants. Corn, wheat, potatoes, turnips, summer squash, and oats are all used in magickal spells for fertility. Portions of this harvest were thrown back onto the still growing fields both as a sacrificial gesture and to induce the autumn crops to continue to thrive.

In some covens (and in synagogues and some churches) a part of the August harvest is placed on the central altar as an offering of thanks to the bountiful deities. When the rites of thanksgiving are ended, the food is taken away and given to the poor.

Lughnasadh has always been a Sabbat where only grains and vegetables were sacrificed, as animal sacrifices were usually reserved for the autumn holidays. But in Romania's Transylvanian Alps, high in the dark Carpathian Mountains, there is a ritual enacted on the first Sunday of every August that has obvious pagan roots and does involve animal sacrifice. At daybreak, a procession of peasants takes a live sow up the steep slopes of Mt. Chefleau where it is ritually slain in thanks for the abundant harvest. The blood of the animal must be allowed to flow into the earth. Then the fingers of the right hand touch the blood on the ground and are used to mark the sign of the cross—for protection and self-blessing—on the forehead. For centuries the local priests in this deeply Catholic land have tried to no avail to put a stop to this odd and ancient ritual. The peasantry, though they now offer their thanks and prayers to the Christian God, are convinced that their next harvest would be blighted should this ritual ever be allowed to go unobserved.

Modern covens that wish to mimic this custom, especially those following Slavic traditions, might choose to bring a pig (even a small guinea pig would do) into the Lughnasadh circle and honor it. Pigs have been sacred to the Mother Goddess in almost every culture on earth, probably because they efficiently convert small amounts of raw grain quickly into large amounts of lean meat, therefore the pig symbolizes abundance just like the Goddess of the Harvest. Use red wine spilled on the ground to represent her blood and mark yourselves with equilateral crosses or pentagrams as a way of self-blessing.

Corn of Plenty

The feast of Lughnasadh is one of the largest of any Sabbat. All the first fruits of the season are consumed, especially any and all grains that have been harvested. The feast is often consumed at least partly inside a ritual circle with generous libations being made to the deities. The Cakes and Ale ceremony, a ritual celebration of earth, water, and the Mother Goddess that accompanies the Esbats, might also be observed, only instead of having the cakes act as moon symbols, they now function as sun symbols. Cookies or flat sheet cakes cut into pentagram or disc shapes are good to use as ceremonial cakes. They can be frosted yellow or orange, and even topped with sun-golden sprinkles in honor of the sun gods.

If you don't have a garden or some other place where you have grown any of these grains and fruits, you may not have to look far to find them. In many places, farm stands spring up along rural roadsides selling the produce of the season. Some of it is so fresh that it was picked the same morning it went on sale.

Corn, or maize as it is sometimes called, is the most well-known and celebrated of the Lughnasadh yield. It has been a major feature of August solar festivals in most of North America and Europe since the sixteenth century, and was revered and celebrated by Native Americans long before then. Though its exact origins remain a mystery, it is known to have been cultivated as early as 7,000 years ago in Mexico and the southwestern United States.

To celebrate the corn harvest, the Native Americans gathered together their large clans and celebrated the Festival of Green Corn in honor of the Corn Grandmother who resides in the corn stalks. The festivities usually lasted for several days at minimum, and featured feasting and games of skill as well as religious rituals.

In the Cherokee language the Green Corn festival was called the Busk, and was a time for the rekindling of sacred fires, offerings of thanksgiving, and for rededicating one's self to personal deities.

Another version of corn personified as deity is seen in the grain mother and grain maiden images of Ceres, Demeter, and Persephone. In ancient Greece these grain goddesses were once focused into the body of a bull (a male symbol that made them a complete fertility image) that was burned as a living sacrifice each August Eve. The Minoans of Crete used to hold a similar but more dangerous rite. They would draw the essence of the harvest deities into a bull, place the bull in a small arena, then take turns attempting to grab it by the horns and vault themselves over its back. This symbolic conquering of the deities was thought to force them to submit to the peoples' will of a successful harvest. In Bardic Wales, a similar practice called Bull Dancing was part of the annual Lughnasadh rites. This is also the origin of the expression, "Take the bull by the horns."

It is common practice among Celtic and English witches to hold back a small portion of the corn harvest to make the Imbolg Corn Dolly. Other grains can be used, and the Dolly's exact name varies with each tradition, but corn is the most prevalent. Use the Dolly made at last Imbolg both as a fertility amulet for this harvest and a ritual centerpiece. Take it out of the place where it has been blessing your home and bring it into the circle or place it on your altar. The Dolly was dressed as a bride at Imbolg, but now it should be dressed as a pregnant woman with a baby in her arms. Use a green cloth to fashion the dress, as this is a color of fertility. Add a ball of stuffing to her stomach. Use a small twist of wheat or ear of baby corn for the child.

You can dry corn shocks—the name for harvested stalks—for the Dolly in the same way you dried herbs at Midsummer. Take the fresh shocks in from the fields, tie them in manageable bundles, and hang them up to dry in a warm place in your home. In autumn, one can often find produce and farm stands selling the dried shocks as autumn decorations.

In Peru, corn is a staple of the rural diet. The Peruvians celebrate its harvest by turning out for a parade in their best clothes. The village elders place small handfuls of corn into everyone's pockets on the parade route. At the end of the procession the corn is either scattered on the fields in a gesture of sacrifice or as a fertility spell, or it is taken into the home and given a place of honor until the next corn harvest. If your coven is in the habit of forming a procession to the Lughnasadh circle, you might adapt this idea to fit in with your own ritual.

Corn is the most well-known and celebrated of the Lughnasadh yield.

The Bretons traditionally cut a pregnant human silhouette from the last sheaf of corn harvested, and kept it in their homes or planted it in the field the day after the harvest was complete. This was clearly an effort at sympathetic magick to ensure the continued fertility of the field, a real concern in the days before pesticides, soil depletion, and crop rotation were general knowledge.

In India, the cotton harvest was treated with the same sacredness given in other places to grain. It is an event still celebrated in that region. The first boll to break through is honored as the Cotton Mother, and becomes the focus of the family or community celebration. It is symbolically fed, ritually honored, and kept nearby until the next harvest when it is burned amid prayers of thanksgiving.

Grain ales made around Lughnasadh were dedicated to the God in his aspect as Harvest Lord. Whiskey, an alcoholic beverage distilled from barley, was once sacred to this Sabbat in Scotland. Other Lughnasadh ales were dedicated to the Moon Goddess and put aside for honoring her at Esbats.

Breads, especially ones made with newly harvested grain, are also a traditional part of this Sabbat's festivities. The baking of sacred and ritual breads is far older than humans realize, and its potent pagan symbolism has been wholeheartedly adopted by both Christianity and Judaism. It represents not only the harvest, but Mother Earth, home, and hearth. Its gentle rising as it bakes is symbolic of growing pregnancy and thriving fields.

In many covens it is traditional to count one's blessings when gathered in the Lughnasadh circle. A ritual loaf of bread is passed clockwise around the circle, and coven members break off portions and consume them after they announce all the things for which they are thankful.

Serve Lughnasadh breads with honey, another sun-associated food. Middle East braided breads such as challah or the Danish julekage are also appropriate and can symbolize the intertwining of Goddess, God, and humans, or the unity of the Triple Goddess. French breads are also a good choice when feeding a large number of people. These breads are easily found ready-made in delis and bakeries.

In North America, cornbread, with its bright yellow coloring, is the most fitting bread symbol of the season, and is often made fresh from the fruit of the harvest. Cornbread mixes can be found in the baking section of any grocery store, though you might want to make your own. If you live in a rural area with a mill nearby, you can purchase fresh ground corn meal and flour.

Cornbread
(Serves four)

¾ cup flour
3 teaspoons baking powder
¾ cup milk
1 tablespoon sugar
½ teaspoon salt
1½ cups yellow corn meal
1 egg
2 tablespoons butter, melted

Preheat a greased 9 x 9 baking pan in a 425° F oven for 20 to 22 minutes. Pour the bread mixture into the hot pan and place it back in the oven for 20 minutes. Serve hot with butter or honey.

Blackberries, a plant sacred to the Irish goddess Brigid and to the Norse thunder god Thor, ripen in July and August, and gentle blackberry wines are made from them and dedicated to these deities before Mabon (See Chapter Nine for Blackberry Wine recipe). In Ireland there was, and still is, a folk taboo against eating blackberries after Mabon. Other regions have similar taboos against eating any summer berries or grapes after that date, but all berries made into wines for a goddess or god have always been permissible to keep and use.

Blackberry pies are also a featured item at this Sabbat feast. Scour gently wooded areas for untapped bushes. They are often easy to find. If you have no luck, check the produce section of large groceries or farm stands.

Brigid's Blackberry Pie
(Makes one nine-inch pie)

4 cups fresh blackberries (thawed frozen is okay)
1½ cup sugar
⅓ cup flour
¼ teaspoon cinnamon
⅛ teaspoon salt
    Unbaked pie crust

Preheat oven to 325°F. Line a deep pie dish with the pie crust, or purchase a commercially-made one. Set aside. Mix all other ingredients together in a large mixing bowl. If it appears too "wet," mix in a little more flour (about 2 tablespoons). Turn the fruit into the pie shell and dot with butter or margarine. You can bake the pie as is, or cover it with another pie crust. If you do this, pinch down the ends to hold it to the other crust. Then score the top several times with a sharp knife. Bake for 1 hour, or until the top crust is a golden brown. (Note: A sugar-free version of this pie can be made by substituting appropriate amounts of artificial sweetener.)

Much lore surrounds the last grain to be cut from each field—not the last for the season, that comes at Samhain—but the last for this Sabbat's harvest. Most pagan cultures required that the last grain be left standing as an offering for faeries or other nature spirits. Native Americans left the last corn stalk in the field for the Corn Grandmother to reside in. Middle Eastern pagans buried the last harvested grain back in the earth so the corn spirit would want to return the following year.

Sacrifice of the first fruit or grain cut is another old Lughnasadh tradition. Almost universally the first cut of the harvest was buried, burned, left in the field, or placed at a ritual or sacred site for the harvest deities to enjoy while the rest of the field was harvested.

Lughnasadh was the traditional time for regicide, or king-killing rites. This practice came from an ancient belief that the king, like the God whose earthly vessel he was, must periodically die and spill his blood on the earth in order for human life to continue. This reflected the belief in most pagan cultures that the God must die at some point in the year before he could be reborn at Yule. Different cultures had different time periods for these rites. Usually they were seven- or nine-year cycles. Kings were acutely aware of this religious duty and never knew which of their trusted advisers was saddled with this unpleasant task. This practice continued until recently in parts of Africa and southeast Asia, where for centuries, no king was allowed to die a natural death.

Beginning in the early Middle Ages, many Western cultures began using scapegoats for this sacrifice, such as a minor prince whose blood had been mingled with the king's in a special ceremony not unlike what children do today to become blood-brothers or blood-sisters. Later, these sacrifices were done wholly symbolically with wine as a substitute for blood. Many believe that these periodic symbolic sacrifices are still continued in secret by the British Royal family.

Harvest Images

Roosters are often present at Lughnasadh festivities because they were long held sacred to the Sun Gods of Europe. In England, roosters figure heavily in nursery rhymes and in children's stories. This one clearly uses harvest images:

> THE COCK'S ON THE HOUSETOP BLOWING HIS HORN,
> THE BULL'S IN THE BARN THRESHING THE CORN,
> THE MAIDS IN THE MEADOW ARE GATHERING HAY,
> THE DUCKS IN THE RIVER ARE SWIMMING ALL DAY.

The threshing of grain, separating the actual grain from the straws, began the day after Lughnasadh and was considered a magickal task. Threshing houses were believed to be guarded by grain deities, and their symbols could be found carved into the walls of the threshing room. The practice of carrying a new bride over a threshold, the wooden floor beam across a doorway that holds the grain inside the threshing house, was an old fertility custom now kept alive in paganism by having a newly handfasted couple jump over a broomstick.

Lughnasadh, like Midsummer, is a great time to have summer gatherings, either pagan or non-pagan, and to celebrate the bounty of the late summer season. Ideas for Lughnasadh parties include a canning party to preserve the bounty of the harvest, family reunions, or simple barbeques with lots of fresh corn on the side. Or you might consider a traditional early American Corn Husking Bee. This was when entire communities joined together to remove the green sheaths from the yellow corn. If one uncovered a red ear he or she was allowed to kiss the person of his or her choice. Even the Puritans followed this old custom which had its roots in pagan fertility rites. What the Puritans did avoid though, because of the sexual symbolism, was the lively folk dance that traditionally ended these Husking Bees.

Other Lughnasadh parties might have farm themes. Have guests come dressed as farmers and bring a pot luck dish made with newly picked vegetables. Play games that use Lughnasadh fruits such as bobbing for corn, or pass the tomato. Make a game out of singing the children's song, "Old MacDonald Had a Farm," and see how many animals you can add to it before the group loses track. Offer baskets of food, fresh ground grains, or packets of seeds to the winners of any games.

You might also try a party with a Native American theme. Play games of skill or endurance, honor the Corn Grandmother, do Native American dances, and tell Indian folk stories around a campfire.

Popcorn is another delicacy given to Europeans by Native Americans, and it is another appropriate food for Lughnasadh. Feature it at parties or at ritual meals. String the corns together with a needle and thread to use as a circle decoration just as many people do at Yule.

Celebrate the First Harvest

August Eve parties are a natural for pagans. Invite your friends and family to help you celebrate the first harvest. Feature not only corn and grain items, but fresh melons. An American corporation called Pumpkin Limited, which makes the Carve-O-Lantern® tools have recently created a similar set of carveable patterns for use on watermelons, called MelonLights®.

Summer vacations are in full swing in August and you can make up travel games with a pagan focus. Have bored travelers make lists as they ride along of bad and good environmental happenings they see. After a time, compare lists and discuss why each thing is bad or good and what can be done about them.

Pagan kids will especially like bingo games with pictures of natural items they are learning to identify.

To make this game you will need stiff cardboard, white poster board, a ruler, a pencil or pen, paste, scissors, several old magazines, and either a can of old buttons or checkers, or some removable stickers to use as markers.

Cut the cardboard and poster board into 12 x 15-inch sections. This will be the size of your playing board, and you will need one for every passenger in your car or van. Some people think bingo games go faster and are more exciting if you are playing many cards at once. If this is your thinking, then make several cards for each player.

Take the poster board and, with a pencil and ruler, make a grid. Leave a three inch bar at the top, then divide the rest into thirty-six 2 x 2-inch sections: six rows of six.

Print the word "Bingo" at the top, and begin to fill in the squares with the names of the items you have chosen to work with. Some cards can have a few items that others don't have. Mix them up so that no two cards are the same, and be sure to print the names of the items small enough at the bottom of each square so that you have room for a pasted picture.

Glue the poster board to the cardboard to provide a firm surface. Place heavy books over them and leave them overnight to bond together.

Meanwhile, look through old magazines for pictures that represent the items you have chosen to work with. Be sure to consider the region where you are traveling when making these decisions. It would be difficult to find cactus in Massachusetts and lakes in New Mexico. If you are traveling through several regions, your bingo cards can reflect this, too.

Cut out the magazine pictures small enough to fit into the 2 x 2-inch squares. When they are all selected you can glue them in place and leave them to dry overnight. If you cannot find enough magazine pictures to represent the items you've chosen, you can draw them above their labels, but magazine pictures are more colorful and help keep children interested. Children, when supervised, can even help select, cut, and glue the pictures.

Use checkers, old buttons, or removable stickers to mark each item as it is seen along the roadside. The first one to make a line up and down, across, or diagonally wins. Or make it a tougher game and require the entire card to be covered.

Another perfect August pastime for pagans is stargazing. The August sky is renowned for its meteor showers and shooting stars, and quietly watching for them is a beautiful way to connect with one's place in the universe.

Shooting stars have long been part of the folklore of many lands which tells us that if we make a wish, it will come true. This lovely bit of folk magick is a nice way for solitaries to end August rituals.

Urban dwellers may have a difficult time seeing much of the night sky since city lights can cause interference for nearly 200 miles. When you have a chance to get out in the country or out on the ocean, look up. An awesome sight awaits, one which is so rare in our time as to inspire an almost immediate response to thank our deities and perform some small ritual in honor of the event.

While it is still warm enough to get out and involved in outdoor activities, your coven might consider getting in on the Adopt a Highway program. This is a program available virtually everywhere in the United States in which civic-minded organizations adopt a stretch of highway—usually two to five miles—and agree to keep it clean by going out periodically and picking up the accumulated litter. It is an excellent way for pagans to practice the environmental messages we preach. If you live outside the United States or are in an area where such programs are not in force, consider organizing such an effort.

After Lughnasadh the sun is noticeably lower in the sky each evening. In some northern regions there is already a nip of fall in the air as we move toward the second harvest.

⇒ 9 ⇐

Mabon:
The Autumn Equinox
September 22

Mabon (May-bone or Mah-boon) is the Autumn Equinox. The Sabbat is named for Mabon, the Welsh God who symbolized the male fertilizing principle in the Welsh myths. Some mythologists equate him as the male counterpart for Persephone.

As a day of balance between light and dark it was not unnoticed by the English and the Celts, but as a Sabbat it went unobserved by them until the Norse invaders brought it into prominence and placed it between Lughnasadh and Samhain as the second of the three harvests. With the number three in these conquered lands associated with the Triple Goddess and with the act of completeness, they adopted this addition wholeheartedly.

In China the day is known as Chung Ch'iu and marks the end of the rice harvest. Judaism celebrates Succoth near this time, another harvest holiday with pagan roots that is often observed by building a temporary outdoor dwelling decorated with fall vegetables and in which all meals are eaten for that celebration. In old Rome the equinox marked the infamous Festival of Dionysus, the God of Wine, whose party lasted for as many days as the revelers could remain upright.

The old Anglo-Celtic festival of Harvest Home, a respite from the work of harvesting and a celebration of thanks, probably once fell on Mabon. In remembrance of that time, Mabon is often referred to as the "Witches' Thanksgiving" and is one of the oldest harvest celebrations in Europe.

Thanksgiving as it is known in the United States and Canada grew more out of the Pilgrims' need to connect with the festivals of their homeland than it did from any religious impulse, and that first Thanksgiving Day had many detractors among the Puritan leaders due to its pagan origins. The Christian hymn "Come, Ye Thankful People, Come," commemorates this festival, and is also an appropriate song for pagans to use at their harvest rites.

If you are interested in using music at your Mabon gathering you might also want to look into "We Gather Together To Ask the Lord's Blessing," "All Good Gifts" (From the musical *Godspell*), "Now Thank We All Our God," and "Thanks Be To God," a hymn set to an old Welsh folk tune. These songs are mainstream but reflect such a universal theme that hardly anyone will object to singing them.

The original Harvest Home festival featured many of the same activities that characterize Mabon. These include cider pressing, grain threshing, dancing, feasting, and the crowning of a Harvest King and Queen that is still done in pagan circles. The King and Queen become the earthly vessel for the God and Goddess to reside in during the Mabon ritual and festivities. The English folk song "Lavender Blue, Lavender Green" was a song that grew out of Mabon observances. Blue is the color of the Harvest Lord and green of the Harvest Lady.

You should feel free to add prayers and songs of thanksgiving to your deities in any Mabon rituals you do. You may also want to observe the "official" Thanksgiving Day in the United States (fourth Thursday in November) and in Canada (second Monday in October). When these holidays were established—in 1863 and 1957 respectively—they were decreed as days to give thanks to our Maker for all our blessings, including the harvest. There is no reason pagans cannot fully be a part of this holiday by expressing their own thanks to whichever deities they worship.

There are many ways to make Thanksgiving, observed either at Mabon or later on with the general population, meaningful to pagans. Those who worship with a coven may choose to meet for a special feast of Thanksgiving separate from their regular gatherings. You could even meet to have a special day to offer thanks to your deities for your many blessings. This could either be a time of your own choosing, or it could be a part of another holiday. Construct a special ritual of thanks as a group.

As a solitary you may simply want to add prayers of thanks to either your Mabon ritual or to your own Thanksgiving Day prayers. If you have family and friends who know of and are accepting of your religious views you may be free to offer these prayers aloud at your family Thanksgiving gatherings when everyone is asked to say a few words.

Whether you are part of a group or on your own, prayers should always come from the heart. Make a list ahead of time, either mentally or on paper, so you know what you want to say thank you for, and let the rest be somewhat spontaneous. To ensure that the spirit of thanks and praise is maintained, avoid asking for favors at this time.

The following is a sample prayer which you should adapt to your own needs:

> *Bountiful Mother Earth, whose dark*
> *womb has brought forth this munificence*
> *we see before us, we humbly thank you*
> *for your gift of sustenance which*
> *nourishes our bodies and minds.*
> *Lord of the Harvest, wise and giving,*
> *we praise your generosity in providing*
> *this feast which gives us strength and endurance.*
> *Lord and Lady, our blessings this year*
> *have been many. We thank you for ...*
>
> (Enumerate your blessings here, whatever
> you wish to offer thanks for. Or, if you
> are in a group, allow everyone to speak
> in turn offering personal prayers.)
>
> *... And for all those blessings and gifts*
> *which in the hustle and bustle of daily*
> *living we have overlooked and taken for*
> *granted, we most gratefully thank you now.*
> *Blessed Lord and Lady, mighty and*
> *powerful, tender and charitable, forever*
> *may your praises be sung by your adoring*
> *and thankful children.*
> *So mote it be!*

In keeping with pagan feasting traditions, it is fitting that you should offer part of your meal in sacrifice. At this time of year the two best ways to do this are by putting something out for the wild animals who will be glad to have it as winter begins to set in, or by giving either time, money, or food to a shelter or social service organization that feeds the homeless and hungry on Thanksgiving. As a solitary, such an investment of your time and caring can be personally rewarding, and if you volunteer as a group you will bridge good public relations with all those who view your loving efforts.

It became customary during Mabon in Ireland, and in parts of western Scotland and Cornwall, to visit burial mounds, called cairns, to honor dead ancestors, particularly female ancestors. This practice may have had two origins. One was to visit the dead and appease them so when they visited the human world at Samhain they would be predisposed toward kindness and good will. The second origin may have been in ancient Ireland where a cult of female ancestor worship based its beliefs on the notion that, upon death, all human souls were reabsorbed into the wombs which bore them, and therefore only women inhabited Tir-na-nog, the Irish Land of the Dead also known by the name "The Land of Women." Women were the ones required to decorate and adorn the graves at Mabon while the men prepared the nearby feasting site.

Cairns and cemeteries were feared by many of our ancestors as places where evil spirits lingered. Approaching such places at Mabon was deemed safe because it was believed that the balance of light and dark would act like an equilateral cross, and offer protection from any negative spirits attracted to the graveyards. Fires were lit at the cairns, or carried in gourds similar to our jack-o'-lanterns, to further frighten away baneful spirits.

Just prior to Mabon, the Druids cut wands from the willow tree, a tree associated with death and also sacred to the Celtic goddesses. These wands were thought to be powerful tools for magick involving the conjuring of spirits they consulted for divinatory purposes.

Some pagans question why there is a focus on death at Mabon, a theme they usually associate with Samhain. Mabon begins the season of autumn when leaves die, and nature, having given forth an abundance of new life-giving foods, withers so that the cycle may begin again. The deities are aging and the God will soon die, as will as the old year. For our pagan ancestors who marked time by the turning of the Wheel of the Year, this was a natural time to reflect on the meaning of death.

Mabon is not only a time when night and day are equal, but all things are in balance for one brief moment. The Goddess and the God are thought to have equal power on this night, as well as the forces of good and evil. It was a time when the old Norse people believed one's fate for the coming year was sealed. The Norse often spent the day and night before Mabon fasting and praying for forgiveness for transgressions. Divinations and vision quests were done to ascertain whether one's life in the last year had been pleasing to the deities.

Mabon marks the end of the second harvest, a time when the majority of crops are gathered. Nuts, apples, and grapes—all autumn crops—are the featured items at this Sabbat feast. Berries, which began to ripen in summer, are ready now to be made into jam, jellies, and wines. In many traditions there is a taboo against eating autumn berries after Mabon unless they were made into wine.

In Scotland and Wales, Mabon wines were poured onto the ground to honor the aging Goddess as she moved swiftly into her Crone aspect. It was also a symbolic sacrifice, as in the spilling of blood, so that the God might live until Samhain.

Wines from the autumn grape harvest have always figured prominently in pagan harvest rites. Drunken orgies were common practice at the equinox in Germanic lands and in Rome and Greece.

The German Ocktoberfest celebrations were once festivals for the wine harvest, particularly in Bavaria, where the equinox was a major Sabbat. Today one can still buy an alcoholic concoction at the Bavarian festivals called Neuweisswein (New White Wine), a milky and potent by-product of the distillation process. The mixture is not bottled, but sold by the glassful from old stoneware crocks resembling tall cauldrons. The milky look of this wine connects it with the Mother Goddess who has entered her croneage at Mabon.

Celtic lands were not as well known for their grape industry as their neighbors to the south, but that did not deter the ingenious Celts. What they developed was a heather wine made from the native flowering plant. Though the end product doesn't have the deep sacred significance of grape wines in other lands, it is a tribute to the bounty of nature and very appropriate for Mabon.

Blackberry wines were another Celtic specialty, especially in Ireland, where the berry was sacred to the goddess Brigid.

Following are two types of wines. An ale-style wine can be made from the Blackberry Wine recipe by adding one package of brewer's yeast to the berries while fermenting. Be extra cautious when storing yeast wines. Tremendous pressure can build in the bottles.

Heather "Wine"
(Makes four bottles)

Gather at least 1 pound of fresh heather. Use the upper stalks and flowers only. Boil the heather with 1 gallon water in a large stockpot until the mixture resembles a dark tea. If necessary, add more stalks and flowers if the color is weak. The mixture should be opaque. Remove the mixture from the heat and strain. Discard the heather. When the mixture has cooled, add:

  4   cups sugar
  ¼   teaspoon nutmeg
  ¼   teaspoon allspice
  ¼   cup lemon juice

Pour the new mixture into casks or bottles. Heather Wine has a gentle, grassy flavor. Serve chilled.

Blackberry Wine
(As with any alcoholic beverage, the making of wine is a lengthy and tedious process. This recipe makes enough for two to three bottles.)

  4   pounds fresh blackberries
  3½   cups sugar
  3¼   cups hot water

Set the berries in a large bowl for about 4 weeks, stirring occasionally. (The berries will smell and may begin to mold.) With a mortar and pestle or blender, crush the berries into a very smooth pulp. Stir in the sugar, then the water. pour into casks for fermentation. Let the wine age at least 8 months. Air the wine every few days to allow gasses to escape. The longer it is kept, the better it will be. This wine has a gentle port-like flavor when finished, and should be immediately dedicated to a deity.

A grapevine wreath decorated for Mabon.

The fermented juices we know as wine figure heavily throughout human history as a drink of the deities. Many cultures limit—or once limited—the making and use of wines to a priestly class, or to certain sacred time periods. Finished wines have nearly always been dedicated to a particular local deity. This practice is the reason Jewish law insists on the use of only kosher (ritually correct and pure) wine. They wanted to ensure that their wines had not been inadvertently consecrated to a pagan deity, and even today they carefully guard the making of their wines which are dedicated to their own version of God.

Vines also figure heavily in Mabon symbolism. They are used as decorations for altars, as raw material for the making of wreaths, and as head crowns for Mabon worshipers. Unadorned grapevine wreaths came to symbolize Mabon in many parts of Europe. The vine was a symbol of the season and its emptiness represented a completed harvest.

One large, sturdy grapevine wreath can carry you through the whole year and beyond if you change its decorations to correspond to each Sabbat. Another can be reserved as head wear for the actual Mabon ritual. A full range of sizes, from two to thirty inches across, can be found in any craft shop. If you wish to make your own, you can buy lengths of vine and weave them together yourself. Soak them in warm water until they are pliable enough to mold. When they dry, their shape will hold.

Another type of vine is a garland. A little-known Irish festival called Garland Sunday was observed on the first Sunday in September, and still is celebrated in some parts of western rural Ireland. Many pagans believe the traditions surrounding Garland Sunday grew out of the older Mabon tradition of making pilgrimages to burial grounds to honor the dead.

Garlands were constructed of native vines and apples by a village's unmarried women and taken by them, along with all unmarried men, to a churchyard. If an apple fell during the procession, it was a bad omen since apples often stood as symbols for the human soul and for the Goddess. At the churchyard, the garland was then broken apart and strewn over the graves amidst loud keening. Feasting and dancing near the cemetery followed, and it was obligatory to show hospitality to strangers on this evening.

I have observed this beautiful old rite whenever possible at the small country cemetery in rural Indiana where my family has been buried for generations. If you wish to follow this custom it is best to find a secluded, country cemetery where you are unlikely to be noticed. If you are seen, people will naturally be more than a little curious as to why you are parading and picnicking in a graveyard, and you may draw an unwanted crowd or be asked to leave.

Such celebrations in cemeteries are still features of autumn worship in many cultures including modern Mexico, Central America, China, Hong Kong, Korea, Vietnam, and Thailand.

You can make your own garland out of any greenery you like if you have access to an abundance of it without harming trees and plants. To begin, you will need to go to a craft store to purchase several yards of dried grape vine. The length will depend on how many people you will have in your procession. Estimate that you will need at least three feet, or one yard, per person. You will also need some small wires or twist-ties. These can also be obtained at craft stores and will be used to attach the greenery to the vine.

Gather your greenery and, with the wires, attach them to the vine until it is as full as you like. To attach the apple you may need something stronger, like string or twine.

Another idea, and a smarter one in this time of environmental concern, would be to purchase an artificial garland from a store that specializes in supplying artificial flowers and foliage for weddings. There is absolutely no reason for this garland to be made all-natural since it is not being used as a direct catalyst for magick. An artificial one would harm no living thing and could be used year after year. You could attach fresh apples to it each year. It could even be brought out at other Sabbats, decorated appropriately, and used to outline your circle.

The Mabon feast is a rich one, full of all the bounty of the earth. Many people take the berries and fruits harvested at Mabon and make them into jams and jellies for the ritual bread, a lengthy and messy process. A simpler bread topping which is still in keeping with the season is apple butter. The first crop of autumn apples is ripe at Mabon, and apple butter can be purchased in groceries or orchard stores throughout September, but it is always nice to make your own.

An easy method of making apple butter is to mix 1 gallon chopped apples with 1 cup vinegar, 6 cups sugar, 12 ounces bottled red sugar, and 20 ounces of cinnamon candy. In a stockpot, bring all ingredients to a boil and let simmer for 30 minutes. Let cool and spoon into jars.

Baked apples are another tasty way to enjoy the season. The following is my father's recipe.

Baked Apples Indiana-Style
(Makes 16 oz.)

12-14	large apples
1	cup granulated sugar
¼	cup flour
¼	cup tapioca
¾	cup warm water

Peel, core and quarter enough apples to fit comfortably in a 9x13 baking pan. Corningware or Pyrex pans are better than metal ones for cooking apples. Preheat oven to 375° F. Place the apples in the baking pan. Mix the remaining ingredients and pour over the apples. Sprinkle with cinnamon and nutmeg. Bake for 45 to 50 minutes. Serve with a scoop of ice cream.

The nut harvest also begins at Mabon. Nuts are fertility symbols, but they have a masculine rather than feminine focus. To incorporate nuts into your Sabbat feast try an old Texas favorite—Pecan Pie!

Texas-Style Pecan Pie
(Makes two pies)

2 deep-dish unbaked pie shells
6 beaten eggs
½ cup butter, melted (The real thing is best. If you use margarine, add ⅛ teaspoon salt to the recipe.)
2 cups brown sugar, packed
1¾ cups corn syrup
2¼ teaspoons vanilla
2½ cups chopped pecans

Preheat oven to 350° F. Slowly and thoroughly mix together the eggs, butter, brown sugar, corn syrup, and vanilla. Pour the mixture into the two pie shells. As this mixture will not "rise" like some pies, you can fill the shells higher than usual, but not so high that they boil over and leave a sticky, burned mess in your oven. Cover the pie with the pecans. Bake for about an hour.

Rattles were made from autumn nuts in nearly all Native American and Polynesian traditions. These rattles were used in ritual to frighten away evil spirits, to purify ritual space, to drive out sickness, and to honor and invite ancestors to participate in the rituals. Rattle hulls were colorfully painted with medicine symbols to seal their function, and many were further adorned with feathers or beads. It was not unusual for the leaders of the tribe to have dozens of rattles, a special one for each holiday, ritual, and magickal purpose.

You can make your own rattles by one of two methods. You can use the modern method of papier-mâché, or you can hollow out autumn gourds. With papier-mâché you can create the exact size and shape you want, and make the handle as long and thick as you please. With the gourd you are stuck with what nature gives you, but this is the traditional way rattles were made. Hollow out the gourd, fill it with nuts, and seal it again using a

The symbolic Horn of Plenty.

leather patch or papier-mâché. Use craft paints to decorate them any way you like.

The Horn of Plenty, used to represent Thanksgiving, is another symbol of Mabon. It is both a phallic symbol and, when stuffed with the fruits of the harvest, a womb gushing forth its autumn bounty.

Horns of Plenty often contain Indian corn, another potent Mabon symbol. Indian corn is actually a type of corn known as pod corn. Its colorful appearance and durability come from the fact that each kernel is encased in its own tiny husk which helps preserve it for an unusually long period of time. It is this longevity which helps make it a Mabon symbol among the death images of the autumn Sabbats.

Modern Mabon activities for pagans and non-pagans can include hay rides, a custom that grew out of riding the full hay wagon back home after it had been fully loaded with the day's harvest. This ride eventually took on a party atmosphere as families sang together and enjoyed the autumn countryside while they rode home to partake of the fall bounty. Though hay rides have become popular Halloween activities, it is warmer to do them at Mabon in many regions. Add a pagan-style feast to your hay ride by concluding with a cookout around an open bonfire.

You might also decorate your home or rented space like an old barn and host a barn dance. This was another European custom that grew out of the pagan celebration of the completion of the harvest, one which continued in lands colonized by Europeans.

On a smaller scale, you might prefer to throw a First of Fall Party featuring fall foods, cider, and wine. Instead of watching sporting events, play them together. You can tailor them to have a pagan focus, or at least a pagan outcome, by having each member of the losing team contribute to a kitty that will be sent to aid an environmental cause, or to a shelter to feed the hungry. Both are good ways to share the richness of the season's harvest with others less fortunate.

If you make or collect wines, you could host a wine tasting party in honor of the grape harvest. Serve wines the traditional way with bland crackers, yeast breads, and cheese. To really feel a part of this season, you could make this an annual event you, your friends, and family can look forward to each year.

Quilting Bees were also fall events. With the cold nights of winter on the way, women remembered the need to craft new blankets to keep their families warm. To combat the tedium and loneliness of this art, women began getting together in groups to work on one woman's quilt at a time. Many of the tried and true quilt patterns that have been popular for centuries hold pagan symbolism, and may have in fact grown out of long-forgotten pagan designs of protection. Stars are popular quilt patterns, especially those with four points (as in a Sun Wheel) and those with eight points (the number of the Sabbats).

Quilting is a skill that takes time to learn, and would make a good winter project. Call some of your local craft and fabric shops to inquire about classes. Men shouldn't be shy about signing up for these classes, too. Over the past several decades men have taken up needle arts in record numbers because it is a relaxing and satisfying pastime.

Mabon, like its polar opposite, Ostara, is a time of balance. Only now, instead of looking outward to the coming summer, we begin looking inward, preparing ourselves for the winter to come. Now is a good time to adopt a pet if you wish to have one, cut firewood for the coming winter, and

Many of today's quilt patterns have grown out of pagan designs of protection.

seek out reading material for the dark, cold nights ahead. Plan your winter craft projects now so you will be ready with them when the air turns crisp once more and you are again moved indoors.

Except for a few items still in the fields, Mabon is the end of the harvest season. After this night of balance darkness will again overcome the light, and the power of light will give way to the powers of darkness. In the patriarchal world this darkness inspires fear and thoughts of evil. Pagans have always honored the dark as being simply another part of the light, as the light is merely another part of the dark. They are each half of a whole and neither is inherently good or bad.

The old God is also preparing for winter by readying himself for his sacrifical death at Samhain. The Goddess is entering cronehood, storing up more wisdom which comes with age, though deep inside her, her Maiden aspect carries the impregnated seed of the God who will be born again at Yule as the Wheel of the Year eternally turns.

⊲◄ ►⊳

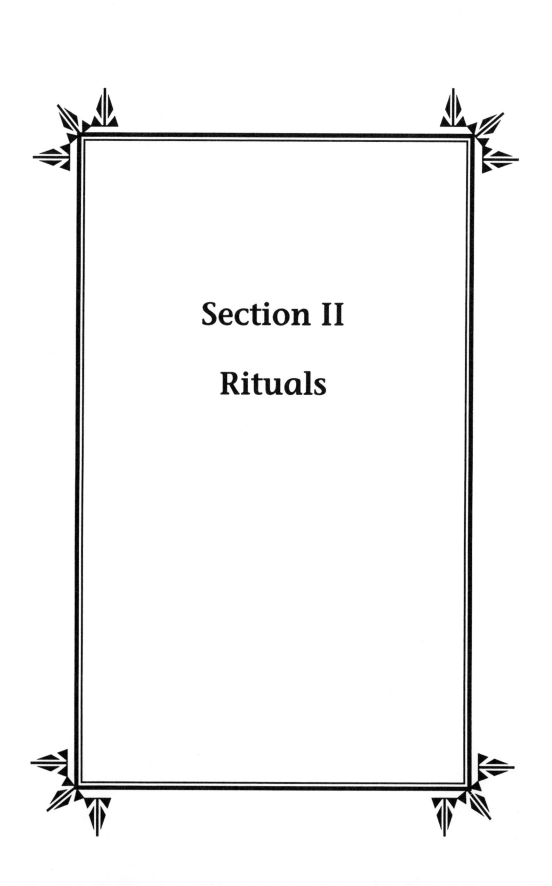

Section II

Rituals

Sabbat Rituals for Groups

No attempt is made in any of the following rituals to coerce or otherwise dictate coven structure and policy to the readers of this book. The way you form and organize your coven, grove, or spirituality group is up to you. Since I feel that hierarchies harm rather than help pagan efforts, I use the word "Acting" before designating the roles of the High Priest and Priestess in all of following rituals. Your leaders, whether they revolve or remain the same, will assume these roles.

Unless it is absolutely necessary to the ritual, the words to be spoken by the High Priest and/or High Priestess are left marked as "Priest/ess" so that they can be assigned to either leader. All-female or all-male covens can assign these roles as they see fit.

The word "Covenor(s)" is used in this text to describe all individuals in the group who are functioning in non-leadership roles. I choose this term because, to me, it reflects the sanctity and safety of the circle. The word "coven" comes from the same word as "covenant," a term meaning "a bond or compact," or "an agreement or promise of honor," and this is what the relationship of one covenor to another ought to be.

Generic labels such as "Goddess" and "God" have been used for the deities rather than giving them specific names. You are encouraged to name these deities according to your tradition. The name for the Land of the Dead is given by the popular appellation "Summerland." Feel free to call this place by the name you know it best.

Respect your circle and its meaning, remembering that once cast, a circle is sacred space, and that also means it is a "safe" space. Everyone should be free to be themselves and to speak their minds without fear of censorship or ridicule. You have created a space into which you have invited deity. It is no place for quarrels or pettiness, for ego or any form of self-aggrandizement.

Some traditions call for the High Priest and/or Priestess to cast the circle all alone and then call the coven into it through a doorway "cut" by the athame. If this is your practice, please feel free to alter the rituals to accommodate this. Otherwise, the rituals written in this book call for the circle to be cast once everyone is inside the ritual space.

Where you place your altar and your balefire is a personal choice. Sometimes these placements are directed by your tradition, other times by the individual coven. But the altar should always be inside the circle, near one of the cardinal points. The balefire may be in the circle, either in the south (the direction represented by fire) or sitting just outside the actual circle area. Some traditions call for the balefire to be at the center of the circle, but this is usually impractical due to space considerations. Balefires can also be placed in a fireplace if you are holding indoor rituals. All placements are correct and good. The choice will have to be made by your group.

For these and all another rituals, do as much preparation as possible beforehand. Assign roles, memorize passages, and even have a dress rehearsal if you like to ensure that everything will go smoothly. There is nothing more disconcerting than being halfway through a ritual and realizing you have forgotten an important item or to assign a role. Meet with your coven to rewrite any portions of the ritual you wish to change, and to discuss which games, food, seasonal poetry, divinations, etc., will be a part of your observance, and to assign those who will be responsible for seeing that those needed items get to and from the working site.

Before you even think about beginning, all decorations should be in place on the altar, and the altar itself set with all the items you wish it to hold. When the coven has gathered, place all other materials that will be needed (ones individuals were asked to bring) inside the area where the circle will be cast. (For instructions on casting a circle, see Chapter One.)

Samhain Group Ritual

For Samhain rituals you might wish to use jack-o'-lanterns rather than candles to mark the directional quarters of your circle. If you wish to have a balefire this can be either inside or outside of your circle. In most of North America it can be fairly cold at Samhain, and many autumn rituals are likely to be indoors. You can still have a balefire in a fireplace by dedicating it as a ritual fire when you light it. You can also toss herbs associated with the Sabbat or its deities into the fire to further make it a part of the holiday. (See Appendix VI: Sabbat Correspondences for a complete table.)

Altar decorations for Samhain traditionally include acorns that represent male fertility, and are often used by Celtic covens to symbolize the hopes for the God's rebirth. Autumn leaves, gourds, and bare twigs are other possibilities. Apples, symbols of the Crone Goddess, are also often used both as decorations and as end-of-ritual treats.

In the Celtic tradition, Samhain marks the time of the New Year. This text acknowledges this fact. If you are of a tradition which celebrates the New Year at Yule, a similar acknowledgement will be provided for you in that ritual. In the meantime, simply eliminate this part of the ritual from your Samhain observances.

For this ritual you will need to ask everyone to bring photos of loved ones who have passed over. These should be placed on the altar before the ritual begins. In place of ritual jewelry you might choose instead to wear a piece of jewelry that belonged to a deceased relative or friend. You will need to have your altar arranged with the ritual tools your tradition chooses to use, and you will also need a cauldron partially filled with water. If you do not have a cauldron you can substitute a pitcher, fish bowl, or other capacious, womb-like vessel. The cauldron, representing the primal melting pot where life begins, ends, and is reborn, is often the central item during Samhain worship. You will also need to have two candles on the altar before the ritual begins. One of these will be designated a God candle (red or orange), and the other a Goddess candle (white or black).

You will need to assign the following ritual roles: High Priestess, High Priest, the Crone Goddess, and the Dying God.

> (When all members of the coven are assembled and the circle is cast, the ritual can begin.)

Acting High Priest/ess:

> *Welcome Friends!*

Covenors:

> *Welcome!*

Acting High Priest/ess:

> *The Wheel of the Year turns on and on, bringing us to*
> *and from each season, and from and to another. What*
> *will be is. What was will be. All time is here and now*
> *inside this sacred space. We pause briefly now to watch*
> *the Wheel turn, and we gather on this blessed eve so that*
> *we might celebrate this season of Samhain. In this*

moment between time, we come to praise the wise
Goddess and her aged consort who is soon to pass into
the Summerland, opening the veil which makes our
world and the world of spirit thin.

(The High Priest/ess will now begin to invoke the directional energies. Beginning with the direction used in your tradition, s/he walks to the altar, picks up the tool representing that direction, and carries it to that edge of the circle. For the purpose of clarity one direction has to be first. Since I am of the Irish tradition, I start this ritual with the west.)

Acting High Priest/ess (holding up the directional tool):

Guardians, Spirits, Elementals, and Powers of the West
and of Water, we ask your flowing, ever-changing pres-
ence at our circle tonight. Join us in honoring this sacred
season and our Goddess and our God.

(Some traditions call for the intoning of a bell as the directions are called. Add this if you like.)

Covenors (turn to face the direction being called):

Welcome, Powers of the West.

Acting High Priest/ess (Priest/ess returns to the altar and lays down the tool. S/he may continue on with the other directions, or these roles may be assigned to others. Words for calling on the other three quarters are given below.)

(North): *Guardians, Spirits, Elementals, and Powers*
of the North and of Earth, we ask your sturdy, comfort-
ing presence at our circle tonight. Join us in honoring
this sacred season and our Goddess and God.

(East): *Guardians, Spirits, Elementals, and Powers of the*
East and of Air, we ask your breezy, cleansing presence at
our circle tonight. Join us in honoring this sacred season
and our Goddess and God.

(South): *Guardians, Spirits, Elementals, and Powers of*
the South and of Fire, we ask your fiery, transformative
presence at out circle tonight. Join us in honoring this
sacred season and our Goddess and God.

Acting High Priestess (takes the chalice from the altar and raises it upward):

> *Blessed Lady Goddess, we humbly ask your presence at our circle tonight as we honor you at this season.*

Covenors:

> *Blessed be the Lady.*

Acting High Priest (takes the athame or sword from the altar and raises it upward):

> *Blessed Lord God, we humbly ask your presence at our circle tonight as we honor you at this season.*

Covenors:

> *Blessed be the Lord.*

> (All of the above, with the exception of the Acting High Priest/ess' speech stating the purpose of the rite, constitutes the opening ritual which will be used for all the Sabbats. Please refer to this text for the opening sequence for all other rituals in this book.)

Acting High Priest/ess:

> *Tonight is a night of death, when our blessed God passes into the Summerland.*

Covenors:

> *Blessed be the God, beloved of the Summerland.*

Acting High Priest/ess:

> *Tonight is also a night of life, when we honor our wise old Goddess who will see us through this ever-darkening season to life renewed.*

Covenors:

> *Blessed be the Crone, bringer of death and giver of life.*

> (The Acting High Priest and Priestess now approach the altar and pick up the God and Goddess candles each according to their gender.)

Acting High Priest/ess (the two Priest/esses hold the candles so their flames are united):

> *Tonight Goddess and God are a part of two different worlds. They are separated from one another.*

(The two Priest/esses remove the candles from one another, and the Priest blows out the God candle to symbolize his death. The Priest/esses replace them on the altar. The two covenors who have been selected to be the Crone Goddess and the Dying God now move into the center of the circle. Traditionally these roles are given to the oldest members present. The Dying God lies on the ground with the Crone kneeling beside him. She should make a gentle keening noise to affect her mourning.)

Covenors:

> *Farewell, Blessed Lord. Safe be your journey into the*
> *Summerland. Wise Old Goddess, may the loving comfort*
> *of your people ease your sorrow.*

(The Acting High Priest, who is in essence a representative or a vessel of the God on earth, will have no more speaking roles in the main body of the ritual to further signify to all present that the God is dead.)

Acting High Priestess:

> *As our beloved Lord passes through the veil which sepa-*
> *rates our world from the world of spirit, that veil is for a*
> *brief moment cast aside. Those who have already passed*
> *over wish to seek their loved ones once again. We will*
> *call to them that they may join in our festivities.*

(The Acting High Priestess now calls out to the loved one whose photo she has brought with her to place on the altar. She should also call the loved one of the High Priest who is now ritually silent. When she has done this she should step in front of the covenor to her left and raise her arms skyward. As Priestess she must act as a channel to take the energy of each covenor's call to the spirit world. The covenor should face the Land of the Dead to make this evocation. The Priestess should continue clockwise around the circle until all covenors have called out to their loved ones. The calls should always be in the covenor's own words. When the Priestess returns to her position the circle should fall silent, each member trying to sense and commune with the presence of the spirits.)

Acting High Priestess:

> *Friends and friendly spirits. Blessed be the New Year.*

Covenors:

> *Blessed be spirit and flesh.*
> *Blessed be the ever-turning Wheel.*
> *Behold, the Summer's End.*
> *Behold, a New Winter.*
> *Blessed be the New Year.*

Acting High Priestess (takes a wand or any other tool she prefers for manipulating energy and walks with it to the center of the circle):

> *Farewell, blessed summer!*

Covenors (this next line is said as the Priestess makes the sign of the banishing pentagram before herself. This may be done either with a forefinger or with any ritual tool):

> *Farewell, season of warmth and light.*

Acting High Priestess:

> *Welcome to winter—start of our New Year.*

Covenors (the following is said as the Priestess draws an invoking pentagram before herself):

> *Welcome winter, season of cold and dark.*

Acting High Priestess (moves to the altar, and turns to face the group):

> *The Wheel of the Year has made yet another transit. We are poised at a time which is an ending, and yet is also a new beginning. As it was and ever shall be, we pause to look back at times remembered, and we look forward to times yet to come.*

Covenors:

> *What will the new year hold?*

Acting High Priestess:

> *Approach the cauldron of the Crone and seek your answers.*

(The coven gathers around the cauldron and joins hands. Together everyone—including the silent God—will scry for answers to the future. The Priestess will decide when to break this contact by releasing the hands of the two persons beside her. The rest of the coven should follow her example.)

Acting High Priestess:

> *We have seen where we are traveling, for it is where we*
> *have been. We are all one with all that is. Who is Goddess?*

All Women:

> *I am Goddess.*

Acting High Priestess:

> *Who is God?*

All Men:

> *I am God.*

Acting High Priestess:

> *Who are Goddess and God?*

Covenors:

> *All living beings are Goddess and God.*

Acting High Priest/ess:

> *And who are we?*

Covenors:

> *We are the children of deity. And we are deity.*
> *We are a part of the creative life forces which move the*
> *universe. We are microcosm and macrocosm.*
> *We are part of all that is.*

(Acting High Priest/ess continues now with whatever seasonal celebrations the coven chooses to have. The reading of ritual or seasonal
poetry, either borrowed or written by members of the coven, is a
nice touch. Feasting may also take place within the circle, though it
can be left for later. On Samhain part of the feast is to be shared with
the spirits. Leave them their portion on a plate. When you are ready
to close the circle, ground it in whatever manner you have chosen to
do so, and then continue on.)

Acting High Priestess:

> *Though we are apart, we are ever together for we are one*
> *in the spirit of our Goddess and our God. Merry meet.*
> *Merry part.*

Covenors:

> *And merry meet again.*

Ancient Welsh Dirge

Music to accompany the Samhain group ritual

All:

> *Blessed Be!*

(It is customary in most traditions to ring a bell, or make some other loud, grounding noise as the ritual is completed. A sharp hand clap or a pound of the gavel are also good. Covenors do not have to leave just because the circle is opened. You may talk, visit, sing, eat, or participate in Samhain acts such as conducting a past-life regression. In some covens it is also customary to take a portion of the Samhain fire home to use to brighten windows to guide the spirits. Do this only if it can be safely done.)

Yule Group Ritual

Yule marks the New Year for virtually all pagan traditions, except the Celtic ones. This is reflected in the following ritual. For those following any of the Celtic paths, simply eliminate this section from the working.

Adorn your circle with lots of red candles, preferably ones with a cinnamon scent. Both the color red and the spice cinnamon are symbols of the Sun God who is reborn on this night. Holly, mistletoe, and evergreen may also grace your altar. Having a Yule tree nearby is another nice touch, especially if it is one which has been decorated by the coven.

For this Yule ritual you will need to arrange for everyone to draw names for a gift exchange. You may set limits on the amount to spend if you like. These gifts will be given in the pagan way—in memory of loved ones, and the sentiment is more important than the cost. You will also need a Yule log with the traditional white, red, and black candles, and something that can function as a cauldron. An optional item in this ritual is a bit of flash powder available in novelty and magic (illusion, not occult) shops.

Preassign the following roles: Acting High Priestess, Acting High Priest, the Holly King, the Oak King, the Virgin Goddess, the Mother Goddess, and the Crone Goddess.

> (When all members of the coven are assembled and the circle is cast, the ritual can begin. Keep the circle area in relative darkness until everyone has gathered. A single candle only—a Goddess candle represented by a taper of white—is recommended unless more light is needed for safety's sake. The one single candle is representative of the one creative life force, and for the maiden Goddess who is alone, but who will soon be joined by her consort as she gives birth to him again. You will also need plain white candles for everyone present. You might want to cut small circles of paper to put the tapers in so hot wax won't drip.)

Acting High Priest/ess:

> *Welcome friends.*

Covenors:

> *Welcome.*

Acting High Priest/ess:

> *The Wheel of the Year turns on and on, bringing us to and from each season, and from and to another. What will be is. What was will be. All time is here and now inside this sacred space. We pause briefly to watch the Wheel turn, and we gather on this blessed eve so that we might celebrate this season of Yule. In this moment between time, we come to praise the bountiful Goddess and her child-lover who is about to be born again. We wish to give thanks, and to feel ourselves a part of the relentlessly turning wheel of life, death and rebirth. Let all who would honor the Goddess and her consort enter into her protective circle.*

[Acting High Priest/ess will now call upon the directional energies. See the Samhain Group Ritual for this text.]

(The Acting High Priestess should lift the single candle from the altar and hold it in front of herself.)

Candle drip catcher

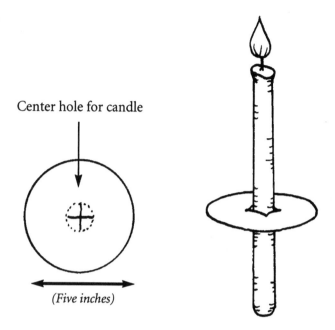

Center hole for candle

(Five inches)

Acting High Priestess:

> *This candle is representative of the life force which is our beloved Goddess. From her the light of the sun is birthed into the world, and from her symbol we will light our Yule circle. Tonight we celebrate the longest night of the year. And though it be our season of winter, tonight our darkness will end. Even though all about us appears in slumber and death, we are not forgotten. Our blessed Goddess carries in her young womb—that womb which has birthed all things into being—a son, her consort, our Lord God.*

(She raises her candle upwards and calls out.)

> *Blessed Lady, turn the wheel once more that the sun, your child and lover—our beloved God—will return to warm us anew.*

Covenors:

> *Blessed be the Lady, giver of life!*
> *Welcome Lord, bringer of warmth!*

Acting High Priest:

> *Tonight darkness has reached the limit of its power. Now*
> *the light of our God is victorious over darkness.*

(He picks up the lighted God candle from the altar and places it
into the flame of the Goddess candle and lights it. The flames are
held joined together.)

Acting High Priest and Priestess:

> *Tonight our God is born.*

(They move the flames apart.)

Covenors (face the direction your tradition views as the direction of the
land of the dead. This is usually the north or west. This is to acknowledge that the reborn God has just come from there):

> *Blessed be the Lady, giver of life!*
> *Welcome the God, Lord triumphant!*

(Covenors face the center of the circle again. The Acting High Priest
and Priestess should approach the altar again and pick up the God
and Goddess candles according to their gender.)

Acting High Priestess:

> *Tonight Goddess and God are reconciled. Together again*
> *these children set out on another journey through the*
> *eternal year.*

Acting High Priest:

> *Together they will bring life anew to our barren earth.*

(The two Priest/esses place the candles together so the flames merge
as one. This is a mimicry of the Great Rite which will be done in
spring Sabbat rituals. The feeling now is that these youngsters are
not ready for this type of union and the merging of the candles is
performed instead. All covenors will now approach the altar, pick up
an unlit candle, and light it from the joined flame.)

Covenors (Each covenor should say the following. Light the candle as the
last line is spoken):

> *Blessed be Goddess and God.*
> *Blessed be creation.*
> *Blessed be the darkness.*
> *Blessed be the light.*

(The Yule log should now be lit by the three pre-chosen women from the coven. Each one lights one candle—the Maiden white, the Mother red, and the Crone black. It is also best if these three women are dressed for their parts.)

Maiden Aspect:

> *Blessed be the Maiden, the little girl Goddess, wide-eyed*
> *and eager, innocent and fresh.*
> (She lights the white candle.)

Mother Aspect:

> *Blessed be the Mother, loving and protective, proud and*
> *fertile.* (She lights the red candle.)

Crone Aspect:

> *Blessed be the Crone, powerful and wise, guardian of the*
> *great cauldron of death, life and rebirth.* (She lights the
> black candle.)

(The three Goddess aspects dip their right hands into the Crone's cauldron which contains salted water and they pass around the circle clockwise, touching each covenor as they pass. The Maiden touches the feet, the Mother the stomach, and the Crone the forehead. This is a symbolic Goddess blessing with the maiden blessing the pathway of your feet, the mother blessing the reproductive regions, and the crone blessing the head wherein wisdom resides. When the circle is complete all the covenors can extinguish their hand-held candles and place them in a designated spot. When everyone has returned to their places, you may continue on.)

All:

> *May the log burn,*
> *May the wheel turn,*
> *May evil spurn,*
> *May the Sun return.*

(Just as this old rhyme is finished, the chosen Oak King and Holly King leap to the center of the circle and begin to fight. In their struggle they may use whatever ritual tools they choose. The covenors should cheer the Oak King until he is victorious. At that time the Holly King will fall to the ground in an imitation of death.)

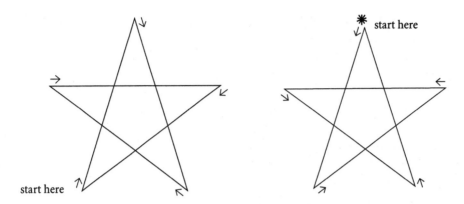

Banishing and invoking pentagrams.

Oak King (places a foot on the stomach of the Holly King in the manner of a victor):

> *I am the Oak King, God of the Waxing Year. Fear not on this dark night of winter, for I have come again to guide you on to summer and all its blessings.*

Covenors:

> *Blessed be the Oak King, King of the Waxing Year.*

Acting High Priest/ess:

> *The Holly King is slain.*
> *The Oak King reigns.*
> *Our Goddess is young once more.*
> *A new young God is born to us.*
> *Tonight, on this darkest night of winter, we turn to the light—the Sun God reborn and we say …*

All:

> *Blessed Be!*

Acting High Priest/ess:

> *Blessed be the New Year.*
> (Takes a wand or any other tool s/he prefers for manipulating energy and walks with it to the center of the circle):
> *Farewell, old year, the Wheel*
> *has banished you to history.*

Covenors (this next line is said as the Priest/ess makes the sign of the banishing pentagram before him/herself):

> *Farewell, old year. Go in peace.*

Acting High Priest/ess:

> *Welcome to winter—start of our New Year.*

(Priest/ess draws an invoking pentagram before him/herself. To further symbolize the returning sun, the other Priest/ess can light a bit of flash power over the God candle. This is optional and very dramatic.)

Covenors (the following is said as the Priest/ess draws an invoking pentagram before him/herself):

> *Welcome winter—season of our New Year.*

Acting High Priest/ess (moves to the altar and turns to face the group):

> *The Wheel of the Year has made yet another transit. We are poised at a time which is an ending, and yet is also a new beginning. As it was and ever shall be we pause to look back at times remembered, and we look forward to times yet to come.*

Covenors:

> *What will the new year hold?*

Acting High Priest/ess:

> *Approach the cauldron of the Triple Goddess and seek your answers.*

(The coven gathers around the cauldron and joins hands. Together scry for answers to the future. The High Priest and Priestess will decide when to break this contact by releasing their hands.)

Covenors:

> *We have seen where we are traveling, for it is where we have been. We are all one with all that is.*

Acting High Priestess:

> *Who is Goddess?*

All Women:

> *I am Goddess.*

Acting High Priest:

> *Who is God?*

All Men:

> *I am God.*

Acting High Priest and Priestess:

> *Who are Goddess and God?*

Covenors:

> *All living beings are Goddess and God.*

Acting High Priest and Priestess:

> *And who are we?*

Covenors:

> *We are the children of deity. And we are deity.*
> *We are a part of the creative life forces which move the*
> *universe. We are microcosm and macrocosm.*
> *We are part of all that is.*

Acting High Priest/ess (calls on one covenor to approach the altar):

> *Did you bring a gift to pass on a memory?*

Covenor:

> *I did.*

> (The covenor takes the gift s/he has brought to the circle
> and hands it to the person whose name s/he has drawn.
> The giver stands before the receiver as the present is
> unwrapped.)

Covenor who received gift:

> *In whose memory do I accept this token of love?*

> (The Covenor who gave the gift will tell who the gift is in memory
> of, and will tell why that person was meaningful to their lives.)

> *Thank you, friend. I will cherish both the gift and the*
> *memory as do you.*

(This process will continue on until everyone has passed out their
gifts. The Acting High Priest/ess then continues on with whatever
seasonal celebrations the coven has chosen to have. The reading of
ritual or seasonal poetry, either borrowed or written by members of
the coven, is a nice touch.)

[While there are thousands of songs that can used used or adapted
for use in pagan rituals, one such song literally cries out to be sung
at this time. "Auld Lang Syne," an old Scottish folk tune with words
by Scotland's poet laureate Robert Burns, is always heard at main-

stream New Year's festivities. The Gaelic words of the title are roughly translated to mean "for old time's sake."]

(When you are ready to close the circle, ground it in whatever manner you have chosen, and then continue.)

Acting High Priest/ess:

> *Though we are apart, we are ever together for we are one*
> *in the spirit of our Goddess and our God. Merry meet.*
> *Merry part.*

Covenors:

> *And merry meet again.*

All:

> *Blessed Be!*

(It is customary in most traditions to ring a bell, or make some other loud, grounding noise as the ritual is completed. A sharp hand clap or a pound of the gavel are also good. Covenors do not have to leave just because the circle is opened. You may talk, visit, sing, eat, etc. Feasting may also take place within the circle, though it can be left for later. Storytelling and pathworking are traditional Yule circle pastimes which can now be observed. You may also sing Christmas songs whose words have been altered to reflect a more pagan meaning.)

Imbolg Group Ritual

An Imbolg altar should hold whichever natural objects of the coming spring can be found in your climate. You might also want to give the Grain Dolly a place of honor on the altar, which should also contain a profusion of candles (as many as are safe) to represent increasing warmth, the Bride's Bed, and Sun Wheels. The candles on the altar and at the directional quarters should all be white, and should remain unlit for the time being. Have only enough firelight so you can all easily see what you are doing.

In the Irish tradition this is a Sabbat which almost singularly honors the goddess Brigid, and her name should be used in place of the word "Goddess" in this working. In Greece and Rome, Venus, Diana, and Februa were similarly honored, and those following the Greco-Roman tradition should venerate them.

Norse covens may wish to meet on a crossroads if such a thing is possible. Perhaps a coven member owns a large spread of land with roads on it. If such a place is not available, you can mimic the crossroads at your circle site by marking a large cross through it with dirt or corn meal. Light small balefires at the points in between or, if you are indoors, use fire contained in censers or in oil lamps.

For this Imbolg ritual you will need a single white candle for each person present, one equipped with wax drip catchers (see Yule Group Ritual for instructions on making these), a besom, and a Candle Wheel (see instructions for making one in Chapter Four).

Roles to be assigned are High Priestess, High Priest, the child God, and the Virgin Goddess.

> (When all members of the coven are assembled and the circle is cast, the ritual can begin. The woman portraying the Virgin Goddess will not be in the circle at this time, but will be in hiding out of sight of the gathering.)

Acting High Priest/ess:

> *Welcome friends.*

Covenors:

> *Welcome.*

Acting High Priest/ess:

> *The Wheel of the Year turns on and on, bringing us to*
> *and from each season, and from and to another. What*

will be is. What was will be. All time is here and now
inside this sacred space. We pause briefly to watch the
wheel turn, and we gather on this blessed eve so that we
might celebrate this season of Imbolg. In this moment
between time, we come to praise the young Maiden
Goddess and her child-lover who was and will be the
father of our harvest bounty. As it was and ever shall be, we
wish to give thanks, and to feel ourselves a part of the
relentlessly turning wheel. Let all who would honor the
Goddess and her consort enter into her protective circle.

[Acting High Priest/ess will now call upon the directional energies.
See the Samhain Group Ritual for this text.]

Acting High Priest/ess:

Tonight is a night when heat overcomes cold.

Covenors:

Blessed be the Virgin Goddess.
Blessed be the child God.

Acting High Priest/ess:

Yule is past, and the young God, like his symbol the sun,
is returning to his Lady Earth. As she turns the great
wheel, she brings him nearer, and soon she will offer her
self as his bride.

All:

Virgin Goddess, innocent and fresh, we beseech you,
bring the sun of spring to warm us once again.

(You may play or sing music as the Virgin Goddess, dressed as a
bride, comes to the edge of the circle with her Candle Wheel either
in her arms or on her head. She should stand at the quarter where
your tradition perceives the Land of the Dead to be. The High Priest
or Priestess will cut a doorway in the circle and allow the Goddess to
enter. Everyone should greet her in their own way. This can be done
verbally, with raised arms, a nod, a bow, etc. The Goddess should
walk three times clockwise around the inside of the circle, and come
to a stop before the altar and kneel before it. Three represents her
Triple aspect, and is a sacred number in many Western traditions. If
you have another number which is sacred to you, you should use

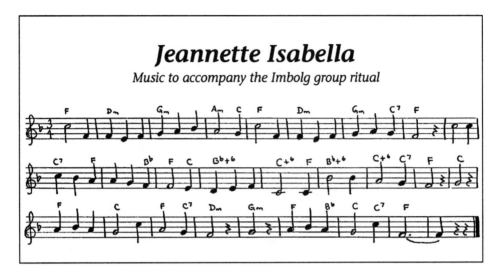

Jeannette Isabella

Music to accompany the Imbolg group ritual

that one. The covenors should walk in single file to the altar starting with the person to the altar's right. This will make the procession head clockwise. Each covenor will take a candle and light it from the Virgin Goddess' Candle Wheel. They will take that flame and light a few of the candles on the altar and whatever others are assigned to them, and proceed clockwise to their starting point. When everyone is back in their places holding their lighted candles, the ritual can continue.)

Acting High Priest:

> *Behold the light. The God has returned for his bride.*

Covenors:

> *Blessed be the light which warms.*
> *Blessed be the God.*
> *Blessed be the wheel which turns.*
> *Blessed be the Goddess.*

(The child God steps out from among the rest and stands before the bride. He bows to her and she to him. They then do a few flowing dance steps around the circle without touching each other, but conveying the idea of an awakening sexuality. You may play or sing music for their dance if you wish. When they are finished, they lift the besom from its resting place near the altar. The Goddess should hold the straw part and the God the stick. They should make sure that they do not physically come into contact with each other while they do this.)

Acting High Priest/ess stands in front of the besom and takes it from them by grasping it firmly with both hands. The Goddess and God step back to take their place with the rest of the coven):

> *With Imbolg we sweep away the last vestiges of winter.*

(The Priest/ess moves counterclockwise around the circle behind the covenors, sweeping from the center outward. The covenors should face outward as this is done. As the Priest/ess passes each covenor he or she should voice either aloud or silently all the things he or she wishes to have swept from their lives. When this is finished, the Virgin Goddess and child God step forward again and take the besom from the Priest/ess in the same manner in which it was given. They take it together to set it where they first picked it up.)

Acting High Priest/ess:

> *The God has claimed his Goddess bride and the Wheel of the Year turns on.*

Acting High Priestess:

> *Who is Goddess?*

All Women:

> *I am Goddess.*

Acting High Priest:

> *Who is God?*

All Men:

> *I am God.*

Acting High Priest and Priestess:

> *Who are Goddess and God?*

Covenors:

> *All living beings are Goddess and God.*

Acting High Priest and Priestess:

> *And who are we?*

Covenors:

> *We are the children of deity. And we are deity.*
> *We are a part of the creative life forces which move the*
> *universe. We are microcosm and macrocosm.*
> *We are part of all that is.*

(Acting High Priest/ess continues now with whatever seasonal celebrations the coven chooses to have. The reading of ritual or seasonal
poetry, either borrowed or written by members of the coven, is nice.
When you are ready to close the circle, ground it in the manner you
have chosen, and then continue.)

Acting High Priest/ess:

*Though we are apart, we are ever together for we are one
in the spirit of our Goddess and our God. Merry meet.
Merry part.*

Covenors:

And merry meet again.

All:

Blessed Be!

(It is customary in most traditions to ring a bell, or make some
other loud, grounding noise as the ritual is completed. A sharp hand
clap or a pound of the gavel are also good. Covenors do not have to
leave just because the circle is opened. You may talk, dance, visit,
sing, eat, etc. Feasting may also take place within the circle, though
it can be left for later. Fire divinations are a part of Imbolg and can
also be observed here.)

Ostara Group Ritual

This Ostara ritual is written for a night working, but some covens celebrate
this spring Sabbat in the daylight. If this is your practice, alter the words to
reflect this preference.

An Ostara altar might contain early spring flowers and symbols of balance, such as Sun Wheels and/or painted eggs.

For this ritual you will need at least one colored egg for each person in
the circle. You can use wooden or plastic ones, but it is better to have real
hard-boiled eggs dyed with spring colors. Place these inside a cauldron, or
some other womb-like vessel, near or on the altar. You will also need dance
music of some sort, either played, sung, or prerecorded. Celtic dance music
works well for this purpose.

In this ritual the music for a very old Irish folk jig called "The Cookoo's
Nest" is given. It makes a spritely dance tune for Ostara. Repeat it as many
times as needed for your ritual dance.

Roles to be assigned are High Priestess and the High Priest.

(When all members of the coven are assembled and the circle is cast, the ritual can begin.)

Acting High Priest/ess:

> *Welcome friends.*

Covenors:

> *Welcome.*

Acting High Priest/ess:

> *The Wheel of the Year turns on and on, bringing us to and from each season, and from and to another. What will be is. What was will be. All time is here and now inside this sacred space. We pause briefly to watch the wheel turn, and we gather on this blessed eve so that we might celebrate this season of balance known as Ostara. In this moment between time, we come to praise the bountiful young Goddess and her son-lover for their blessings of fertility, warmth, and life renewed. We wish to give thanks, and to feel ourselves a part of the relentlessly turning wheel of life, death, and rebirth. Let all who would honor the Goddess and her consort enter into her protective circle.*

[Acting High Priest/ess will now call upon the directional energies. See the Samhain Group Ritual for this text.]

Acting High Priest/ess:

> *This is a night of balance. Dark and light come to each other as equals, as do our young deities.*

Covenors:

> *Blessed be Goddess and God.*

Acting High Priest/ess:

> *But the wheel turns on. After tonight the light will conquer the darkness.*

Covenors:

> *Blessed be the darkness.*
> *Blessed be the light.*

The Cookoo's Nest

Music to accompany the Ostara group ritual

Acting High Priest/ess:

The mythology of our pagan ancestors tells us many stories of our deities whose lives began anew at Ostara when they were restored to us from the dark underworld which had captured them. Tonight we celebrate the renewal of our Mother Earth, and the renewal of our own lives at this sacred spring season. But before we can be reborn we must know death. We must venture into underworld of darkness before we can be reborn into the newness of light.

(The Priest/esses extinguish all the fires lighting the ritual area with the exception of a balefire. If you have no balefire, then keep the Goddess and God candles on the altar burning so that you can see where you are going. Walking toward the quarter of the circle that your tradition views as the one corresponding to the Land of the Dead, the Priest cuts a doorway in the circle and the Priestess leads the coven single file out of the circle. The Priest then closes the opening behind them and remains inside the circle. The Priestess leads the coven slowly counterclockwise around the dark outside perimeter of the circle. Heads should be bowed and, as much as is possible, the mind cleared of all extraneous thoughts. The covenors should view themselves as passing through the underworld of darkness. When the Priestess returns for the third time to the place where she left the circle, the Priest will cut the door for her again and admit her. He hands her the cauldron containing the eggs, and she turns and motions the covenors back inside the circle. As they file in, the Priestess hands each of them an egg, a symbol of life renewed, and the Priest leads them all three times clockwise around the inner perimeter of the circle. The pace is brisker than it was outside of the circle, and heads are held high. The Priestess should close the doorway behind the last person to reenter the circle. When everyone is back at their starting points, the music should begin.)

Acting High Priest and Priestess:

Join us in the dance of joy, the dance of life restored.

Covenors:

Join us in the dance of joy, the dance of life restored.

(The coven should dance in a manner that has been decided upon. Most prefer to have everyone dance as couples to symbolize the sexual awareness of the deities, but this is not always possible. Dancing in a circle, or having each person take a turn showing off in the center are good alternatives. Keep the pace lively, and the attitude as one of reckless abandon. Move in any way you feel moved. No one should be ridiculed for their self-expressions. This is a Sabbat which celebrates life, and all offerings of gladness are right and good. Allow the dancing to continue until everyone is exhausted. The Acting High Priest/ess should stop the music and allow everyone to stand for several minutes in complete silence. It will take some time for the high of dancing to wear off, and you may hear some spontaneous giggles during this quiet time. Just accept and ignore them. It is natural and good that your coven should feel this way. When everyone has had a chance to center themselves a bit, you are ready to continue. The High Priest and Priestess move to the altar and, with the Goddess and God Candles, light the other fires around the circle. They then put these candles in their place, and turn to face the coven.)

Acting High Priest:

> *Behold the light of the God.*

Covenors:

> *Blessed be the God.*
> *Blessed be life renewed.*

Acting High Priestess:

> *Blessed be the turning to light.*

Covenors:

> *Blessed be the Goddess who turns the wheel.*
> *Blessed be life renewed.*

Acting High Priest/ess:

> *The eggs you hold in your hands have been venerated as*
> *symbols of life renewed for as many millennia as*
> *humans have walked this earth. They are now charged*
> *with the life energy we have raised in this sacred circle.*
> *Honor their ancient meaning.*

(In some traditions the eggs are taken home and placed on home altars, in others they are buried to promote the fertility of the land. Covenors should do with the egg what feels right to them.)

Acting High Priestess:

> *Who is Goddess?*

All Women:

> *I am Goddess.*

Acting High Priest:

> *Who is God?*

All Men:

> *I am God.*

Acting High Priest and Priestess:

> *Who are Goddess and God?*

Covenors:

> *All living beings are Goddess and God.*

Acting High Priest and Priestess:

> *And who are we?*

Covenors:

> *We are the children of deity. And we are deity.*
> *We are a part of the creative life forces which move the*
> *universe. We are microcosm and macrocosm.*
> *We are part of all that is.*

(Acting High Priest/ess continues now with the seasonal celebrations the coven chooses to have, perhaps reading ritual or seasonal
poetry either borrowed or written by members of the coven. When
you are ready to close the circle, ground it in whatever manner you
have chosen, and then continue.)

Acting High Priest/ess:

> *Though we are apart, we are ever together for we are one*
> *in the spirit of our Goddess and our God. Merry meet.*
> *Merry part.*

Covenors:

> *And merry meet again.*

All:

> *Blessed Be!*

(It is customary in most traditions to ring a bell, or make some
other loud, grounding noise as the ritual is completed. A sharp hand
clap or a pound of the gavel are also good. Covenors do not have to
leave just because the circle is opened. You may talk, dance, sing,
visit, etc. Feasting may also take place within the circle, though it can
be left for later. Ostara is a time to celebrate romantic love and it is
fitting that Handfastings be performed or celebrated.)

Bealtaine Group Ritual

Whenever possible, Bealtaine rituals should take place outdoors in the full
light of day. After all, this is a Sabbat that celebrates life, fertility, and the
start of the growing season. It is also the beginning of the Celtic summer, a
fact acknowledged in the text of the ritual. For those of you who do not wish
to make mention of this, simply eliminate it from the working.

A Bealtaine altar might contain early spring flowers and painted eggs.
Dispense with candles—except for the Goddess and God candles on your
altar—and have a balefire instead. Even if you have to be indoors you can

light a fireplace, or use an oil lamp or censer with a contained fire as large as can safely be managed.

For this Bealtaine ritual you will need all your usual ritual tools, and two chaplets of flowers to be placed on the heads of the Priest and Priestess at the appropriate time.

Roles to assign are High Priestess, the High Priest, the Priestess's Handmaiden, and the Priest's Handmaster. Because this is a day to enact the Great Rite, it works best if the High Priest and Priestess are an established couple.

> (When all members of the coven are assembled and the circle is cast, the ritual can begin. Because of the sexual nature of this Sabbat, arrange your covenors around the circle as near as possible to male, female, male, female, etc.)

Acting High Priest/ess:

> *Welcome friends.*

Covenors:

> *Welcome.*

Acting High Priest/ess:

> *The Wheel of the Year turns on and on, bringing us to*
> *and from each season, and from and to another. What*
> *will be is. What was will be. All time is here and now*
> *inside this sacred space. We pause briefly to watch the*
> *Wheel turn, and we gather on this blessed day so that we*
> *might celebrate Bealtaine—the start of the fertile sum-*
> *mer season. In this moment between time, we come to*
> *praise the bountiful Goddess and her God consort who*
> *unite today in sacred marriage. We wish to give thanks,*
> *and to feel ourselves a part of the relentlessly turning*
> *wheel of life, death, and rebirth. Let all who would*
> *honor the Goddess and her consort enter into her*
> *protective circle.*

> [Acting High Priest/ess will now call upon the directional energies. See the Samhain Group Ritual for this text.]

Acting High Priest:

> *Tonight is the lusty eve of May.*
> *Blessed be the fertile Goddess.*

Acting High Priestess:

> *Tonight is the lusty eve of May.*
> *Blessed be the Great Horned God.*

Covenors:

> *Tonight is the lusty eve of May. Blessed be the sacred*
> *marriage which manifests all creation.*

(The Handmaiden and Handmaster walk to the altar and the Handmaiden picks up the chalice, and the Handmaster the athame. They carry these to the Priest and Priestess, and the Handmaiden hands the chalice to the Priestess, and the Handmaster hands the athame to the Priest. These are the tools they will use to enact the Great Rite, the symbolic sexual union of the deities.)

Covenors (as the Priestess holds high the chalice with both hands):

> *Behold, the womb of the Great Mother.*
> *The great cosmic egg from which all life flows.*

(As the Priest holds high the athame with both hands):

> *Behold, the phallus of the Father God.*
> *The fertilizing principle of the universe.*

Acting High Priest and Priestess:

> *Blessed be the one divine life force in all its many forms.*

(The Handmaiden and Handmaster step out and place the two chaplets of flowers on the heads of the Priest and Priestess. This is to signify that they now wear the mantle of deity during this rite.)

Handmaiden (as she crowns the Priestess):

> *Blessed are you among women tonight.*

Handmaster (as he crowns the Priest):

> *Blessed are you among men tonight.*

(In ancient times, long before the male role in procreation was recognized, a woman's body often comprised the altar for pagan rites. This was not an act of degradation, but one in which the woman chosen became the earthly vessel of the great Mother Goddess herself, and it was upon her fertile belly that fertility rites took place. The Great Rite is such a rite. The Priestess will lie down in the circle, in the center if there is no balefire there, or else toward the eastern edge. The east is the direction of sunrise, therefore symbolic of new beginnings. She is assisted by her Handmaiden. A decorative pillow can be placed under her head if it is desired. With both hands the Priestess holds the chalice resting over her womb. Her legs may be closed or spread, again depending on how your group feels about this rite. The Handmaiden should make this and any other adjustments in the Priestess' position, depending on what the coven has decided. The Priest stands at the Priestess' knee, either standing over her legs, or in between them. He raises the athame over her, its tip pointing downward. All the members of the coven should close their eyes for a moment and visualize the life energy of the deities filling their two leaders. When the High Priest speaks again, they may all open their eyes.)

Acting High Priest:

> *Blessed be you, my Goddess, my holy bride of heaven and earth. Let me unite with you in the ancient rite of sacred marriage.*

Acting High Priestess:

> *Blessed be you, my God, my holy groom of heaven and earth. Let me unite with you in the ancient rite of sacred marriage.*

Acting High Priest and Priestess:

> *As we become one, so we are one.*
> *As we are one, so we become one.*

(The Priest kneels and brings the blade down into the chalice. The Priest and Priestess' eyes should be locked, and they should feel the deities within themselves merging to become one whole and complete being. The coven should remember this rite is not only an act of fertility magick, but also the primal act of creation from which all life comes. Allow a few moments for these thoughts. The Handmaiden and Handmaster will decide when this is to end. They move forward to the Priest and Priestess and take the ritual tools from them without allowing their contact to be broken. Together they take these, still united, to the altar and set them down. They then return to help the Priest and Priestess to their feet. The Priest and Priestess will remain standing side by side, keeping themselves in

The Old English Morris Dance
Music to accompany the Bealtaine group ritual

physical contact. They will also be ritually silent until the circle is closed. Their roles will now be assumed by the Handmaiden and Handmaster.)

Handmaiden:

> *By this act of love, all life comes to be.*

Handmaster:

> *By this act of faith, we proclaim our belief in our place*
> *on the eternal cycle of life.*

Handmaiden and Handmaster:

> *Blessed be the Great Rite.*
> *The Lord and Lady reign eternal.*

(Dancing is very much a part of the Bealtaine Sabbat. The coven should all join hands and do a joyous clockwise dance around the silent High Priest and Priestess. The Handmaiden leads the dance, and everyone should follow her footsteps. Likewise, she will decide when this is to stop.)

Handmaiden:

> *Who is Goddess?*

All Women:

> *I am Goddess.*

Handmaster:

> *Who is God?*

All Men:

> *I am God.*

Handmaiden and Handmaster:

> *Who are Goddess and God?*

Covenors:

> *All living beings are Goddess and God.*

Handmaiden and Handmaster:

> *And who are we?*

Covenors:

> *We are the children of deity. And we are deity.*
> *We are a part of the creative life forces which move the*
> *universe. We are microcosm and macrocosm.*
> *We are part of all that is.*

(The Handmaiden and Handmaster continue now with the seasonal celebrations the coven chooses to have, perhaps reading ritual or seasonal poetry, either borrowed or written by members of the coven. When you are ready to close the circle, ground it in the manner you have chosen, and then continue.)

Handmaiden and Handmaster:

> *Though we are apart, we are ever together for we are one*
> *in the spirit of our Goddess and our God. Merry meet.*
> *Merry part.*

Covenors:

> *And merry meet again.*

All:

> *Blessed Be!*

(It is customary in most traditions to ring a bell, or make some other loud, grounding noise as the ritual is completed. A sharp hand clap or a pound of the gavel are also good. Covenors do not have to leave just because the circle is opened. You may talk, dance, visit, etc. Feasting may also take place within the circle, though it can be left for later. Weaving the May Pole is another time-honored way to celebrate this Sabbat, and you should try to do this if it is at all possible. For instructions, see Chapter Six. One of the reasons for trying to pick an established couple as the Acting High Priest and Priestess for this ritual is so that they can reenact the Great Rite later when they are alone, making the bond between the Goddess and God actual as well as symbolic.)

Midsummer Group Ritual

Even if you celebrate all the other Sabbats of the year in the dark of night, you should try—if at all possible—to hold this observance in the bright light of day. Some covens will choose to rise early and go out as a group to greet the rising sun with their ritual immediately following. This Sabbat is a veneration of the pregnant Goddess and of the sun at its peak, and it is difficult to feel the proper sentiments if you are cloistered in darkness.

A Midsummer altar might contain a chalice of milk, a besom, mistletoe or other summer herbs, nuts, or young food plants.

For this ritual you will need to bring pets or their photos for the pet blessing. If you farm, you can bring one animal to represent your entire flock or herd, or an item symbolic of them. Also bring a small gift for the animal such as a pendant for its collar or a special food treat. If you have no pet, bring a picture of some animals you wish to help, and your gift can be a donation to an animal rights cause or a local animal shelter. You will also need to have a crown, which symbolizes the sun, to crown the Holly King, and a bit of salted water in a cauldron.

Roles to assign are High Priestess, High Priest, the Holly King, the Oak King, and the Pregnant Goddess. Pick a pregnant woman for this last role whenever possible, otherwise have the chosen woman dress the part. Consider having a processional to the Midsummer circle site. The Norse did this with song and blazing torches. Do this only if it can be done safely. When all members of the coven are assembled and the circle is cast, the ritual can begin.)

Acting High Priest/ess:

Welcome friends.

Covenors:

Welcome.

Acting High Priest/ess:

The Wheel of the Year turns on and on, bringing us to and from each season, and from and to another. What will be is. What was will be. All time is here and now inside this sacred space. We pause briefly to watch the Wheel turn, and we gather on this blessed day so that we might celebrate this season of Midsummer. In this moment between time, we come to praise the bountiful

> *Mother Goddess and the benevolent Sun God who rides*
> *high above us at the peak of his power. We are a part of*
> *them. We are them, and we are their children. We wish*
> *to give thanks and to feel ourselves a part of the relent-*
> *lessly turning wheel of life. Let all who would honor the*
> *Goddess and her consort enter into her protective circle.*

[Acting High Priest/ess will now call upon the directional energies. See the Samhain Group Ritual for this text.]

Acting High Priestess:

> *Blessed be the Golden Sun.*

Covenors:

> *Blessed be the Father.*

Acting High Priest/ess:

> *Blessed be the Fertile Earth.*

Covenors:

> *Blessed be the Mother.*

(The woman assigned to be the Pregnant Goddess steps forward and raises her arms and face upward as if trying to capture the sun. She symbolically bathes in it by rubbing it over her arms, face, and belly. If the sun is not shining, do this anyway as a symbolic gesture.)

Covenors:

> *Great Mother, turn the Wheel once more.*
> *Turn us toward the harvest.*

Pregnant Goddess:

> *Who will be my king as we travel onward?*

(The Holly King and the Oak King both step forward as if to claim the right to stand beside the Goddess.)

> *There can be only one God of the harvest, one King of*
> *the Waning Year.*

(The two Kings symbolically fight as they did at Yule. This time the coven should cheer for the Holly King who eventually emerges victorious. At that time the Oak King will fall to the ground in an imitation of death.)

The Slender Rowan Tree
Music to accompany the Midsummer group ritual

Holly King (places a foot on the stomach of the Oak King in the manner of a victor):

> *I am the Holly King, God of the Waning Year. Fear not the ravages of summer's heat and drought, for I have come again to guide you on to the harvest and all its blessings.*

Covenors:

> *Blessed be the Holly King, King of the Waning Year.*

Acting High Priest/ess:

> *The Oak King is slain.*
> *The Holly King reigns.*
> *Our Mother Earth is heavy with harvest's bounty.*
> *The Sun God rides high above.*
> *Tonight, on this brightest day of summer, we turn to the coming darkness and we say...*

All:

> *Blessed Be!*

Pregnant Goddess (takes the Holly King by the hand and moves with him to the altar, and they turn to face the group):

> *The Wheel of the Year has made yet another transit. We are poised at a time which is a new beginning, and yet is also an ending.*

(She removes the Sun crown from the altar and places it on the Holly King's head.)

> *Be thou my King.*

(The Holly King kisses the Goddess's out-stretched hand.)

All:

> *Blessed be the Father.*
> *Blessed be the Mother.*

(The Goddess and the two Kings take their former places in the circle. The Acting High Priest/ess will give a signal to call or gather the pets who have been invited to the pet blessing.)

Acting High Priest/ess:

> *For many millennia pagans have brought their animals*
> *to the Midsummer circle to receive the special blessings of*
> *life, health, and fertility.*

(In these days of severe animal over-population do not emphasize the fertility aspect unless someone among you raises livestock for a living. The Priest/ess will call the covenors and their animals to the altar one by one. The Pregnant Goddess stands with them. The covenors should state aloud to the pet the particular blessings they wish it to have, and present it with its gift, or state to the animal what gift will be forthcoming. When finished, the Acting High Priest will wave the athame over the pet's head three times clockwise.)

Acting High Priest:

> *I bless you,* (State animal's name or function), *with*
> *health, strength, and well-being.*

(The Pregnant Goddess will place her hands into the cauldron and take a bit of the salted water onto her fingertips. She will then place her hands on the head of the animal.)

Pregnant Goddess:

> *I bless you,* (State animal's name or function), *with fertility, love, security, and peace. May you live a long and*
> *happy life.*

(When all the animals are blessed, the Pregnant Goddess returns to her place in the circle. Many beautiful words have been written about the animals who share with us the planet. You may wish to have someone read such a piece at this point. Below is an excerpt from a letter written by a Native American chief to Grover Cleveland in 1885:)

…What is man without beasts? If all the beasts were gone, man would die of a great loneliness of spirit, for what happens to the beasts also happens to man. All things are connected. Whatever befalls the earth befalls the sons of the earth…

Acting High Priestess:

> *Who is Goddess?*

All Women:

> *I am Goddess.*

Acting High Priest:

> *Who is God?*

All Men:

> *I am God.*

Acting High Priest and Priestess:

> *Who are Goddess and God?*

Covenors:

> *All living beings are Goddess and God.*

Acting High Priest and Priestess:

> *And who are we?*

Covenors:

> *We are the children of deity. And we are deity.*
> *We are a part of the creative life forces which move the*
> *universe. We are microcosm and macrocosm.*
> *We are part of all that is.*

(Acting High Priest/ess continues now with the seasonal celebrations the coven chooses to have, perhaps reading ritual or seasonal poetry either borrowed or written by members of the coven. When you are ready to close the circle, ground it in the manner you have chosen, and then continue.)

Acting High Priest/ess:

> *Though we are apart, we are ever together for we are one*
> *in the spirit of our Goddess and our God. Merry meet.*
> *Merry part.*

Covenors:

> *And merry meet again.*

All:

> *Blessed Be!*

> (It is customary in most traditions to ring a bell, or make some other loud, grounding noise as the ritual is completed. A sharp hand clap or a pound of the gavel are also good. Covenors do not have to leave just because the circle is opened. You may talk, visit, eat, etc. Feasting may also take place within the circle, though it can be left for later. Pieces of unburned balefire wood were once kept as powerful talismans of light during the ever-darkening waning year. The telling and interpreting of dreams should also be a part of your celebration, especially if you follow the Norse tradition.)

Lughnasadh Group Ritual

Lughnasadh rituals are done during the day as often as at night. Those covens who celebrate it primarily as the first harvest festival usually choose evening rituals, and those who celebrate specific sun deities (such as the Irish who honor Lugh) opt for daytime rituals. The choice is yours.

A Lughnasadh altar should hold items from the harvest, particularly corn and other grains. If you choose to honor a sun deity, you may want to add sun symbols such as golden stones or Sun Wheels to the altar.

Because those traditions who celebrate only the harvest at this Sabbat outnumber those who worship sun deities, this ritual will focus on the harvest aspect of the holiday. If you wish to add a part to this ritual to your own sun deity, simply grab a pen and write one in.

For this ritual you will need a large loaf of bread—preferably corn bread—and some sort of juice or wine. You will also need a plate or bowl to remove the harvest offering.

Preassign the roles of High Priestess, High Priest, Coven Spokesperson, the Grain God, and the Corn Mother.

> (You may wish to outline the perimeter of your circle with corn meal, the grain most sacred to this Sabbat. When all members of the coven are assembled and the circle is cast, the ritual can begin.)

Acting High Priest/ess:

> *Welcome friends.*

Covenors:

> *Welcome.*

Acting High Priest/ess:

> *The Wheel of the Year turns on and on, bringing us to
> and from each season, and from and to another. What
> will be is. What was will be. All time is here and now
> inside this sacred space. We pause briefly to watch the
> Wheel turn, and we gather on this blessed eve so that we
> might celebrate this season of Lughnasadh—the first
> harvest. In this moment between time, we come to praise
> the bountiful Goddess and the benevolent God. We wish
> to give thanks for the bounty of the fertile earth, and to
> feel ourselves a part of the relentlessly turning wheel of
> life, death and rebirth. Let all who would honor the
> Goddess and her consort enter into her protective circle.*

[Acting High Priest/ess will now call upon the directional energies.
See the Samhain Group Ritual for this text.]

Acting High Priest/ess:

> *Blessed be the bounty of the harvest, fruit of the womb of
> the Goddess.*

Covenors:

> *Blessed be Mother Earth.*

Acting High Priest/ess:

> *Today we honor our deities in their aspects as the Grain
> God and the Corn Mother.*

(The Priest and Priestess assume a place within the circle, and the
two covenors portraying the Corn Mother and the Grain God will
step to the altar. They should dress their parts by wearing harvest
colors and adorning themselves with sheaves of grain if possible.
Sheaves can be pinned on clothing, woven into belts or headdresses,
or carried. The Corn Mother should pick up the loaf of bread, and
the Grain God the chalice of wine. Substitutions for wine are acceptable, especially if some members of your coven cannot drink alcohol. Moving clockwise around the circle, the Grain God and Corn
Mother stand before each covenor. The Corn Mother hands the loaf
of bread to the first person.)

Corn Mother:

> *Will you count your many blessings on this Sabbat of*
> *bounty?*

(The covenor holds the loaf while s/he recites all the things for which s/he is thankful. Then s/he breaks off a piece of the bread and eats it. Another piece is broken off and is placed on the altar by the covenor. This is a libation to the faeries and deities who have attended this harvest rite and will be left for them later. The covenor returns to his/her spot in the circle and the Grain God holds the chalice while s/he takes a drink. The Corn Mother and Grain God move around the entire circle in this way. When they reach the end they administer this rite to each other, replace the items on the altar, and take their places back in the circle. The Priest and Priestess then walk to the altar. The Priestess picks up the bread which is to be given as a libation and holds it before her.)

Acting High Priestess:

> *Blessed be the harvest, manifestation of the sacred*
> *marriage of the deities.*

Covenors:

> *Blessed be the fruitful Corn Mother.*
> *Blessed be the God of the Harvest.*

Acting High Priestess:

> *To whom does the coven give this offering?*

Coven Spokesperson (steps forward and stands in front of the Priestess):

> *We give this bounty of the land back to whom it came.*
> *We offer it to Mother Earth, and to her consort. And we*
> *ask that it be shared with the faeries of the fields and the*
> *animals of the woodland.*

Acting High Priestess:

> *Who charges you with these words?*

Covenors:

> *We do.*

Acting High Priest and Priestess (she turns to the Priest and together they wrap their hands around as much of the offering as they can):

> *We consecrate this offering back to the Mother from*
> *whom it came, to her consort, her animals, and her faery*
> *beings. Blessed be.*

(The Priest removes the offering to a bowl to be taken out later and laid onto the earth.)

Acting High Priest:

> *Offerings given in love return three times over. Blessed be*
> *this gathering, the givers and the gift.*

Covenors:

> *Blessed be.*

Acting High Priest/ess:

> *All things have their season. Tonight the wheel has*
> *brought us to the season of harvest. A time of beauty and*
> *time of toil. A time to reflect on the summer and a time*
> *to prepare for the winter ahead.*

(Pagans can borrow from many sources to find their inspiration. You may wish to read from the Judeo-Christian Biblical text of Ecclesiastes. There are several excellent passages about everything being in its season. The first section is found in the first chapter which begins, "One generation goes, and another comes...." The other is the famous "A Time for Every Purpose Under Heaven" section which is found in the first eight verses of the third chapter.)

Acting High Priestess:

> *Who is Goddess?*

All Women:

> *I am Goddess.*

Acting High Priest:

> *Who is God?*

All Men:

> *I am God.*

Acting High Priest and Priestess:

> *Who are Goddess and God?*

Covenors:

> *All living beings are Goddess and God.*

Coming Through the Rye

Music to accompany the Lughnasadh group ritual

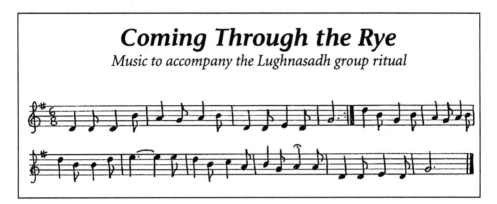

Acting High Priest and Priestess:

> *And who are we?*

Covenors:

> *We are the children of deity. And we are deity.*
> *We are a part of the creative life forces which move the*
> *universe. We are microcosm and macrocosm. We are*
> *part of all that is.*

(Acting High Priest/ess continues now with the seasonal celebrations the coven chooses to have. The reading of ritual or seasonal poetry, either borrowed or written by members of the coven, is a nice touch. When you are ready to close the circle, ground it in the manner you have chosen, and then continue.)

Acting High Priest/ess:

> *Though we are apart, we are ever together for we are one*
> *in the spirit of our Goddess and our God. Merry meet.*
> *Merry part.*

Covenors:

> *And merry meet again.*

All:

> *Blessed Be!*

(It is customary in most traditions to ring a bell, or make some other loud, grounding noise as the ritual is completed. A sharp hand clap or a pound of the gavel are also good. Covenors do not have to leave just because the circle is opened. You may talk, sing, visit, eat, etc. Feasting may also take place within the circle, though it can be left for later. The feast of Lughnasadh is one of the largest of any of the Sabbats. All first fruits of the season are consumed, especially any and all grains which have been harvested.)

Mabon Group Ritual

A Mabon altar might contain autumn leaves, a Horn of Plenty, nuts, apples, or any other bounty of the harvest. Grapes, because they are deeply associated with this Sabbat, should also be present.

If you live in a rural area and are not likely to be seen, you might consider holding this ritual during the daylight hours in a country cemetery. Do not go into a cemetery at night, simply because most cemeteries are officially closed at sundown and most people might be upset to see witches parading around in graveyards. We can work to change the latter, but the first is a matter of private cemetery policy and we have no business attempting to change it.

For this ritual you will need a deep chalice or glass of wine or juice (apple juice is an excellent substitute for wine), and an apple for each person present. You will also need two grapevine wreaths to crown the Harvest King and Queen.

Preassign the roles of High Priestess, High Priest, God of Wine, Harvest Queen, and Harvest King.

> (You might consider processing to the circle site in the Irish way with your apples tied to a garland. See Chapter Nine for instructions. When all members of the coven are assembled and the circle is cast, the ritual can begin.)

Acting High Priest/ess:

> *Welcome friends.*

Covenors:

> *Welcome.*

Acting High Priest/ess:

> *The Wheel of the Year turns on and on, bringing us to and from each season, and from and to another. What will be is. What was will be. All time is here and now inside this sacred space. We pause briefly to watch the Wheel turn, and we gather on this blessed eve so that we might celebrate this season of Mabon—the time of the second harvest. In this moment between time, we come to praise the bountiful aging Goddess and her consort, our God of the Wine Harvest. We wish to give thanks, and to feel ourselves a part of the relentlessly turning wheel of life, death and rebirth. Let all who would honor the Goddess and her consort enter into her protective circle.*

[Acting High Priest/ess will now call upon the directional energies. See the Samhain Group Ritual for this text.]

Acting High Priest/ess:

> *Tonight all things are in balance. Night and day are equal. Goddess and God are equal. Life and death are equal. But tonight darkness conquers the light, taking us into the dark of the year, a time to reflect on those passed over, and on those who are yet to come.*

(Picks up the vessel containing the apples. It is good if this is a cauldron, but often one large enough to hold enough apples for an entire group cannot be afforded. Use what you have available. S/he reaches in and lifts out one apple.)

> *Before you, you see a symbol. This small red fruit is a symbol of the harvest season, of the Crone Goddess, and of the life force which animates deity. You see a fruit which gives life, but you also see a fruit whose seeds give death. As it was and ever shall be, two halves of a whole, beginnings and endings—all are one.*

(One by one the covenors come to receive an apple handed to them by the Priest/ess.)

Acting High Priest/ess (the Priest/ess asks this of each one who stands before him/her):

> *Whom do you mourn?*

(Each covenor answers in his or her own way, and then s/he returns to their place back in the circle and facing outward. When the entire coven is back in their places the Priest/ess continues):

> *Tonight we mourn the loss of life and the loss of light. But just as the apple you hold in your hands gives both life and death, so do our beloved deities. Those who are passed shall return as surely as shall the light. Pour your troubles, mourning, and worries into this ancient symbol.*

(The covenors should spend some time doing this and then the apples should be tossed away, collected for disposal later, or buried on the spot if such a thing is possible at your meeting site. In the meantime covenors should feel free to mourn and give in to their feelings of sorrow.)

Acting High Priest/ess:

> *Just as we have sorrow, we also have joy. For this is the*
> *time of the wine harvest.*

(The covenors should turn back in to face the center of the circle.
They should cheer loudly for the wine harvest, quickly shaking off any
gloom felt by the previous part of the ritual. The persons chosen to be
the Harvest King and Queen and the God of Wine come forward. The
God of Wine dances his way to the altar. He is to adopt a spritely and
playful demeanor. He lifts up the wine chalice in his left hand and the
athame in the right. He hands the chalice to the Queen who stands on
his left, and the athame to the King who stands on his right.)

God of Wine:

> *I crown you the King and Queen of the Harvest.*

(He takes the grapevine crowns from the altar and crowns them.)

> *Deity now resides in you. Will you bless*
> *the harvest wine?*

(The Queen moves the chalice towards the King and he places the
athame inside it.)

Harvest Queen:

> *I bless this wine of the harvest in the name of the*
> *Crone Goddess.*

Harvest King:

> *I bless this wine of the harvest in the name of the*
> *Harvest God.*

God of Wine:

> *Follow me in merry measure to celebrate the fruit of*
> *the vine.*

(The God of Wine should lead the King and Queen around the circle in a dance that is frolicking and fun, and also quite sensual. He
will decide when this is to end. When it does, the King and Queen
should take their places in the circle again. The God of Wine
approaches the High Priestess first and offers her the chalice with a
rakish bow.)

God of Wine:

> *Milady, will you offer a toast to the season?*

Boat to Avalon

Music to accompany the Mabon group ritual

(She will make a toast in whatever words she chooses and then drink
a bit of it before offering some to the deities of the season. For ways
in which this can be done, see Chapter Nine. The God of Wine will
continue clockwise around the circle and address all the women as
"Milady" and all the men as "Milord" until everyone has had a
chance to offer a toast. Then he begins again, this time moving
counterclockwise. This time he is to pose a ridiculous, unintelligible
question to each covenor, which they are to answer in the silliest way
they can. He then hands them the wine glass again for another
drink. This can continue on for as long as you like. It is proper to
feel the giddiness and sheer sense of fun the God of Wine represents.
When this is done, the Harvest King and Queen move to the altar
and ask everyone to join hands.)

God of Wine (addressing the coven):

> *Does this company still mourn the loss of their light?*

All (speaking loudly):

> *No!*

Harvest Queen:

> *Tonight we move into darkness, we allow it to envelop us
> in its loving arms. We welcome it joyously.*

Harvest King:

> *Tonight we move into darkness, knowing it is but
> another part of the light. We welcome it joyously.*

Covenors:

> *Blessed be the darkness, bringer of introspection, bringer
> of cold, bringer of death and resurrection.*

Harvest King and Queen:

> *Blessed be the season of darkness. Blessed be the time of night.*

Covenors:

> *Blessed be this Mabon.*

Acting High Priestess:

> *Who is Goddess?*

All Women:

> *I am Goddess.*

Acting High Priest:

> *Who is God?*

All Men:

> *I am God.*

Acting High Priest and Priestess:

> *Who are Goddess and God?*

Covenors:

> *All living beings are Goddess and God.*

Acting High Priest and Priestess:

> *And who are we?*

Covenors:

> *We are the children of deity. And we are deity.*
> *We are a part of the creative life forces which move the universe. We are microcosm and macrocosm.*
> *We are part of all that is.*

(Acting High Priest/ess continues now with the seasonal celebrations the coven chooses to have. The reading of ritual or seasonal poetry either borrowed or written by members of the coven is a nice touch. When you are ready to close the circle, ground it in a manner you have chosen, and then continue.)

Acting High Priest/ess:

> *Though we are apart, we are ever together for we are one in the spirit of our Goddess and our God. Merry meet. Merry part.*

Covenors:

> *And merry meet again.*

All:

> *Blessed Be!*

(It is customary in most traditions to ring a bell or make some other loud, grounding noise as the ritual is completed. Covenors do not have to leave just because the circle is opened. You may talk, sing, dance, visit, eat, etc. Feasting may also take place within the circle, though it can be left for later. This is a good night to attempt spirit contact as a group or to attend a wine tasting party. Whatever you do, try to keep the atmosphere one of joy and thanksgiving.)

Sabbat Rituals for Solitaries

Just because you are a solitary practitioner does not mean you have to lead an insular life, shut off from the joy of the Sabbats. Read carefully the chapters on each of the Sabbats for ideas on how to host celebrations for your non-pagan family and friends. Only the worship aspect of your spiritual life need be done alone.

Ritual by its very nature contains a certain amount of repetition. Those of you working alone, either by choice or chance, have an opportunity to make meaningful changes in the text of your rituals that can reflect the subtle changes in yourself over the years. This does not mean that you should not preplan your rituals with the same care and effort that a group would do. Planning and memorizing a ritual is part of its working, and is necessary to its success, maybe even more so in solitary practice where you do not have group dynamics and energy to help sustain the momentum. Don't leave things to chance and find that, when you are in the middle of everything, you have left some important item out of the circle or forgotten your lines.

The solitary rituals in this guide appear mostly as raw outlines that suggest rather than dictate practice. You should use these as guides only, and write your own rituals after careful study of the meaning and purpose of each Sabbat.

The sections marked off in parentheses are suggestions for actions, and the italic passages are suggestions for speaking roles. Speaking roles will generally be short and few since the nature of solitary practice is to feel your intent, to project the inner energy outward, instead of speaking the words out loud as you would to a group.

Solitaries should rely heavily on ritual or seasonal poetry and music to enhance their rituals. Music is an excellent mood setter, and poetry can be used to add to an invocation, or just to honor the Sabbat at hand. Find the poetry in books and pagan publications, and either play, sing, or prerecord your music. Make sure these are in the circle with you before you begin a ritual. Double check that your musical intruments are in working order and/or that your tape player has fresh batteries. (Check Appendix IV: Resources and Merchants Guide for sources of pagan music and poetry.)

You should arrange your solitary altar with all of your working tools just as a coven would. Be sure to include a Goddess and a God candle in all your workings. They will be used throughout these rituals. For ideas on how to decorate your altar or ritual space for each holiday, read the chapters on each of the Sabbats, and the opening sections of the group rituals. Have all of these decorations in place before your ritual begins.

If you are neither part of a large coven or a solitary, you should know that solitary rituals are most easily adapted to the working of two people. Many pagans work this way. Their covens consist of only two people, usually a Handfasted couple or two best friends. To design rituals proper for the two of you, you should combine the solitary ritual here with the parts you most like from the group workings.

Samhain Solitary Ritual

For this ritual you will need to have on hand several photos of passed over loved ones, one unlit candle, and matches. If you wish to do divinations or spirit contact after your ritual, you should bring all the items you will need for this into the circle with you.

> (When you are ready to begin you should cast your circle, call your directional energies, and invite your deities. See the Samhain Group Ritual for the words and actions that accompany this.)

> *Blessed be the season of Samhain.*
> *The time of the wise Crone Goddess.*
> *The night of the death of the God.*
> *The night to celebrate the nearness*
> *of the spirit world.*

> (Spend a few moments standing quietly inside your circle allowing your thoughts to dwell on the meaning of this Sabbat. Move to the photos of your passed over loved ones and stand before them.)

> *Dearest loved ones, tonight the passing of our God makes the veil which separates us thin. Come now to my circleside and join in the celebration.*

(Light the unlit candle on your altar to light the spirits' way to you. Spend a few moments sensing their presence. Now address each one individually. Say the things to them you wish to say, and then fall silent to try and feel their response. If you are of a Celtic tradition you should next take your athame and banish the old year and invoke the new one in the same manner as in the Group Ritual. Take the athame and walk to the center of your circle.)

Farewell Old Year.
Farewell to the season of summer.

(Make the sign of the banishing pentagram. For instructions on how to make this and the invoking pentagram, see the Samhain Group Ritual.)

Welcome the New Year.
Welcome the season of winter.

(Make the sign of the invoking pentagram. When you are done, replace the athame on the altar. Next, take your Goddess and God candles and hold them before you, the Goddess candle in the left hand, and the God in the right.)

Tonight the Goddess and God belong to separate worlds, divided by the thin veil which separates the world of the living from the land of the dead.

(Blow out the God candle to signify his death, and then replace both candles on the altar as far apart as they can be.)

Blessed be the Crone Goddess,
sorrowful in her mourning.
Blessed be the Aged God,
beloved of the Summerland.

(You may stay in your circle for as long as you like communing with your loved ones. This is the perfect night for you to try divination, spirit contact, past-life regression, or a simple meditation. Engage in at least one of these events before ending your ritual. When you are finished you may close the circle in whatever manner you choose. See the introductory chapter of this book for suggestions.)

The circle is open, but unbroken.
Blessed be.

(Take the candle you lit during the ritual and place it where it can guide the spirits on their way. Also leave out a bit of your private feast for them.)

Yule Solitary Ritual

For this ritual you will need a bowl of salted water placed on your altar. You should also have some holly and mistletoe. Place the holly on your altar, and have the mistletoe ready, but not conspicuously visible. Artificial herbs are fine for this ritual. You may also have a Yule Log, but this is optional.

(When you are ready to begin you should cast your circle, call your directional energies, and invite your deities. See the Samhain Group Ritual for the words and actions which accompany this.)

Blessed be the season of Yule.
Blessed be the young Virgin
Goddess who gives to her people
tonight a newborn God.
Blessed be the newborn God.

(If you are of a non-Celtic tradition you should next take your athame and banish the old year and invoke the new in the same manner as did the Group Ritual. Take the athame and walk to the center of your circle.)

Farewell Old Year.
Farewell to the Holly King.

(Make the sign of the banishing pentagram.)

Welcome the New Year.
Welcome the Oak King.

(Make the sign of the invoking pentagram. When you are done, replace the athame on the altar. Remove the holly from the altar and place it out of sight. Place the mistletoe, the symbol of the Oak King, on top of the altar in a place of honor.)

Blessed be the King of the Waxing Year.
I pray you will guide your
children safely through to the
season of warmth and light.

(Take the Goddess candle in your left hand and the God candle in your right.)

*Tonight Goddess and God are
reunited. Tonight life begins
anew, and light begins anew.
Blessed be the one light.
Blessed be the divine force
of creation.*

(Move the candle flames together so that they are one. Spend a moment reflecting on its meaning, and then replace the candles side by side on the altar. Next, light the Yule Log if you have one. Follow the instructions below for lighting it.)

Blessed be the Virgin, innocent and fresh.

(Light the white candle.)

Blessed be the Mother, fertile and loving.

(Light the red candle.)

Blessed be the Crone, powerful and wise.

(Light the black candle.)

Blessed be the Triple Goddess.

(Go to the vessel of salted water and place your fingertips into it. Anoint your feet, belly, and head. This is the blessing of the Triple Goddess. If you wish to add words to these gestures, then repeat the ones used while lighting the Yule log. The Virgin at the feet, Mother at the belly, and Crone at the head. You should spend time in your circle space singing seasonal songs whose words you have changed to reflect a pagan meaning. Think about the gifts you want to give this season, and in whose memory they will be given. When you are finished you may close the circle in any manner you choose.)

*The circle is open, but unbroken.
Blessed be.*

Imbolg Solitary Ritual

For this ritual you will need to have a Candle Wheel and plenty of white candles on your altar—as many as are safe. Light only the Goddess and God candle and the Candle Wheel. Keep all the other candles out until the appropriate time. You will also need a Grain Dolly dressed as a bride, some nuts, and a Bride's Bed.

(When you are ready to begin you should cast your circle, call your directional energies, and invite your deities. See the Samhain Group Ritual for the words and actions which accompany this.)

Blessed be this season of Imbolg,
Blessed be the Goddess, waiting
bride of the returning Sun God.

(Take your athame and press it to the heart of the Grain Dolly.)

Bride of heaven and earth, bless this ritual which honors you.

(Point the blade upward towards the sun. Do this even if it is night.)

Groom of heaven and earth,
come now to claim your waiting bride.

(Kneel before your altar, and with the candles of the Candle Wheel, light all the others around you. This symbolizes the young Goddess turning the Wheel of the Year back to spring.)

From this union comes the light of the world. Be fruitful,
oh Bride, and turn our earth gently again to spring.

(Toss the nuts into the bed with the bride. Nuts are a fertility symbol and will seal the words you have just spoken.)

Blessed be the Sun God, coming back to us tonight.

(Lift the Candle Wheel and carry it several times clockwise around the circle, then replace it on the altar. Spend a few moments quietly singing to the bride and groom. When you are finished you may close the circle in whatever manner you choose.)

The circle is open, but unbroken.
Blessed be.

Ostara Solitary Ritual

For this ritual you will need to have a small basket filled with painted eggs. You may use artificial ones, but the real thing is best.

(When you are ready to begin you should cast your circle, call your directional energies, and invite your deities. See the Samhain Group Ritual for the words and actions which accompany this.)

Blessed be Ostara, night of the equinox, night of balance. Tonight all
things stand as equals: Goddess and God, Life and Death, Light and

Dark. But tonight the light will conquer the dark and new life will burst forth on the face of Mother Earth.

(Lie down with the basket of eggs and place as many of them around you as possible. Put yourself in the position of the pentagram with arms and legs spread. Visualize yourself infused with the primal life force symbolized by the eggs. Sense the balance of the night within yourself.)

Blessed be the youthful Goddess.
Blessed be the lusty God.

(Sit up and replace the eggs back in the basket. Visualize the basket as the vessel in which totality of being resides. See the eggs as energizing this life center. Now get up and dance, happily and sensually, expressing the great delight all living creatures feel at the first moment of spring. When you are finished you may close the circle in the manner you choose.)

The circle is open, but unbroken.
Blessed be.

Bealtaine Solitary Ritual

For this ritual you will need to have on hand your usual ritual tools, and some spring flowers. Having a chaplet of flowers for yourself is optional. If you have one, leave it on your altar until indicated. Instructions for making or buying a chaplet are included in Chapter Six.

(When you are ready to begin you should cast your circle, call your directional energies, and invite your deities. See the Samhain Group Ritual for the words and actions that accompany this.)

Blessed be this day of Bealtaine,
wedding day of the Goddess and God.
Holy day of sacred marriage, holy
night of sacred union.

(Some traditions insist that a pagan working alone cannot properly perform the Great Rite. Since the act is a symbolic one, there is no reason you cannot make it part of solitary worship. Take your athame in your right hand, and your chalice in the left. Hold them in front of you. See them as the earthly vessels of deity.)

Tonight I witness the marriage of my Goddess and God. May the union be fruitful.

(Place the athame inside the chalice and feel the union of the deities.)

As they are one, they become one.
As they become one, they are one.
And I, too, am one with them.

(Raise the athame and chalice, still united, to your forehead to honor this union of the three of you. You may also now crown yourself with the chaplet of flowers. This will signify that you are a Queen or King, just like the deities with whom you have joined. Take some of the flowers from the altar and dance with them. They are manifestations of the union of the deities. If you follow the Greco-Roman tradition you may want to offer your praises to Flora, the Goddess of Flowers. When you are finished you may close the circle in whatever manner you choose.)

The circle is open, but unbroken.
Blessed be.

Midsummer Solitary Ritual

For this ritual you will need to have holly and mistletoe, and a vessel containing salted water. The mistletoe should be on the altar, and the holly near it just out of sight. You may use artificial herbs if you prefer. If you have a pet or Familiar, you can give it a special Midsummer blessing in this ritual.

(When you are ready to begin you should cast your circle, call your directional energies, and invite your deities. See the Samhain Group Ritual for the words and actions that accompany this.)

Blessed be this season of Midsummer. The sun rides at his peak in the skies above. The Goddess is heavy with pregnancy. Today I celebrate the light, for tomorrow that light will wane. Today I acknowledge the end of the waxing year, and the beginning of the waning time.

(Take your athame and raise it in front of you pointing up.)

Farewell to the waxing year,
Season of fertility and growth.
Farewell to the lusty spring
and the time of planting.

(Make the sign of the banishing pentagram.)

Welcome to the waning year,
Season of harvest and wisdom.
Welcome to the bounty of autumn.

(Make the sign of the invoking pentagram. Set the athame back in its place on the altar, then switch the mistletoe with the holly. The holly is the symbol of the Holly King who now reigns over the waning year. Midsummer is a good time to reenact your self-dedication. Take your salted water from the altar and hold it upward with both hands.)

O blessed Lady, whose belly quickens with the harvest bounty, fill this vessel of your womb with your holy presence that I might rededicate myself to your service. Great Mother of heaven and earth from whom I and all life was born. Womb to whom we all return to be born again, as did my ancestors so long ago, I stand before you today to acknowledge you as the Great Mother, giver of all life.

(Hold the chalice in your left hand and, with your right, reach in to wet your fingertips. Bend down and anoint your feet.)

Bless my feet as I seek to walk your ancient pathway. Steer them in the direction of right and light.

(Take some more water and anoint your heart area.)

Bless my heart which humbly turns to you in love, and is given to you freely. Help me to love unconditionally all my fellow living things.

(Take more water and anoint the area near your eyes; be careful not to get any water in them.)

Bless my eyes that they may be open to the wonders of your world; that I may see you in all your guises; that I may see the unseen and know all "truths" through them.

(Take more water and anoint the crown of your head.)

Great Mother, bless my mind that it will always be open to you, and guard it that it not conceive to do harm to any fellow living creatures. May I always remember and follow the Pagan Rede. I know that if through your path I bring harm to any living creature that I will experience the same three times over. As all living things are one, as I harm others, I also harm myself. May I always seek a spiritual path in

*this earthly incarnation, and come joyfully to you when my earthly
time is done.*

(Hold the chalice upward again with both hands.)

*Blessed Lady of many faces, you who are warrioress, protectress,
instructress, inspirer, innocent Virgin, Wise old Crone, and Great
Mother. I present myself to you as your child, (state craft name), and
ask that you accept my dedication to you. So Mote it Be. Blessed Be!*

(If you do not have a craft name, you should look for one you would
like to adopt. This is an old pagan tradition. As you assume a new
life, you should also assume a new name. Deity names are popular
choices, as are names taken from nature. Keep an ear and an eye
open for the right one for you. Spend a few moments in quiet meditation on the meaning of the dedication ritual you have just completed. If you wish to bless your pet hold it in your arms and tell it
what you wish for it. You may seal the ritual by giving it a gift if you
like. When you are finished you may close the circle in whatever
manner you choose.)

*The circle is open, but unbroken.
Blessed be.*

Lughnasadh Solitary Ritual

For this ritual you will need one loaf of bread and your Grain Dolly.

(When you are ready to begin you should cast your circle, call your
directional energies, and invite your deities. See the Samhain Group
Ritual for the words and actions that accompany this.)

*Blessed be this season of Lughnasadh, time of the first harvest, time of
the earth's bounty born. The womb of the Goddess is opened, and out
spills the grain which sustains us.*

(Take the bread from the altar.)

*Many blessings I have been given. I count them now by this bread of
the grain of Mother Earth.*

(Name all the things you are thankful for one by one. With each
thing you name, break off a piece of the bread and eat it. When you
are finished doing this say:)

Thank you, Great Mother. I ask that you humbly accept my offering of this bread. May it be used to feed your loved ones in nature.

(Put the bread aside so that when you are finished with your ritual you can place it outdoors as a libation to the faeries and animals. Take the Grain Dolly from the altar and hold it in your arms as you would a baby.)

This child of nature is the promise of the deities fulfilled. The fruit of the union the Great Mother and her consort, the Grain God. Blessed be the Great Mother whose womb contains and births all life. Blessed be the Grain God whose seed plants that life. Blessed be the grain of the earth.

(Replace the Dolly on the altar. If you are outdoors and it is night, star-gaze. This is a great way to feel connected to the deities and the wondrous mysteries of the universe. When you are finished you may close the circle in whatever manner you choose.)

The circle is open, but unbroken.
Blessed be.

Mabon Solitary Ritual

For this ritual you will need an apple and a chalice of wine or juice. Grape or apple juices are excellent choices if you cannot drink alcohol. If it is at all possible, this ritual should take place in a secluded cemetery. If this is not possible, you should try to visit a cemetery where your loved ones are buried and leave apples to wish them a quick rebirth.

(When you are ready to begin you should cast your circle, call your directional energies, and invite your deities. See the Samhain Group Ritual for the words and actions that accompany this.)

Blessed be this season of Mabon, time of the second harvest, the harvest of fruit and wine. Tonight all things are in balance: Goddess and God, Life and Death, Light and Dark. Tonight the darkness will conquer the light, leading us ever deeper into the waning year.

(If it is possible, you should arrange to be in a cemetery near the markers of loved ones. If you cannot do this, visualize their resting places in your mind. Take the apple and hold it in front of you at heart level.)

Ancient symbol of life, death, and rebirth, take away my mourning.
Help me to be assured that death is not a permanent parting, but a
new and joyful beginning.

(If you are in a cemetery you should place the apple in front of the grave of a loved one. The apple symbolizes reincarnation. If you are not in a cemetery you should save the apple to bury in the earth later to symbolize your hope for the rebirth of all life. With the somber portion of the ritual over, you should turn yourself to gladness and honor the God of Wine and the aging Crone Goddess. Take the chalice of wine and hold it upward.)

Blessed Crone, thank you for bringing me safely to this season.
God of Wine, thank you for your gift of the grape.

(Now make a game of offering a toast to whomever or whatever you wish, taking a sip of wine after each. Feel free to make these toasts as silly as you like. This is a Sabbat where it is perfectly fine to feel a little giddy. Just do this wisely and in a way where you will not endanger yourself or others. When you have made all the toasts you care to, replace the chalice on the altar.)

Blessed be Mabon, season of bounty.

(Spend some time in your circle meditating or singing songs of autumn. When you are finished you may close the circle in whatever manner you choose.)

The circle is open, but unbroken.
Blessed be.

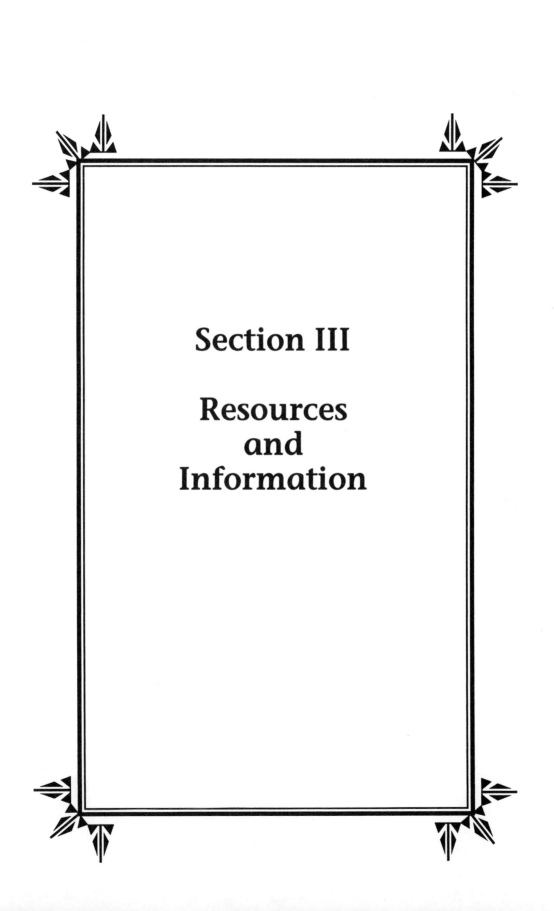

Section III

Resources
and
Information

⇥ Appendix I ⇤

Outline for Ritual Construction

Below is a step-by-step guide for creating pagan rituals that can be adapted to almost any need, and can work for either covens or solitaries.

1. If you wish to use an altar, adorn it with items of the season. Acorns, apples, and gourds in fall; flowers in spring; herbs, fruits, or greenery in summer; holly and evergreen in winter, etc. The direction your altar faces is up to you. Every coven and solitary has their own views on this. Many change directions with the seasons. If you are undecided, place the altar in the center of your circle facing north until you work out your own system.

2. Cast a circle of protective energy with an athame, your creative mind, your forefinger, or with any other ritual tool you feel comfortable using. See it clearly in your mind as a perimeter of protective blue-white light.

3. Invite, but never command, friendly spirits, faeries, or elementals to join you as you wish. In some traditions it is common to invite ancestors to join you, especially during the dark days from Samhain to Imbolg when it is believed that the portal between our dimensions is at its thinnest.

4. Call on the directional quarters or other sentient energies if you wish, and light a candle to honor them. This is often done by ringing a bell in each direction and asking that the spirits of that quarter join you. However, remember that bells frighten away faery beings. If you want faeries at

your ritual, forgo the bell. Be sure to walk clockwise as you call the quarters. The direction you choose to begin with is a personal one, though some traditions dictate one for you. The Celtic traditions usually begin with the west where it is believed that the Land of Death and Rebirth is. Middle Eastern traditions and the Alexandrian tradition both begin in the east, the direction of the rising sun. The English, Welsh, and Norse traditions usually begin rituals in the north, the dark land where, in the northern hemisphere, the sun never travels.

5. Use a candle to honor each deity you invite into your circle. Goddess candles are traditionally white and God candles are orange or red. Or you can use a white, red, and black candle for the Triple Goddess. Once again, this is a matter only you can decide. If you only have white candles available, then use them for both the God and Goddess, marking them with male and female symbols for distinction.

6. State aloud the purpose of your ritual—sabbat observance, personal enrichment, rite of passage, honor of a deity, magick, or whatever. Sing, dance, chant, meditate, and/or offer praise and thanks to your deities. Let the words come from your heart. Singing (feel free to make up your own words and melodies as you go) can quickly tap your inner states of consciousness, and dancing can raise your personal power and energies. You can write out and memorize your rituals or you can speak spontaneously as would have been customary in many ancient rituals. You can use certain set phrases, but be creative and celebrate with feeling. You will get more out of your ritual by being spontaneous than you will with most prepared speeches. And if you find you have done something you really like, then by all means, write it down after you have closed the circle.

7. If you choose to work magick, have with you whatever materials you need for your spell. Once a circle is cast it is unwise to break it until it is grounded. Making a "hole" in the protective energies allows the energy you've worked to raise seep out, and can allow practically anything to enter. When I began my path in witchcraft I tended to ignore the sanctity of the circle, feeling myself too rational to believe some nasty entity was waiting to get in. I had a few surprising and unpleasant experiences. Don't learn the hard way. The energy you raise will attract things you don't want around. With your circle properly cast they can't get in, and they will go when the energy they are attracted to is grounded. Respect your circle.

8. If your purpose is a rite of passage, then you should have already worked out with the family of those involved what words, gestures, or materials will be used. Keep these as simple as possible without losing the meaning of the event.

9. Raise and send your cone of power if you wish. If you have no magickal need for it you might send it out to heal the polluted and ailing Mother Earth. If you have just celebrated a rite of passage then you can send loving energy to the persons or spirit involved. But remember that magick is generally not worked on a Sabbat unless absolutely necessary.

10. If it is a Sabbat, enact whatever drama you wish to honor the holiday, and use whatever seasonal rituals seem appropriate. The Great Rite is appropriate at all spring Sabbats, but can be done at all of them if you wish. At Samhain many circles enact the death of the God and mourn for him. At Yule we celebrate the rebirth of the God. Adapt seasonal songs for these holidays, and thank the Goddess for the bounty of the earth at all seasons.

11. There is no rush to close the circle once you have finished your ritual. You may sit inside it and sing, meditate, scry, or just feel in communion and at peace with nature and your deities. If you are with a group you can eat, tell stories, or play circle games. Don't dismiss the circle until you feel ready. Simply being in this sacred space has a healing effect on the mind and body.

12. When you are ready to close the circle, thank the elementals and spirits who have joined you, and thank your deities especially. If you have called the quarters, then dismiss them in a counterclockwise movement. Dismiss all whom you have called upon with the traditional phrase, "Merry meet, merry part, and merry meet again."

13. Ground the energy from your circle—always! See it dissipate and return to the earth.

⇒ Appendix II ⇐

The Elements of Spell Construction

T hough no work—magick included—is traditionally to be done on the Sabbats, in times of emergency or extreme circumstances there may be a need for magickal aid. Also, it is permissible to work magick prior to the Sabbat in order to take advantage of the waxing energies caused by growing anticipation of the holiday by pagans worldwide. The following is a list that outlines the basic steps for creating magickal spells. This is by no means an all-inclusive guide, but the many intricacies of spellwork lie beyond the scope of this book. Check the Bibliography for the names of books that go into depth on spell work.

Magick has long been understood by its practitioners as the manipulation of forces and energies not yet understood by science. For example, an internal combustion engine would have been an awesome manifestation of magick several hundred years ago, but for those of us who understand the factual scientific principles on which it runs, it is not "magickal" at all.

Pagan religions have few hard and fast rules, but there are two laws which it acknowledges. The first is commonly called the Pagan Rede:

AS YE HARM NONE, DO WHAT YE WILL.

Memorize this Rede and call it to mind each time you begin a power ritual or magickal working. This law prohibits a witch from doing anything that might harm any other living being, and most significantly prohibits us from violating any living being's free will. And this law also applies to the self. You have an obligation to keep yourself from harm. If one chooses to do anything magickally which might cause harm one should remember the second law: the Threefold Law.

The Threefold Law

Witches believe that any energy sent out, either good or bad, will be revisited on the sender three times over. This is a karmic law, and a good one to keep in mind if you doubt that your spells are entirely harm free.

Some witches will add a line to their incantations such as "as it harms none," or "as all will it freely," or something similar to insure that they are not violating the Rede. Love magick is especially vulnerable to this law. Many witches wish to work a love charm to draw a specific person to them. Nothing could be more against the Pagan Rede, or more dangerous. If you want to draw love into your life, make a charm or construct a ritual which draws "the right person for me now," or "the person who seeks me as I seek them." Don't even risk manipulating another person through magick; the consequences are too great.

In an earth religion a spell can use virtually anything that comes from nature. Remember that the power is not as much in the object as within the mind of the witch, intimately connected to his/her deep needs and desires. Remember too that elemental representations are less a concern than the will and force of the magician who draws on them.

Once you decide to create a spell for any need, follow these basic steps:

1. Clearly understand and define your magickal goal. Begin to invest the spell and the desired outcome with emotion.

2. If you wish to use a specific element, then decide which one is most appropriate and collect items to represent that energy.

3. Gather candles, stones, or whatever else you intend to use to focus and send the energy you will raise. Empower those items with your personal energy as you focus upon your goal.

4. Decide upon your words of power. You may write them out, or simply remember the key phrases you wish to use as you improvise.

5. If you wish to use a special deity in your magick, decide on which one or ones, and on how you will petition, connect with, and honor them. You may wish to write out special prayers and invocations and memorize them.

6. If you wish to use a faery or elemental being in your magick, decide which one you would like to call on, and have ready its favorite foods or other items that will induce it to stay and help you.

7. Plan how you will visualize your goal. This is the essence of the magick and very important to your outcome. The moment you start visualizing the resolution of a magickal need is the moment you begin to create the changes in your deep mind necessary for the magick to manifest. Don't skimp on visualization. Enjoy it!

8. Decide when and where you want to do the spell. Where will depend largely on your own resources. When can be anytime you like or need the magick, or you may take into consideration astrological influences and moon phases.

9. At the appropriate time gather what you will use and go to the place where you will perform the spell. This can be at your altar, outdoors, or anywhere else that feels appropriate.

10. Cast your protective circle or use some other form of protection that you can count on.

11. Your ritual is now beginning. Invite whatever elementals, faeries, spirits, or deities you wish to have present as you work. They should always be welcome, but they are not necessary for spell work. If you wish to use them for spell work, then have a speech prepared telling them what you'd like from them.

12. Clear your mind and begin clearly visualizing your goal.

13. Raise energy within yourself and pour it into the magickal object(s).

14. Use your words of power, light your candles, charge your stones, dance, or sing. Do whatever you have decided to do to focus your attention and raise energy. If you are working with other beings, encourage them to raise energy with you. Get them to dance and infuse the area outside of your circle with as much energy as possible.

15. Take advantage of natural phenomena that can help you raise energy. A storm, for instance, is an excellent source of energy which any witch can draw on to help feed a spell. Feel yourself becoming a part of the storm, psychically drawing on the storm's vast stores of energy as you seek to raise your own energies or cone of power.

16. When you feel you have put as much energy into the spell as you can, send the energy out to do your will. Relax, throw up your arms, raise a tool, kneel, or do whatever else makes you feel the energy being sent. Be sure to direct it out from you visually as well. Also send out any energy raised for you by other entities at your circle side.

17. You should finish your spell with words such as "So Mote It Be." Mote is an obsolete word for "must." These words are synonymous with "Amen," "So It Is," and "It is Done." It is a statement of completion and an affirmation that you know your magick is successful. All magick is worked from the point of view that the desired goal is already manifest—it will not come to be, but IT IS. Always phrase your magickal desires in the present tense such as, "I have love in my life now," or, "My bills are now paid in full." Talking of magick happening in the future will keep it forever in the future, always out of reach.

18. Meditate briefly on your goal. Visualize it as already manifest. Smile, and know the magick is at work.

19. Thank and dismiss all faeries, spirits, and deities who have come to witness or aid in your magick.

20. Ground your excess energy and open your circle.

21. Record your spell in your Magickal Diary or Book of Shadows with the date, time, weather conditions, and any astrological data you wish to include. This will be useful later when you have done enough spells to look for patterns. For example, you may see that your most efficient spells were done on Sundays or when it was cloudy or snowing or when you had gnomes present, or when you burned green candles or when the moon was full. Everyone has different affinities. These patterns will help you pick the best times for your own spell work.

⇥ Appendix III ⇤

Glossary

Aboriginal—The pagan tradition(s) of the native peoples of Australia.

Akasha—A Hindustani word which refers to the "fifth element" of spirit. Also see **Elements**.

Alchemy (Al-kem-ee)—A branch of High Magick developed in the Middle Ages which sought to magickally and/or chemically turn base metals into gold. Part of its focus was the elevation of the human soul to a more God-like existence through the role of creation. Alchemists have always referred to the practice of their tradition as "The Great Work."

Alexandrian—The pagan tradition named for its founder Alexander Saunders. This tradition combines the teachings of the Hebrew Kaballah with those of Anglo-Celtic witchcraft. Also see **Kaballah**.

Amulet—A natural object which is reputed to give protection to the carrier. Amulets are such things as stones or fossils and are not to be confused with person-made talismans.

Arthurian Tradition—Pagan tradition from Wales and Cornwall based upon the Arthurian myths surrounding King Arthur, Merlin the Magician, and Queen Guinevere.

Aspect—The particular principle or part of the Creative Life Force being worked with or acknowledged at any one time. For example, Brigid is a Mother aspect of the one Goddess, Thor is one aspect of the God, and both are merely single aspects of the Creative Life Force.

Astral Plane—A place which is generally conceptualized as an invisible parallel world which remains unseen from our own solid world of form. The vast majority of pagans believe this plane can be entered through conscious effort with practice.

Astral Projection—The art of "leaving one's body" or "lucid dreaming" whereby someone in a trance state visits other locations, realms, or times. This is often referred to as traveling on the **Astral Plane**, a place which is generally conceptualized as an invisible parallel world unseen in our own world of form.

Astrology—The study of and belief in the effects the movements and placements of planets and other heavenly bodies have on the lives and behavior of human beings.

Athame (Ath-aah-may)—The ritual knife often associated with the element of air and the direction of the east, though some traditions attribute it to fire and the south. The knife was traditionally black-handled, but many modern pagans now prefer handles of natural wood. In some circles the athame is called the **Dagger** or **Dirk**.

Aura—The life-energy field surrounding all living things.

Automatic Writing—A form of divination where the channeler uses a pen, paper, and an altered state of consciousness to receive messages.

Autumn Equinox—See **Mabon**.

Balefire—The traditional communal bonfire of the Sabbats. The name is derived from the Anglo-Saxon word "boon," meaning a "gift" or "something extra." Even in modern times balefires play a major role in both pagan and non-pagan holidays and folk celebrations. The modern word "bonfire" is synonymous with balefire, though it often has no religious significance.

Baltic Traditions—The pagan traditions of the Baltic region of northeastern Europe. Here the Slavic, Russian, and Teutonic traditions all met and melded into a unique path which is being actively revitalized today. Also see **Slavic Tradition**.

B.C.E.—"Before Common Era." This is a designation scholars often use to denote dates synonymous with B.C., but without the biased religious implications. It is also sometimes abbreviated BCE, without the periods in between.

Bealtaine (Beel-teen)—Also called Beltane (Bell-tayn). This Sabbat, celebrated on May 1, is rich with fertility rituals and symbolism, and is a celebration of the sacred marriage of the Goddess and the God.

Beltane—See **Bealtaine.**

Bells—Often used as ritual tools in paganism. They are used to invoke directional energies, to ring in the sunrise on many Sabbats, and to frighten away faeries and baneful spirits.

Besom (Bee-sum)—The witch's broomstick. European folklore has witches riding their brooms through the sky, which many feel is an uninformed explanation of astral projection. As a tool, the broom is used to sweep a sacred area, ground a circle, or to brush away negative influences. Besoms were often mounted and "ridden" over crops in fertility rites.

Black Magick—A name applied to any negative magickal working. Persons who regularly indulge in this practice are said to be on the "left-hand path."

Black Mass—Negative and destructive rites that have nothing to do with paganism. These rites are performed by those who claim to follow the Christian anti-God called Satan, and they are nothing more than a perversion and mockery of Catholic religious practices.

Book of Shadows—Also called Book of Lights and Shadows, is the spell book, diary, and ritual guide used by an individual witch or coven. Some say the name came from having to hide the workings from church authorities, and others say it means that an unworked spell or ritual is a mere shadow, not taking form until performed by a witch.

Brujeria (Brew-har-ee-ah)—This is a tradition from Mexico which combines the old Aztec religion with Catholicism. Its practitioners are called *brujas* or *brujos.*

The Burning Times—The time from the the Spanish Inquisition through the last outbursts of persecution and witch killings in the mid-nineteenth century (though murderous persecutions began as early as the twelfth century). The last known capital sentence for witchcraft in the west took place in Scotland in the early 1800s. Figures vary on how many were killed during this hysteria, estimates range anywhere from 50,000 to as many as 9 million.

Candlemas—A Christianized name for Imbolg.

Cauldron—Linked to witchcraft in the popular mind, this is a primal Goddess image used like a chalice or cup. This was a common magickal instrument in the Celtic traditions because it was a practical object as well, one which could be used for cooking or washing as well as making brews and magick potions. In many of the mythological stories from Ireland and Britain, the cauldron is symbolic of the womb of the Mother Goddess in which all life begins, ends, and regenerates.

C.E.—"Common Era." This term is often used by scholars to denote time which is synonymous with A.D., but without a religious bias. It is sometimes abbreviated as CE, without the periods in between.

Celtic Traditions, The—The collective and individual pagan traditions of the old Celtic lands of Ireland, Scotland, Cornwall, Man, Brittany, and parts of Wales and England. Though many groups and individuals take practices from all these lands under the heading of a single Celtic tradition, they are actually distinct traditions in their own right even though they share many common elements.

Ceremonial Magick—A highly codified magickal tradition based upon Kaballah, the Jewish-Gnostic mystical teachings.

Chakra—This term comes from Hindustani and is used to define the sacred energy centers of the human body. The seven principal centers are located at the base of the tail bone, at the navel, the solar plexus, the heart center, the breast bone, the throat, the Third Eye (between the eyebrows), and just above the crown of the head. These centers can be energized to promote good health, spirit contact, psychicism, and a host of other physical and spiritual benefits.

Chalice—The chalice or cup as a ritual tool represents water and the west, and it is also representative of the feminine principle of creation.

Channeling—Allowing one's self to be used as a vessel for a discarnate being or spirit to speak through. This practice is not popular in all pagan traditions.

Chaplet— A crown for the head usually made of flowers and worn at Bealtaine. Chaplets can also be made of vines and other natural material.

Charging—The act of empowering an herb, stone, or other magickal object with one's own energies directed towards a magickal goal. Charging is synonymous with enchanting or empowering.

Circle—The sacred space wherein all magick is to be worked and all ritual contained. The circle both contains raised energy and provides protection for the witch, and is created and banished with her/his own energy. Many books on magick go into circle lore and practice heavily, and it is recommended that students of paganism study these carefully.

Collective Unconsciousness—A term used to describe the sentient connection of all living things, past and present. It is synonymous with the terms "deep mind" and "higher self." This is believed to be the all-knowing energy source which is tapped during divination.

Coming of Age Ritual—At age thirteen for boys, and at the time of a girl's first menses, pagan children are considered to be spiritual adults. They join with other pagans to celebrate their new maturity with rituals and parties and are permitted full membership in covens. This is also the time when ritual tools are given to them as gifts, or else they are allowed to choose their own.

Conscious Mind—That part of the brain which we have access to in the course of a normal, waking day. It is the part of the mind which holds retrievable memory and other easy to recall information.

Corn Dolly—See **Grain Dolly**.

Coven—A group of witches who worship and work together. A coven may contain any number of witches, both male and female, but the traditional number of members is thirteen which reflects the thirteen moons in the solar year, or three persons for each season plus a high priest/ess.

Covenstead—An obsolete name for the area encompassed by an individual coven. In the days when paganism was the only religion, one would meet in covens with persons who lived within a particular covenstead.

Crone—That aspect of the Goddess that is represented by the old woman. She is symbolized by the waning moon, the carrion crow, the cauldron, and the color black. Her Sabbats are Mabon and Samhain.

Cross-quarter Days—A name sometimes given to the Sabbats not falling on the solstices or equinoxes.

Dagger—See **Athame.**

Deity—An inclusive name for a Goddess or God.

Deosil (Jes-l)—The act of moving, working, or dancing in a clockwise motion. This is the traditional direction one works with for creative magick. Deosil is also called sunwise.

Devil—The Christian and Islamic opposite of God. The Devil as an entity was the result of the mistranslation of a Hebrew word appearing in the Old Testament, "ha-satan," which simply means "adversary." The term was personified by the early Christian Church and its image taken from the Great Horned God of Europe as a means of frightening people away from the religions of witchcraft. Some Christians contend that all pagans worship the Devil, but since he is a creation of Christian theology (one adopted whole-heartedly by Muslims) one must necessarily be of those faiths to believe in or worship him.

Dianic—A tradition of the craft which is made up largely of women. They primarily worship the Greek Goddess Diana.

Dirk—The ritual knife of the Scottish tradition.

Discarnate—See **Ghost.**

Discordian—A pagan tradition which bases its philosophy on the chaotic nature of the universe. They believe that the natural laws which appear to govern the universe are not truly a constant, and that those inconsistencies provide a powerful framework for magick and ritual. Despite their chosen name, Discordianism is *not* a negative path. The tradition was named for Discordia, Roman Goddess of Folly, Mischief, and Moral Blindness.

Divination—The act of divining the future by reading potentials currently in motion. Divination can be done through meditation, scrying, astral projection, with cards, stones, or any one of a myriad of means. The most popular forms of divination today are tarot, runes, pendulums, scrying, and the controversial Ouija™ board.

Drawing Down the Moon—Ancient pagan ritual enacted at the Esbats to draw the powers of the full moon, in her aspect as Great Mother Goddess, into the body of a female witch. Esbats and Sabbats can co-exist, but these conjunctions are rare.

Drawing Down the Sun—This is a lesser-known and lesser-used companion ritual to Drawing Down the Moon, in which the essence of the Sun God is drawn into the body of a male witch.

Druids—Much speculation still continues on the role of the Druids. They were the priestly class of Celtic society, the magicians and writers, poets and royal advisors. Their power flourished from the second century BCE to the second century CE. They are credited with creating the Celtic Tree Calendar, communicating with faeries, and possessing powerful divination skills that required living sacrifices. Their eventual insistence on the superiority of males as religious leaders and teachers helped pave way for the Roman church's victory over the British Isles.

Druidic Tradition—The pagan tradition which seeks to reconstruct and practice the pagan ways of the Druids.

Duality—The opposite of polarity. Duality, when used as a religious term, separates two opposites such as good and evil and places those characteristics into two completely separate God-forms.

Earth Plane—A metaphor for your normal waking consciousness, or for the everyday, solid world we live in.

Eclectic Path—The name applied to covens or individuals who create their own pagan tradition by borrowing from many different sources. In the United States and Canada, this blending of paths is probably the most widely accepted form of organized pagan practice.

Elements, The—The four alchemical elements once thought to make up the entire universe. These are Earth, Air, Fire, and Water plus the fifth element of pure spirit in, of, and outside them all. Each pagan tradition has their own, slightly differing directions, tools, and correspondences for each of these.

Elementals—Archetypal spirit beings associated with one of the four elements. Elementals are sometimes called Faeries.

Elven—A secretive tradition of the craft which works closely with elemental beings.

Enchanting—The act of empowering an herb, stone, or other magickal object with one's own energies directed towards a magickal goal. Enchanting is synonymous with charging or empowering.

Eostre's Eggs—The colored and decorated eggs of the Ostara and Bealtaine Sabbats which are named for the Teutonic Goddess Eostre. Her name is the derivation of the Christian holiday of Easter.

Esbat—The monthly pagan holy time which coincides with the full moon. The word is from the French *esbattre* meaning "to gambol or frolic."

Evocation—The act of summoning the presence of deities, friendly spirits, or elementals to your circle or home.

Familiar—A witch's non-human coworker. Animals are the most common Familiars, thus the popularity of the witches' cat. But Familiars can also be discarnate spirits, spirit guides, or elementals. The choice of having a Familiar or not is a personal one, and must also be the conscious choice of the other being involved.

Faery—See **Elemental**.

Faery Burgh—Also erroneously called a Faery rath (a circular enclosure). This is a mound of earth which covers a faery colony's underground home. They can be found all over Europe and they are numerous throughout Ireland and Scotland.

Floralia—Roman pagan holiday corresponding to Bealtaine which celebrates Flora, Goddess of Flowers.

Folklore—The traditional sayings, cures, fairy tales, and folk wisdom of a particular locale which is separate from their mythology.

Folk Tale—See **Myth Cycle**.

Gardnerian—The pagan tradition named for English witch Gerald Gardner. His books on the craft appeared shortly after the repeal of the British anti-witchcraft laws in the early 1950s, and have had a profound impact on the neo-pagan movement.

Gaulish Tradition—The lost pagan tradition of ancient Gaul. Very little survives from this tradition except a few deity names, some vague writings, and the remnants of a calendar, and much of these fragments are difficult to translate even for the most adept scholars. Gaul, founded in 121 BCE, was a Roman outpost in what is now the southern half of modern-day France and Austria. The Gauls were also a cousin-race of the Celts and it appears that the Gaulish tradition probably shared elements of both the Roman and the Celtic paths.

Germanic Tradition—The pagan tradition of the southern Teutons, also sometimes called the Gothic tradition. The pagans who followed this path came from the regions now occupied by modern day Germany, Switzerland, Austria, and Denmark. Also see **Teutonic Tradition**.

Ghost—The intact, sentient spirit or soul of a deceased human, often referred to in paganism as a "human discarnate." Many pagan believe these spirits can be contacted by various means such as through seances or deep meditations.

Gaian (Guy-an)—The pagan tradition named after the Greek Earth Mother, Gaia. This path is very environmental minded and attracts a following comprised largely of eco-feminists.

God—The masculine aspect of deity.

Goddess—The feminine aspect of deity.

Gothic—See **Germanic Tradition**.

Grain Dolly—The figure usually woven at Imbolg from dried sheaves of grain collected at the previous harvest. At Imbolg she represents the Virgin Goddess and is usually dressed as a bride. She is dressed as a pregnant woman at Midsummer and Lughnasadh, and as a crone in the autumn. The Dolly is traditionally burned in the Yule fire and a new one made the following Imbolg. The Dolly is often given various names depending upon what material she is created from. She is also frequently called the Corn Dolly.

Great Rite, The—The symbolic sexual union (also sacred marriage) of the Goddess and God that is enacted at Bealtaine in most traditions, and at other Sabbats in many others. It symbolizes the primal act of creation from which all life comes. The sexual union is symbolized by ritually placing the athame, a phallic symbol, inside the chalice or cauldron, a womb symbol.

Greco-Roman—The name of pagan tradition which worships the old deities of the Greek and Roman pantheons.

Grimoire (Greem-warr)—A book of magickal spells and rituals. Some claims to their antiquity are highly suspect, and those that are truly ancient contain much apocryphal material. However, this does not invalidate the spells or rituals in the newer ones, it merely means they are not old. Any Book of Shadows can also be a Grimoire.

Gris-gris (Gree-gree)—The name of a popular and potent amulet from the Voodun tradition. The contents of the gris-gris bag depend upon the desired outcome of the amulet's magick.

Grounding—To disperse excess energy generated during any magickal or occult rite by sending it into the earth. It can also mean the process of centering one's self in the physical world both before and after any ritual or astral experience.

Grove—A term synonymous with coven. Which one a coven uses to refer to itself is often a matter of tradition or personal tastes.

Gypsy Tradition—See **Romany Tradition.**

Handfasting—Pagan marriage, traditionally contracted for a specific period of time depending on one's tradition. It is renewed only if both parties agree.

Herbalism—The art of using herbs to facilitate human needs both magickally and medically.

Hermetic Tradition—Though this term is often used in conjunction with the practices of Ceremonial Magick, pagans following the old Egyptian ways also refer to themselves by this term.

Higher Self—That part of us which connects our corporeal minds to the Collective Unconscious and with the divine knowledge of the universe. It is often visualized as being connected to the Crown Chakra, the energy center located just above the head.

Hiving Off—This term is used for a small coven which splits off from a larger one. Sometimes this is done to keep the gatherings of a manageable size, other times covens split over philosophical differences.

Horned God—This God-image is the most prevalent in all of paganism. His image has been seen drawn on cave walls in the Middle East and India that date to 5000 B.C.E. As Cernunnos, Pan, and Robin Goodfellow, he is still revered in the European pagan traditions. The Horned God's image was demonized by the early Church, and he became the prototype for their Devil.

Imbolg (Em-bowl/g)—Also known as Candlemas, Imbolc, or Oimelc. Imbolg, observed on February 2, is a day which honors the Virgin Goddess as the youthful bride of the returning Sun God.

Incense—Ritual burning of herbs, oils, or other aromatic items to scent the air during acts of magick and ritual, and to better help the witch attune to the goal of the working.

Initiation—Modern practice of admitting a witch to a coven or specific pagan path. Every tradition has its own method, but it is also quite acceptable to initiate yourself by personal dedication to the deities. Many books on paganism contain ritual texts for initiation ceremonies.

Invisibility Spells—This type of magick has been widely misunderstood. Though the Celtic Druids did purport to have spells called *fith fath* which rendered them invisible, most of the magic relates to working magick backward in time to change present situations. The idea of this kind of magick gained popularity during the Burning Times when witches did not want to be seen going to meet their covens by night. This is also probably a metaphor for astral projection.

Invocation—The act of drawing the aspect of a particular deity into one's physical self. The rite of Drawing Down the Moon is an example.

Jewitch—A name coined by some pagans of Jewish origin who are actively seeking out the pagan roots of their birth religion.

Kaballah—The body of mystical teachings from the Jewish-Gnostic tradition upon which both Ceremonial Magick and the Alexandrian pagan traditions base their practice. While the principles of Kaballah are ancient, its codification as a system of religious study dates only to the medieval period. Also transliterated from the Hebrew as Qabala and Caballa.

Kalends—An old name for the Roman pagan new year which may have, at one time, coincided with Yule. Our modern English word "calendar" is derived from Kalends.

Karma—A Hindustani word which reflects the ancient belief that good and evil done will return to be visited on a person either in this life or in a succeeding one. Also see **Reincarnation**.

Lammas—See **Lughnasadh**.

Law of Responsibility, The—This is an often repeated corrolary to the other laws of paganism. It simply means that if you inadvertantly violate someone's free will or harm them in any way, you will accept responsibility for your action and seek to make restitution. This, of course, does not apply in cases where you have used magick to protect yourself from someone seeking to harm you. Also see **Pagan Rede** and **Threefold Law**.

Libation—A ritually given portion of food or drink to a deity, nature spirit, or ghost.

Lughnasadh (Loo-nas-sah)—Also known as Lammas and August Eve. This Sabbat celebrates the first harvest. The date is August 1 or 2, depending upon your tradition.

Mabon (May-bone)—Sabbat named for a Welsh God associated with the Arthurian myth cycles. This is the Sabbat observed at the Autumn Equinox and celebrates the second harvest, wine, and balance.

Magick—Spelled with a "k" to differentiate it from the magic of stage illusions. The best definition of magick was probably invented by infamous Ceremonial Magician Aleister Crowley: "Magick is the science and art of causing change to occur in conformity to will." Magick is work, and work is forbidden at the Sabbats.

Male Mysteries—A pagan study which attempts to reclaim the power and mystery of the old Gods for today's pagan males.

Matrifocal—Also Matricentric. This is a term used to denote pre-patriarchal life when familial clans centered around and lived near one clan matriarch. While in temperate regions these female-led tribes were exceptionally peaceful and egalitarian, others were not. Generally, tribes and clans living in colder regions were more war-like. Anthropologists site the seasonal inavailability of vital natural resources as a possible reason for this differentiation.

May Pole—The sexual symbol of Bealtaine representing the phallus and birth canal of the deities in copulation.

Meditation—A deliberate attempt to slow the cycles per second of one's brain waves to generate a consciously controlled sleeping state.

Middle Eastern Traditions—A generic name which lumps together the many varying traditions of the Middle East. Among these traditions are the Hebraic, Sumerian, Babylonian, Assyrian, Caananite, and the Egyptian.

Midsummer—The Sabbat observed at the Summer Solstice which honors the Sun God at the height of his power, and the Goddess as the pregnant mother-to-be.

Monotheism—The belief in one supreme deity who has no other forms and/or displays no other aspects. I.e.; Judaism and Islam are monotheistic.

Mother—One of the aspects of the Triple Goddess. This aspect represents motherhood, mid-life, and fertility. She is represented by the full moon, the egg, and the colors red and green. Her Sabbats are Midsummer and Lughnasadh.

Myth Cycles—The body of lore about any land or people that makes up their mythology. The word "myth" does not mean something false, but rather it means a "theme" or "a traditional story."

Native American Traditions—The neo-pagan traditions based in the old indigenous religions of the Native Americans. Within this broad classification are many different expressions of their religious beliefs.

Neo-pagan—Name applied to the various pagan movements after the repeal of the British anti-witchcraft laws in the early 1950s. Neo is a prefix meaning "new" or "reformed."

New Age—While this term is usually used to describe persons interested in applying metaphysics to everyday living experiences, it is also a tradition of paganism which adopts these practices and beliefs.

New Religion, The—A pagan term used in reference to Christianity, but it can also be applied to all other non-pagan religions. These New Religions are sometimes referred to as the Patriarchal Religions because of their exclusive, or nearly exclusive, focus on a male deity.

Norse Tradition—The pagan traditions from Scandinavia, also sometimes called the Nordic Traditions, and includes the beliefs and practices of the early Vikings and Lapps.

Nursery Rhyme—Cute doggerels or poems supposedly written for the amusement of children. Much pagan lore was hidden in these ditties during the years of witch persecutions.

Occult—The word occult literally means "hidden" and is broadly applied to a wide range of metaphysical topics which lie outside the accepted realm of mainstream theologies. Such topics include, but are not limited to,

divination, hauntings, spirit communication, natural magick, Ceremonial Magick, alternative spirituality, psychic phenomena, alchemy,
astrology, demonology, the study of the spiritual practices of ancient
civilizations, and the study of any of the above mentioned topics as
applied to mainstream religions.

Occultist—One who practices and/or studies a variety of occult subjects.

Ogham—The Celtic equivalent of the Teutonic runes. This was the ancient
alphabet of the Celtic people, used today for sacred writing and divination.

Oimelc—See **Imbolg**.

Old Religion—A name for paganism, particularly as practiced in Britain
and Ireland.

Ostara (O-star-ah)—The Sabbat observed at the Vernal Equinox, and often
referred to simply as the Spring Equinox. This Sabbat celebrated the sexual union of the Goddess and God in the Norse traditions before the
Celts influenced this event to Bealtaine. It is a time to celebrate new life
and emerging sexuality. Ostara is symbolized by the egg.

Pagan—Generic term for anyone who practices an earth or nature religion.
The word is sometimes used synonymously with Witch. But not all
pagans are known as witches, only those of the Anglo-Saxon, Brythonic,
and Celtic traditions. However, all witches are pagans.

Paganing—Also called Wiccaning or Wittaning. This is when a baby is presented in circle to the Goddess and God, and given a craft name which
he/she will keep until they are about thirteen years old and can choose
their own at their Coming of Age celebration.

Pagan Rede, The—This is the basic tenet of witchcraft. "As ye harm none,
do what thou will." The Rede prohibits pagans from harming any other
living thing, or from violating anyone's free will. Also see THREEFOLD
LAW and LAW OF RESPONSIBILITY.

Pantheism—The belief in many deities who are really one because they are all
merely aspects of the single creative life source. Paganism is pantheistic.

Passing Over Ritual—A ritual observed when a loved one has died.
Depending upon one's tradition this ceremony includes keening and
candle lighting, feasting and revelry, sitting up with the body, ritualized
farewell speeches, drinking, and storytelling.

Past-life Regression—The act of using meditation or guided meditation to pass through the veil of linear time and perceive experiences encountered in a previous existence.

Pathworking—Though the term comes to paganism from Ceremonial Magick, pagans use it to define a guided journey into the realm of the unconscious, or astral plane, for the purpose of acquiring a lasting change on both the conscious and subconscious mind of the seeker. The term is synonymous with Guided Meditation. Good storytelling often leads the listener on an unconscious pathworking.

Patriarchial—A term used to apply to the world since the matrifocal clans that worshiped Goddesses were supplanted by codified religions that honor an all-male deity(s).

Pendulum—A divination tool which uses a weight on the end of a string or chain. Answers are discerned either by the movement of the pendulum itself, or by its pointing to pre-set groups of items, words, or letters.

Pentacle—A pentagram surrounded by a circle and carved on a circlet of wood or other natural object. The pentacle is used in some covens to represent the earth element, and is also called a Disk or Shield. It can, and often is, embellished with other carvings of significance to the witch or coven who owns it.

Pentagram—The five-pointed star that has come to symbolize Western paganism. It is an ancient symbol with multiple meanings. It is always seen with its apex up. It can represent the four elements headed by the fifth element of spirit, or it can represent a human with arms and legs spread to represent mind over matter. It can also represent the creative principle over all creation. Sometimes it is encased in a circle and then it is properly called a Pentacle. Satanist cults often take the pentagram and invert it to signify matter over spirit in much the same way that they pervert the meaning of the Christian cross. Pentegram is an alternative spelling.

Pecti-Wita—The solitary path of the pre-Celtic Scottish Highland people known as the Picts. The beliefs and practices of this path were recorded by Raymond Buckland in his 1991 book *Scottish Witchcraft*. Since no culture exists in a vacuum, Celtic pagans will find much in this tradition that is familiar to them.

Polarity—The opposite of duality. Polarity means that everything has two sides or two forces within it that are not wholly separate. For example, we can draw power from our Gods for either good or evil as these diverse powers are not contained in two separate entities, but in one.

Polynesian—A broad inclusive term for the many pagan traditions of the central and south Pacific islanders. Within this wide classification are dozens of diverse pagan paths such as the Maori, Hawaiian, Sulu, and Tonganese. Shamanic practices and leadership play a large role in the social structure and day-to-day religious life of these people. Also see **Shamanism**.

Polytheism—The belief in the existence of many unrelated deities each with their own dominion and interests who have no spiritual or familial relationships to one another. Paganism is often erroneously characterized as polytheistic. But polytheism does not acknowledge a single source or force of creation, as most pagans do.

Poppets—Anthropomorphic dolls used to represent certain human beings in magickal spells. These have been associated with the negative aspects of Voodoo, but they also serve positive purposes such as healing.

Radical Fairy—A tradition of the Craft that seeks to blend paganism with modern alternative lifestyles.

Reincarnation— A basic tenet of paganism. The belief that the souls of human beings return to the earth plane in another human body, or even in another life-form, after death. There are many theories of how reincarnation works, but the largest division is between those who believe that all our lives are lived in one great omnipresent now, and those who believe we live a linear succession of many lives.

Ritual—A systematic, formal or informal, prescribed set of rites whose purpose is to imprint a lasting change on the life and psyche of the participant.

Ritual tools—A general name for magickal or ritual tools used by a witch or magician. These tools vary by tradition and usually represent one of the elements. Among these are the Sword or Athame, the Staff or Wand, a Chalice or Cauldron, and some earth symbol such as Salt, Stone, or a Pentacle. Ritual tools can also be called Magickal Tools or Witch Tools.

Romany Tradition—This is the highly syncretized religion of the people we call Gypsies. Romany combines magick and religion from the Basque region with those of Italy and eastern Europe. The emphasis of this tradition is more on spell casting and divination than on religious ritual. In modern times, a good deal of Catholicism has found its way into the Romany beliefs.

Runes—The ancient writing of the Teutonic people. Today it is considered a magickal alphabet among pagans and is used for writing in one's Book of Shadows and for divination.

Russian Tradition—A broad inclusive term for the various pagan traditions of what is now Russia. Pagans in western Russia were influenced by other European Slavs, those of the southeast by the Asian traditions and philosophies, while Siberia boasted its own unique path of paganism. Of course, all of these traditions developed their own expression throughout the centuries of living within the diverse Russian culture.

Sabbat—Any of the eight solar festivals or observances of the pagan year. The word is derived from the Greek word "sabatu," meaning "to rest."

Salt—Is often used in Western paganism to represent the element of earth and the direction north. Salt may be used interchangeably with clay, earth, or stones. Because of its grounding abilities it is often eaten after strenuous ritual, astral projection, etc., to assure reconnection with the earth plane.

Samhaim (Sow-een, Sow-in, Sam-hayn, or Sav-ain)—Sabbat celebrated at what is now called Halloween, October 31. Samhain marked the beginning of winter for the Celts and was also their New Year's Day. It is a day to honor the Crone Goddess and the dying God who will be reborn at Yule. Samhain also marks the end of the harvest season.

Santeria (San-tah-ree-ah)—This tradition was born in the black cultures of the Caribbean. It combines African practices and beliefs with those of the natives of the Caribbean and blends them with Catholicism.

Satanist—Those who purport to worship the Christian anti-God, Satan, or the Devil. Witches do not believe in the existence of this entity and therefore cannot worship him.

Saturnalia—See **Yule**.

Saxon Tradition—A Germanic tradition practiced by the people of Saxony. The Saxon path also shares some common elements with the Celtic traditions, including a veneration of trees. The best-known champion of this path is pagan leader and writer Raymond Buckland who, many years ago, started his own pagan seminary that teaches Seax-Wica, his name for the craft of Saxony.

Scourge—This is a small device made from leather or hemp which resembles a whip and is used in flaggelation rites within some traditions.

Scrying—The divinatory act of gazing at an object or candle until prophetic visions appear.

Shaman (Shay-men)—The word "Shaman" comes from an extinct Ural-Altaic language called Tungus. They are the priests and medicine men of old tribal societies worldwide. Shamans, and also Shamanesses, practice in every known culture, and many are still active today. In many vernaculars the native word for Shaman roughly translates into "walker between the worlds."

Shamanism—A religious practice in which one attempts to work in the physical, spiritual, and underworld simultaneously. Shamanic practice has been part of all pagan traditions. Also see **Shaman**.

Shillelagh (Shah-lay-lee)—The magickal tool corresponding to the staff in other traditions. They are traditionally made from blackthorn wood.

Skyclad—Ritual nudity, common practice within the Gardnerian tradition of Wicca. Contrary to popular belief, going skyclad is not the norm among most pagans working in group situations. Going skyclad is a personal choice, and it should not be made mandatory, especially since there is little or no evidence to suggest that this was common practice in ancient paganism. Gerald Gardner got the idea from an Italian monograph written in the late medieval period by a pagan woman. While it may be warm enough in sunny Italy to run around naked most of the year, that was and is not the case in most of northern and western Europe and was probably not a part of their general practices.

Slavic Traditions—A generic label for the traditions of not only the Slavic lands, but also, if somewhat erroneously, to the Baltic region's traditions as well. Within this broad classification are many varying practices and individual traditions, the most well-known and accessible to westerners being the Lithuanian tradition.

Solitary—A pagan who works and worships alone without the aid of a larger coven. This is sometimes a matter of personal choice, and other times because the pagan knows no one else with whom to work.

Sorcerer/Sorceress—Terms sometimes applied loosely to both pagans and Ceremonial Magicians which most feel has negative connotations.

Spell—A specific magickal ritual designed for the purpose of obtaining, banishing, or changing one particular thing or condition. See Appendix II: The Elements of Spell Construction for a complete outline for constructing spells. Synonyms for making spells are Spell Weaving, Spellcraft, Casting, and Spell Spinning.

Spring Equinox—See **Ostara**.

Staff—Ritual tool which corresponds to the wand or athame. A staff is usually used in traditions from mountainous regions because it was a practical device.

Stang—A ritual tool from pagan Rome which resembles a two-pronged trident. It is often used in place of the wand or staff, and also marks the entrance and exit points of the circle. The stang is sacred to the two-faced Roman God, Janus.

Strega Tradition—An Italian Tradition which dates its organization to the fourteenth century, the time of the Black Plague in Europe. It bases itself on the teachings of Aradia, a mythical witch queen.

Subconscious mind—That part of the mind which functions below the levels we are able to access in the course of a normal, waking day. This area stores symbolic knowledge, dreams, and the most minute details of every experience ever had by a person. In paganism this is sometimes referred to as the Super-conscious Mind.

Summerland, the—The Wiccan Land of the Dead, somewhat similar to Tir-na-nog in Ireland, Avalon in Wales, Valhalla in the Nordic lands, and Gresholm in the southern Germanic. Summerland has recently become a wildly accepted generic term for the Land of the Dead.

Sympathetic Magick—A concept of like attracts like. The best example of sympathetic magick was in the hunting dances of Native America. Hunters would dress as the animals they sought and enact their own slaying. Sympathetic magick is the most common way spells are worked.

Talisman—An object which is reputed to offer protection or other magickal service to the carrier. It differs from an amulet by being constructed and charged by the witch rather than being found in nature.

Tarot—A set of cards containing potent symbols which can be read by the subconscious in order to do divination. The origin of the cards is unknown, but some guess that they originated in the Middle East around 3,000 years ago.

Teutonic Traditions—Today the Teutonic tradition is often thought of as being only the southern Germanic traditions, but in reality it also encompasses the Norse tradition.

Threefold Law, the—The karmic principle of paganism. It states that any energy released by the witch or magician (or anyone else), either positive or negative, will return to the sender three times over. Also see **Pagan Rede** and **Law of Responsibility**.

Torches—Fire perched atop tall staves. Torches were often used in the Norse and Teutonic traditions at the warmer Sabbats in lieu of balefires.

Tradition—The branch of paganism followed by any individual witch or coven. There are hundreds of these traditions, most drawn along ethnic or cultural lines, but several are modern amalgamations. The word traditions in this case is synonymous with path. I.e.; Wicca is one tradition of paganism.

Triple Goddess—The one Goddess in all of her three aspects: Maiden, Mother, and Crone. This triple theme of feminine deity has been found in nearly every known culture.

Vikings—The warrior class of the ancient Norse people. Their eventual insistence on the superiority of the male as a ruler and fighter helped pave the way for paganism's fall as the principal religion of the region.

Virgin—The youngest aspect of the Triple Goddess, also known as the Maiden. She is represented by the waxing moon, and the colors white and blue. Her Sabbats are Imbolg and Ostara.

Voodun—Also spelled Voodoo and Voodun. This is the New World translation of the practice of African Shamanism which flourished in the black sub-cultures of the Caribbean and the American South from the seventeenth to the early twentieth centuries. Voodun places a heavy emphasis on compulsive magick and obligatory ritual sacrifices to deities. Though Voodun became heavily influenced by Catholicism in the mid-nineteenth century, it seems to be reversing itself now, with a trend toward recovering the older African ways.

Wand—Another ritual tool brought in to the craft through Ceremonial Magick. A wand can symbolize either the element of air and the direction of east, or of south and fire.

Warlock—An antiquated term often misused in reference to a male witch. Warlock is a Scottish word akin to the word "sorcerer" and is generally not used in modern paganism. Some male pagans even find the term offensive.

Wheel of the Year—The conceptualization of the eternal cycle of time. In pagan mythology the Goddess turns the Wheel of the Year bringing everything to its season. The Wheel of the Year is symbolized by either a wreath, a ring, a snake holding its tail in its mouth, or an eight-spoked wheel.

Whitsuntide—A Christianized term for Midsummer.

Wicca—A tradition of witchcraft with a huge following among neo-pagans. Wicca is an Anglo-Saxon word meaning "wise one," a term which came to label the craft as it was practiced in England, Wales, and the continental region once known as Saxony. Today, Wicca has become a term generally used to refer to any of the pagan traditions of western and northern Europe. Wiccans are also known as witches.

Wicce—Wicce is synonymous with Wicca. Wicca is an Anglo-Saxon word, and is the older of the two. Wicce is the Old English version of the same word, but it is sometimes used to refer to an English tradition where the Saxon influences have been eliminated wherever possible.

Widdershins—This word is from the Teutonic tradition. It means to go backwards, and is the act of moving, working or dancing counterclockwise in order to banish, diminish, or counter some negative force.

Witch—Pagans of the Wittan (Celtic-Irish), Witan (Celtic-Scottish), or Wiccan (Anglo-Breton-Welsh) traditions of the craft.

Wita—The witchcraft tradition of Celtic Scotland. The term Wita is a Gaelic-ized version of the older Anglo-Saxon word Wicca.

Witta (Weed-ah)—The witchcraft tradition of Celtic Ireland. The term Witta is a Gaelic-ized version of the older Anglo-Saxon word Wicca.

Wizard—A name sometimes applied to male Ceremonial Magicians, but rarely to pagans unless they are part of the secretive Elven tradition which uses this label freely.

WomanSpirit—A feminist tradition of the craft which focuses exclusively on female deities.

Yggdrasil—One of the world's best known Tree of Life symbols. This tree, also called the World Tree, unites all of existence from the Underworld, to the Physical World to the Spiritual. It comes from the Norse tradition.

Yoruba—A popular pagan tradition from West Africa which is the parent religion of Santeria.

Yule—Sabbat celebrated at the Winter Solstice. Most of its traditions come from the pagan Roman holiday, Saturnalia. The Norse and Teutonic traditions held this as one of their most important Sabbats, and it was their New Year's Day. This Sabbat celebrates the return of the Sun God to the earth.

⇥ Appendix IV ⇤

Resources and Merchants Guide

T he following businesses sell items of interest to pagans. When contacting any of them by mail be sure to enclose a self-addressed stamped envelope (SASE), or an International Reply Coupon (IRC) when addressing mail to a foreign country. At the time of this writing all of the following organizations were active and all of the merchants in business. But keep in mind that groups and businesses can move, and even the best of them can occasionally fail. Call directory assistance or the Better Business Bureau in the cities listed if you need further assistance.

Herbs and Ritual Oils

American Herb Association
P.O. Box 353
Rescue, CA 95672
This umbrella organization does not sell herbs, but instead seeks to promote knowledge of and use of herbs. They can recommend reliable herb dealers throughout the United States.

Capriland's Herb Farm
Silver Street
Coventry, CT 06238
Write for free price list of dried herbs and herbal books. Capriland also holds special classes on herb use and has herbal lunches at various times throughout the year. Reservations are a must!

Companion Plants
7247 N. Coolville Ridge Rd.
Athens, OH 45701
Catalog $2.00.

Herbal Endeavors
3618 S. Emmons Ave.
Rochester Hills, MI 48063
Catalog $2.50.

Indiana Botanical Gardens
P.O. Box 5
Hammond, IN 46325
Sellers of herbs, teas, charcoal blocks, herbal medicines, and some books on alternative health care. Request free catalog.

Mountain Butterfly Herbs
106 Roosevelt Lane
Hamilton, MT 59840
Write for current information and prices.

Leydet Oils
P.O. Box 2354
Fair Oaks, CA 95628
Sellers of fine essential oils. Catalog and price list is $2.00.

Sandy Mush Herb Nursery
Rt. 2, Surrett Cove
Lancaster, NC 28748
Has over 800 in-stock herbs, dye plants, and other foliage. Catalog contains helpful herbal tips and recipes. Catalog $4.00, refundable with first order.

Stones and Stone Information

Lapidary Journal
P.O. Box 80937
San Diego, CA 92138
This is a publication for rock collectors that contains information on stone origins and their lore. It also has ads from companies which sell stones, tumblers, jewelry mountings, etc. Write for subscription information.

Music Sources

Music Circle
P.O. Box 219
Mt. Horeb, WI 53572
Circle sells printed and recorded music written by and for pagans. Request a sample copy of their excellent periodical for more information. Sample copy $4.50.

Postings
Dept. 654
P.O. Box 8001
Hilliard, OH 43026-8001
Send $3.00 for a year of video and audio catalogs. They are sellers of videos and off-beat audio tapes and CDs. Their audio catalog usually includes a good selection of folk and ethnic music.

Southern Music Company
1100 Broadway
San Antonio, TX 78212
(512) 226-8167
Publishers and sellers of printed music, including folk and ethnic music. They don't publish a catalog, but stock virtually everything that's in print. Contact by phone for information on placing orders.

Winners!
Valley of the Sun Publishing
P.O. Box 683
Ashland, OR 97520-0023
Publishers and sellers of New Age music and of mind-body video and audio tapes, including tapes to aid meditation, past-life recall, and astral projection. First copy of their mag-a-log is free upon request, and will continue be sent free for up to a year if you order from them.

Pagan and Metaphysical Books

Llewellyn's New Worlds of Mind and Spirit
(Formerly *New Times*)
P.O. Box 64383
Dept. 269-663
St. Paul, MN 55164-0383
This informative catalog is produced by one of the world's largest and old-est sellers and publishers of books on metaphysics, magick, paganism, astrology, and alternative spirituality. This mag-a-log contains book reviews, articles, interviews, and a list of upcoming events, as well as order forms for their large line of excellent publications. One year's subscription $10.00.

Pyramid Books
P.O. Box 3333, Altid Park
Chelmsford, MA 01824-0933
Sellers of metaphysical, pagan, and magick books. Also beautiful pagan jew-elry and statuettes. Catalog $2.00.

Magickal, Ritual, and Pagan Supplies

Craft of the Wise
45 Grove Street
New York, NY 10014
Sellers of herbs, oils, books, tapes, magickal tools, and other occult para-phernalia. Request free catalog.

Isis Metaphysical
5701 E. Colfax
Denver, CO 80220
(303) 321-0867
Write for information, catalog price varies. Isis carries jewelry, incense, oils, herbs, books, and periodicals. They carry a wide stock of books on all meta-physical topics, and what they don't carry they will gladly order for you. It is also a pleasant gathering center for local pagans and other "New Age"

thinkers. Be sure to obtain a list of their upcoming workshops, lectures, and classes. A few years ago Isis was the target of arson by an unknown party. As Isis continues to grow as a gathering place for those seeking alternative spiritualities, the threat of repeat violence is likely. Any protective energy you can send their way would no doubt be greatly appreciated.

The Magic Door
P.O. Box 8349
Salem, MA 01971
All manner of magickal and ritual supplies. Request free catalog and ordering information.

Moon Scents and Magickal Blends, Inc.
P.O. Box 1588-C
Cambridge, MA 02238
Sells all manner of magickal paraphernalia and books. Request free catalog.

Sacred Spirit Products
P.O. Box 8163
Salem, MA O1971-8163
Sellers of books, magickal tools, herbs, incense, and other occult items. Catalog $3.00.

Candles

Most gift shops carry candles in various colors and scents. Two large chains usually found in shopping malls throughout North America are "Wicks 'n Sticks" and "Candles 'n Stuff." Also look for craft shops in your area that teach candle-making.

Corndles
P.O. Box 35537
Albuquerque, MN 87176
(505) 836-2148
Corndles are candles made to look like ears of corn—perfect for burning at the Lughnasadh Sabbat.

Pagan Periodicals

Circle Network News
P.O. Box 219
Mt. Horeb, WI 53572
This quarterly pagan publication is nothing less than excellent. It is full of well-written articles and contacts. Circle sponsors pagan gatherings throughout the year and helps pagans all over the world connect with each other. At this writing, a one-year subscription is $13 by bulk mail to USA addresses, $17 first class to USA, Canada, and Mexico, and $24 elsewhere. Payment must be in U.S. funds. Send a SASE for other subscription information, or request a sample copy currently priced at $4.50.

The Cauldron
Caemorgan Cottage
Caemorgan Rd.
Cardigan, Dyfed
SA43 1QU
Wales
Send one IRC for updated subscription information on this quarterly which covers many nature spirituality paths.

Changing Men
306 N. Brooks St.
Madison, WI 53715
Finally, a magazine on men's spirituality! And one which is well worth looking into. Publishes quarterly. Subscriptions, $24. Sample copy, $6.00.

The Green Egg
P.O. Box 1542
Ukiah, CA 95482
This was the reigning queen of pagan periodicals in the early 1970s, and has been successfully revived. Contains beautiful artwork and well-researched articles. Subscriptions to this quarterly are $15 in the USA and $21 in Canada. Write with SASE for other subscription information. Sample copy, $4.95.

Llewellyn's New Worlds of Mind and Spirit
(Formerly *New Times*)
P.O. Box 64383
Dept. 269-663
St. Paul, MN 55164-0383
See under previous heading of Pagan and Metaphysical Books.

Rocky Mountain Pagan Journal
P.O. Box 620604
Littleton, CO 80162
Send SASE for subscription information. This periodical seeks to provide support and contacts for pagans in the non-coastal west.

SageWoman
P.O. Box 641
Point Arena, CA 95468
This is a journal of women's spirituality. One year subscription is $18. California residents must add current state sales tax. Send SASE for other subscription information.

Woman of Power
P.O. Box 2785
Orleans, MA 02653
This is a well-organized magazine covering feminist spirituality. Sample copy, $8.00. Write with SASE for foreign rates and other subscription information.

Yggdrasil
% Freya's Folk
537 Jones St. #165
San Francisco, CA 01772
Cost is $15 per year, 8 issues; $2.50 for a sample copy. This pagan journal focuses on the Teutonic tradition of the Craft. Checks should be made payable to Freya's Folk. Write with SASE for other subscription information.

Animal Rights and Environmental Organizations

Clean Water Action Project
317 Pennsylvania Ave., SE
Washington, DC 20042
(202) 745-4870
This organization has chapters all over the country seeking to clean up and protect water resources.

Earth First!
P.O. Box 5871
Tucson, AZ 85703
(602) 662-1371
Publishes *Earth First* Magazine. Involved with many environmental causes.

The Humane Society of the United States
2100 L Street, NW
Washington, DC 20037
HSUS seeks to stop abuse of all animals, domestic and wild.

Greenpeace
1436 U Street, NW
Washington, DC 20009
(202) 462-1177
This is a world-wide organization concerned with all aspects of the environment. They are a non-violent, but highly aggressive organization which has done a lot to increase popular awareness of our environmental woes.

People for the Ethical Treatment of Animals
Box 42516
Washington, DC 20015
(202) 726-0156
This group works to eliminate inhumane treatment of animals and animal exploitation. However, this group has been criticized for advocating breed-specific legislation against certain breeds of dogs.

Ethnic Cultural Societies

These organizations can be found in virtually every city and town in the United States and Canada, and they can be a great help to you in finding out more about the folklore and folk ways of your heritage. Many of them conduct language and cultural literacy classes, and teach native dance and music. To find them, first look in your phone book or the phone book of a nearby city for a contact number. More often though, you will have to keep an eye on the local newspaper for news about where and when the local ethnic organizations meet. If you have no luck there, go to your library and ask a librarian to help you locate them.

Continuing Education

It is possible to pursue a course of study at a reputable center of learning that is relevant to paganism without having to obtain a four-year degree. Most colleges and universities welcome non-degree seeking students. All you need to do is write to or go to a school near you and request a copy of their undergraduate catalog. This will tell you the names of all the courses the school offers, what level of difficulty each are, what, if any, prerequisite classes are required, the cost of the classes, and how to apply for admission as a non-degree student. For the names of classes that are of particular interest to pagans, look for courses under department headings such as Classics, Egyptology, Cultural Anthropology, Religion (especially comparative and aboriginal), Mythology (often found as a subheading to the other departments mentioned), Ethnic Studies (such as Celtic Studies, Russian Studies, Black Studies, Native American Studies, etc.), Philosophy (especially the esoteric), Women's Studies, and Musicology.

Folk Art and Seasonal Decorations

Look in your local newspaper for national craft shows that travel through your area. Also check out gift shops in your area that specialize in folk crafts.

Abbey Press
354 Hill Drive
St. Meinrad, IN 47577
(812) 357-8251

Though Abbey bills itself as "The Christian Family Catalog," it contains many items of interest to pagans. Seasonal lights and decorative accents not seen anywhere else can be found in their catalog. Write or call about getting on their mailing list.

Better Homes and Gardens Craft Club
1716 Locust St.
P.O. Box 10646
Des Moines, IA 50380-0646

Write for information and special introductory offers. BHGCC has quilts, wreaths, baskets, seasonal decorations, and items to make yourself. They also sell instruction books.

Country Folk Art Magazine
8393 E. Holly Rd.
Holly, MI 48442

Look for this bimonthly publication on your newsstand or write to the above address for subscription information. CFAM sponsors the Country Folk Art traveling craft show. Schedules are listed in the magazine.

Country Sampler
P.O. Box 352
Mount Morris, IL 61054-0352

This is another bimonthly magazine which should be available on your local news stand. If not, write to the above address for subscription information. CS sponsors the Country Peddler Show, a traveling folk art and craft show whose schedules are listed in the magazine.

Seasonal/Ritual Art and Poetry

Circle Network News
P.O. Box 219
Mt. Horeb, WI 53572
This periodical features ritual poetry written by readers. Request a sample copy of their excellent periodical for more information. Sample copy $4.50.

Ideals Magazine
P.O. Box 148000
Nashville, TN 37214-8000
Ideals has been publishing beautiful seasonal material since just after World War II. They publish eight standard issues a year plus some specialty issues. Current copies can be found in most bookstores, and back issues in many second-hand bookstores.

Cross-Stitch and Other Craft Supplies

Always look for and patronize local businesses first—they need your support. Look under "crafts" or "fabrics" in your yellow pages for the names of supply stores, or for shops specializing in cross-stitch, quilting, or your area of interest. Be sure to ask about lessons in these various arts if you want or need them. Two large chains that carry almost everything any craftsperson could want are Crafts, Etc. and Ben Franklin. If you cannot find the things you need or want locally, or you simply want to seek out other options, write to the following magazines for information.

Cross Stitch and Country Crafts Magazine
Box 56829
Boulder, CO 80322-6829
A bimonthly magazine featuring cross stitch patterns and other needle crafts complete with instructions. Write for subscription information.

For the Love of Cross Stitch Magazine
104 Riverwood Rd.
North Little Rock, AR 72118
Publishes bimonthly. Has many full-color cross-stitch patterns and instructions. Also sells some supplies by mail. Heavy on seasonal themes. Write for subscription information.

Just Cross Stitch
405 Riverhills Business Park
Birmingham, AL 35242-9948
This bimonthly publication contains very few patterns, but has much coverage on what is currently available. Lots of color pictures. Excellent for those who have no easy access to craft suppliers. Write for subscription information.

Food Preparation

Try your local gift shops for seasonal cookie molds to use with the All-Purpose Holiday Cookie recipe found in the Yule section of this book, or with your own favorite. Hallmark Stores, located in virtually every American town, also sell seasonal cookie molds, as do many larger groceries.

Brown Bag Cookie Art
A Hill Design Company
Rt. 3 A
Hill, NH 03243
(603) 934-2650
This company makes and sells oversized cookie molds for all seasons and in many motifs. These are incredibly detailed molds, and each is sold in a gift bag with a recipe book. Prices vary. Write for information.

American Meade Association
P.O. 206
Ostrander, OH 43061
This organizations promotes and keeps alive the art and lore of meade. Also provides access to various recipes and meade making supplies. Membership is $10 a year.

Of General Interest

Cumberland General Store
Route 3
Crossville, TN 38555
(615) 484-8481

Cumberland is an authentic old-time general store that carries a vast variety of items of interest to pagans: cauldrons, cider presses, corn dryers, wine making and candle making supplies, spinning wheels, craft books, folk instruments, oil lamps, canning supplies, folklore books, seasonal cookie cutters, cook books, hand-hewn bells, baskets, and fire place supplies, including an old-fashioned popcorn pan designed for use over an open flame. Send $3.50 for current catalog.

Pagan Organizations

Council of Magickal Arts
4300 Lafayette St.
Bellarie, TX 77401

An umbrella organization that supports pagans in the Southwest.

The Fellowship of Isis
Clonegal Castle
Enniscorthy
County Wexford, Ireland

This is an international organization of Goddess worshipers with a membership of around 10,000. Send one IRC for response to inquiries.

Pagan Spirit Alliance and Lady Liberty League
% Circle Sanctuary
Box 219
Mt. Horeb, WI 53572

For membership application to PSA, send a SASE to Circle. LLL involves itself in aiding pagans who face legal difficulties due to their religion.

Witches' Anti-Defamation League
c/o Black Forest Publishing
Dept. WADL
Box 1392
Mechanicsburg, PA 17055-1392
Modeled on the very effective Jewish Anti-Defamation League, this group
actively combats discrimination against persons involved in nature reli-
gions. Include SASE for response.

Witches' League for Public Awareness
P.O. Box 8736
Salem, MA 01970
Include a business-sized SASE for response. This organization seeks to edu-
cate the public about nature religions and tackles discrimination issues.

≼ Appendix V ≽

Instructions for Making
Felt Sabbat Calendars

Counting calendars have been a popular part of modern religious festivities since the Victorian era. I first came into contact with them when my mother made one for my brother and me to count off the days until Christmas. This idea adapts very easily to the seasonal focus of pagan practice, and adults enjoy the anticipation and the untying of the buttons every bit as much as their children.

This section is intended as an appendix to Chapter Six, where complete instructions are given for making a Bealtaine Calendar. The method and dimensions for all other calendars will be exactly the same. Below you will find ideas for making and decorating them for the other Sabbats. But be warned that the novelty of these calendars loses its freshness if they are in constant use. Pick one or two of your favorite Sabbats, the ones you, your family, or coven most enjoy, and make its counting calendar a special part of your yearly celebrations.

Samhain Calendar

Use orange felt with black contrast colors, and use pale green for the construction paper. Cut designs of black cats, cauldrons, jack-o'-lanterns, and ghosts for the border design. Use black buttons (30) and orange or black yarn. For an inventive variation, try cutting the entire calendar in the shape

307

of an orange felt pumpkin. Glue the poem on the stem, and let black buttons form the facial features. When you are done, glue the entire thing to heavy cardboard. Begin untying the buttons on the night of October 1.

> THE LIGHTS ARE IN THE WINDOW,
> THE JACK-O'-LANTERNS SMILE.
> HOW LONG MUST IT BE 'TIL SAMHAIN—
> A LONG OR A LITTLE WHILE?
> UNTIE A BUTTON EVERY NIGHT
> BEFORE YOU GO TO BED,
> OCTOBER FIRST TO SAMHAIN EVE—
> GOOD NIGHT, YOU SLEEPY HEAD!

Yule Calendar

Use bright red felt with green and white contrast felt, and white buttons and white yarn. You can use either 21 or 24 buttons, depending on when your family exchanges Yule gifts. Some pagans wait until Christmas because they would rather celebrate the season with the rest of their family than on the actual solstice date. Twenty-one will, in most years, allow you to count from the beginning of the month to the solstice. Twenty-four allows you to begin counting on December 1 and end on Christmas Eve. Have lots of small jingle bells at the top and bottom of the calendar. Use white construction paper for the poem. Cut out Sun Wheels, stars, and Yule Trees as border decorations.

> HOW MANY MORE DAYS 'TIL YULETIDE?
> HOW MANY MORE NIGHTS TO GO?
> HOW MANY MORE DAYS 'TIL THE PRESENTS,
> AND THE YULE LOG'S FRAGRANT GLOW?
> 'TIL GOD IS BORN OF GODDESS...
> OH, IT'S SO AWFULLY HARD TO COUNT!
> SO LET THESE FRIENDLY BUTTONS
> TELL YOU THE EXACT AMOUNT.

Imbolg Calendar

For the Imbolg calendar use pink, white, pale green, or pale yellow as the main color, and use the remaining three as contrast colors and as possible colors for the construction paper. Cut out lots of hearts and flaming candles to adorn the border. Use white buttons (24) and yarn. Begin untying the buttons 24 nights before Imbolg.

In the bitter cold of winter
Spring seems so far away.
How long 'til the Imbolg Candles
Urge the sun to come to stay?
To help you count the nights so long
Are these little buttons white.
Untie one each eve at dream time,
And it will soon be Imbolg night.

Ostara Calendar

The Ostara Calendar can be as multi-colored as you like, just like Eostre's Eggs, but the traditional colors of the holiday are grass green and pastels. Use a pastel as the background color and the green as the contrast. Use another pastel for the construction paper. Buttons (21) can be of any color, but pastels or white look the best. Match the yarn color to the buttons. Cut eggs and rabbits as border designs. Begin untying the buttons on March 1.

The light will soon be coming
To lighten the darkened skies.
But how long must we wait to see the sun
Rise triumphantly on high?
Untie a button every night
When the Sandman weaves his spell,
And Ostara morn will be here
In the tinkling of a bell.

Midsummer Calendar

Use solar colors for this calendar—yellow, orange, and gold. Use browns and tans for additional contrast colors. Buttons (21) should be in a paler version of one of these shades as should the yarn. Cut Sun Wheels and balefires as border designs. For a different look you can cut the felt background in the shape of a large Sun Wheel. Glue the design to heavy cardboard when finished for stability. Glue the poem in the center and place the buttons around the outside. With either calendar, begin untying the buttons on June 1.

If you long to hear the balefire
Crackling in a magick blaze,
To greet with joy the morning sun
Rising through a misty haze.
Then you ask how long 'til Midsummer...

IT SEEMS SO FAR AWAY.
BUT THESE TINY RIBBONED BUTTONS
WILL COUNT DOWN TO THE DAY.

Lughnasadh Calendar

Use corn yellow, soybean green, and other first harvest colors for this calendar. Try using the lighter color as the background and the darker as the contrast. White or yellow buttons (24) will look the best, as will white or yellow yarn. Cut silhouettes of harvest fruits and Sun Wheels for the border design. Begin untying the buttons 24 nights before Lughnasadh.

DO YOU FIND YOUR MOUTH STARTS TO WATER
AT THE THOUGHT OF THE LUGHNASADH FEAST?
DO YOU DREAM AT NIGHT OF CORN PONE,
OF BREADS RISEN HIGH WITH YEAST?
HOW LONG UNTIL THE HARVEST,
'TIL THE FIELDS ARE GATHERED IN?
UNTIE A BUTTON NIGHTLY
TO USHER THE SEASON IN.

Mabon Calendar

The warm earth tones of autumn are the ones you should use here. Try a deep gold or rust background with brown and/or maroon as a contrast color. Use dark buttons (21) and dark yarn. Pick a paler shade of any one of these colors for the construction paper or your poem will not be readable. Cut autumn leaves, grapes, and wine bottles for the border design. Begin untying the buttons on September 1. This is a good calendar to make if you have young children who dislike school because it gives them something special to look forward to at the beginning of the school year.

THE CRISPY NIP OF AUTUMN
IS STARTING TO CHILL THE AIR.
HOW LONG IS IT 'TIL MABON,
WHEN THE HARVEST WE WILL SHARE?
UNTIE A BUTTON EVERY NIGHT
WHEN HOME AND HEARTHSIDE CALL,
AND SOON MABON EVE WILL BE HERE—
THE BLESSED SEASON OF FALL.

⇥ Appendix VI ⇤

Sabbat Correspondences

SABBAT	OTHER NAMES	SYMBOLS	COLORS
Samhain	Halloween	Jack-o'-Lantern	Black
	Hallowmas	Balefire	Orange
	All Hollows Eve	Besom	
	Day of the Dead	Masks	
	Feast of Spirits	The Cauldron	
	Third Harvest	Waning Moon	
	Samonios		
	All Saint's Eve		
	Martinmas		
	Celtic New Year		
	Samhuinn		
	Celtic Winter		
	Samana		
	Festival of Pamona		
	Vigil of Saman		
	Hallowe'en		
	Vigil of Todos		
	Santos		
Yule	Midwinter	Evergreen Trees	Red
	Sun Return	Yule Log	Green
	Alban Arthan	Holly	White
	Pagan New Year	Eight-Spoked	Gold
	Saturnalia	Wheel	

SABBAT	OTHER NAMES	SYMBOLS	COLORS
Yule	Winter Solstice	Wreaths	
	Finn's Day	Spinning Wheels	
	Yuletide		
	Festival of Sol		
	Great Day of the Cauldron		
	Festival of Growth		
Imbolg	Imbolc	Candles	White
	Oimelc	The Bride	Yellow
	Candlemas	Burrowing Animals	Pink
	Disting-tid	Grain Dolly	
	Feast of Brigid	Sun Wheels	
	Festival of Light		
	Feast of the Virgin		
	Festival of Milk		
	Anagantios		
	Feast Day of St. Blaize		
	St. Bridget's Day		
	Candlelaria		
Ostara	Eostre's Day	Eggs	Pink
	Spring Equinox	New Moon	Yellow
	Vernal Equinox	Butterflies/Cocoons	Grass Green
	Alban Eiber		All Pastels
	Bacchanalia		Robin's Egg
	Lady Day		Blue
Bealtaine	Beltane	Eggs	Red
	May Day	Flowers	Green
	Walpurgisnacht	Chalice	White
	Walpurgis Eve	May Pole	Dark Yellow
	May Eve	Butterchurn	
	Rudemas	Flower Chaplet	
	Celtic Summer	May Baskets	

	Floralia	Crossroads	
	The Great Rite		
	Giamonios		
	Bhealltainn		

Midsummer	Summer Solstice	Fire	Gold
	Litha	The Sun	Green
	Alban Hefin	Blades	Blue
	Sun Blessing	Mistletoe	Tan
	Gathering Day	Oak Trees	
	Feill-Sheathain	Balefire	
	Whit Sunday	Sun Wheels	
	Whitsuntide	Faeries	
	Vestalia		
	Thing-Tide		
	St. John's Day		

Lughnasadh	Lammas	Corn	Red
	Lughnasa	All Grains	Gold
	Festival of Green Corn	Bread	Yellow
	First Harvest	Full Moon	Green
	Ceresalia	Wheat	Orange
	August Eve		Citrine
	Elembiuos		
	Feast of Cardenas		

Mabon	Autumn Equinox	Grapes	Brown
	Fall Equinox	Wine	Orange
	Second Harvest	Vines	Violet
	Festival of Dionysus	Garland	Maroon
	Wine Harvest	Gourds	Russet
	Alban Elfed	Burial Cairns	Deep Gold
	Cornucopia	Rattles	
		Horn of Plenty	
		Indian Corn	
		Sun Wheels	

SABBAT	DEITIES	ACTIVITIES	TABOOS
Samhain	All Crone Goddesses The Dying/Dead God	Divination Past-Life Recall Spirit Contact Meditation Drying Winter Herbs	Travel After Dark Eating Grapes or Berries
Yule	Newborn God Triple Goddess	Decorating Yule Tree Gifts in Memory of Deceased Storytelling	Extinguishing Fire Traveling
Imbolg	God and Goddess as Children All Virgin Goddesses	Candle Lighting Searching for signs of Spring Gathering Stones	Cutting or Picking Plants
Ostara	Youthful and virile God and Goddess	Dying Eggs Looking for Spring Growth	None Known
Bealtaine	Marriage/Sexual Union of Deities All Mother Goddesses	Wrapping May Pole The Great Rite Gathering Flowers	Giving Away Fire Giving Away Food
Midsummer	Father Gods Mother Goddesses Pregnant Deities Sun Gods	Jumping Balefire Gathering Herbs Clan Gatherings Well Dressing	Giving Away Fire Sleeping Away from Home Neglecting Animals

Lughnasadh	Sun Gods Mother Goddesses	Baking Bread Gathering First Fruits Astrology	Not Sharing Food
Mabon	Wine Deities	Wine Making	Passing Burial Sites and not honor ing the dead
	Aging Deities	Adorning Graves	

SABBAT	ANIMALS	STONES	FOODS
Samhain	Bats Cats Dogs	Obsidian Onyx Carnelian	Apples Squash Pork
Yule	Stags Squirrels Wren/Robin	Bloodstone Ruby Garnet	Poultry Dried Fruit Egg Nog Pork Beans
Imbolg	Robin Burrowing Animals Sheep Lamb Dragon Deer	Turquoise Amethyst	Milk Honey Poultry Pork Lamb
Ostara	Rabbits Snakes	Aquamarine Rose Quartz Moonstone	Eggs Honey

SABBAT	ANIMALS	STONES	FOODS
Bealtaine	Goats Rabbits Honey Bees	Sapphire Bloodstone	Dairy Foods Sweets Honey Oats
Midsummer	Robin/Wren Summer Birds Horses Cattle	Emerald Jade Tiger's Eye Lapis Lazuli Diamond	Summer Squash Lemons Oranges
Lughnasadh	Roosters Calves	Yellow Diamond Peridot Citrine	Breads Corn Berry Pies Potatoes All First Harvest Foods
Mabon	Dogs Wolves Birds of Prey	Amethyst Yellow Topaz	Wine Grapes Nuts Apples

SABBAT	PLANTS	MEANING
Samhain	Apple Mugwort Gourds Sage Allspice Catnip	Wisdom of Crone Death of God Reflection on Our Place in the Wheel of the Year Honoring of the Dead End of Summer New Year (Celtic) Celebrating Reincarnation

Yule	Holly	Rebirth of God
	Mistletoe	Honor of the Triple Goddess
	Evergreens	Return of Sun and Waxing Year
	Poinsettia	New Year (Non-Celtic)
	Bougainvillaea	
	Tropical Flowers	
	Bay	
	Pine	
	Ginger	
	Valerian	
	Myyrh	

Imbolg	Evergreen	Honor of the Virgin Goddess
	Willow	First Signs of Returning Life
	Rosemary	Festival of Light
	Clover	
	Dill	

Ostara	Crocus	Balance
	Daffodil	New Life/Rebirth
	Jasmine	Goddess and God in Youth
	Irish Moss	End of Winter (Non-Celtic)
	Snowdrop	Light Overtaking Darkness
	Ginger	

Bealtaine	Primrose	Union of God and Goddess
	Cowslip	Sacred Marriage
	Hawthorn	All New Life
	Rose	Fertility for All Living Things
	Birch	End of Winter (Celtic)
	Rosemary	
	Lilac	

SABBAT	PLANTS	MEANING
Midsummer	Oak	Honoring of Sun/God at His Power
	Mistletoe	Saying Farewell to the Waxing Year
	Frankincense	Preparation for Harvest
	Lemon	Honoring the Pregnant Goddess
	Sandalwood	Beginning of Waning Year
	Heliotrope	
	Copal	
	Saffron	
	Galangal	
	Laurel	
	Ylang-Ylang	
Lughnasadh	Corn	Honoring the Parent Deities
	Rice	Honoring the Sun Gods
	Wheat	Celebrating First Harvest
	Ginseng	
	Rye	
Mabon	Vines	Celebrating the Second Harvest
	Ivy	Balance
	Hazel	Honoring the Aging Deities
	Cedar	Honoring the Spirit World
	Hops	Darkness Overtaking Light
	Tabacco	Celebration of Wine

SABBAT	ATTUNEMENT TEAS (Individually or Blended)	RITUAL OILS
Samhain	Apple Cider	Frankincense
	Angelica	Basil
	Catnip	Yarrow
	Indian Hyppo	Lilac
	Sage	Ylang-Ylang
	Valerian	Camphor
		Clove

Yule	Cinnamon	Rosemary
	Mullein	Myrrh
	Willow Bark	Nutmeg
	Yarrow	Saffron
		Cedar/Pine
		Wintergreen
		Ginger
Imbolg	Chamomile	Jasmine
	Red Clover	Apricot
	Rosemary	Carnation
	Blackberry	Sweet Pea
		Neroli
		Olive
Ostara	Dandelion	Lotus
	Egg Drinks	Magnolia
	Hyssop	Ginger
	Linden	
Bealtaine	Burdock	Passion Flower
	Damiana	Rose
	Hibiscus	Tuberose
	Rose Hips	Vanilla
	Saffron	
Midsummer	Anise	Heliotrope
	Carrot Drinks	Cinnamon
	Lemon	Sandalwood
	Nettle	Lavender
	Orange	Orange
		All Mint Oils
		Lemon
		Saffron
Lughnasadh	Alfalfa	Eucalyptus
	Cornsilk	Corn
	Golden Seal	Safflower

SABBAT	ATTUNEMENT TEAS	RITUAL OILS
Mabon	All Berries	Apple Blossom
	Grape Drinks	Hay/Straw
	Heather	Black Pepper
	Hops	Patchouly
	Sassafras	

SABBAT	MYTHICAL CREATURES	KEY ACTION(s)
Samhain	Phooka	Return
	Goblin	Change
	Medusa	
	Beansidhe	
	Fylgiar	
	Peryton	
	Erlkonig	
	Harpies	
Yule	Phoenix	Meditate
	Trolls	Introspection
	Mermecolion	
Imbolg	Firebird	Plan and Prepare
	Dragon	
	Berometz	
Ostara	Unicorn	Open
	Merpeople	Begin
	Pegesus	
Bealtaine	Faeries	Take Action
	Pegesus	
	Satyrs	
	Giants	

Midsummer	Satyrs	Nurture and Love
	Faeries	
	Firebird	
	Dragon	
	Thunderbird	
	Manticore	
Lughnasadh	Phoenix	Receive
	Griffins	Harvest
	Basilisk	
	Centaurs	
	Speaking Skull	
Mabon	Andamans	Give Thanks
	Cyclopes	
	Gnomes	
	Gulon	
	Minotaur	
	Sphinx	

DEITIES ASSOCIATED WITH THE SABBATS

Samhain Goddesses

All Crone Goddesses	All Underworld Goddesses
Al-Ilat (Persian)	Baba Yaga (Russian)
Babd (Irish)	Bast (Egyptian)
Bebhionn (Irish)	Bronach (Irish)
Brunhilde (Teutonic)	Caillech/Cailleac (Irish-Scottish)
Carlin (Scottish)	Cassandra (Greek)
Cerridwen (Welsh-Scottish)	Crobh Dearg (Irish)
Devanyani (Indian)	Dolya (Russian)
Edda (Norse)	Elli (Teutonic)
Eris (Greek)	Fortuna (Greco-Roman)
Frau Holde (Teutonic)	Frigga/Frey (Norse)

Samhain Goddesses

Hakea (Polynesian)   Hecate (Greek)
Hel (Norse)   Husbishag (Semitic)
Inanna (Sumerian)   Ishtar (Babylonian)
Kali (Hindu)   Kalma (Finnish-Yugoritic)
Kele-De (Irish)   Lilith (Hebrew)
Macha (Irish)   Mara (Persian)
Mari (Hindu)   Mari-Ama (Norse)
Marzana (Slavic)   The Morrigu/Morrigan (Celtic)
Nicnevin (Anglo-Scottish)   Pamona (Roman)
Psyche (Greek)   The Queen of Elphame (Scottish)
Remati (Tibetan)   Rhiannon (Welsh)
Zorya Vechernaya (Slavic)

Samhain Gods

All Death Gods   All Aged Gods
All Underworld Gods   Am-Heh (Egyptian)
Arawn (Welsh)   Corn Father (Native American)
Coyote Brother (Native American) Dis (Roman)
Eite-Ade (Etruscan)   Ghede (Voodun)
Hades (Greek)   Heimdall (Norse)
The Great Horned God (European)   Kronos/Cronus (Greco-Phoenician)
Loki (Norse)   Maderha (Lapp)
Nefertum (Egyptian)   Odin (Norse)
Pluto (Greco-Roman)   Rangi (Maori)
Samana (Aryan)   Sekhet (Egyptian)
Woden (Teutonic)   Xocatl (Aztec)

Yule Goddesses

All Spinning Goddesses   Albina (Tuscan)
Angerona (Roman)   Anna Perenna (Roman)
Befana (Italian)   Brigitte (Voodun)
Changing Woman (Apache)   Eve (Hebraic)
Fortuna (Roman)   Frey (Norse)
Gaia (Greek)   Hannah (Sumerian)
Heket (Egyptian)   Kefa (Egyptian)
Lilith (Hebraic)   Lucina (Italian)

Ma'at (Egyptian)
Nox (Roman)
Pandora (Greek)
Shekinah (Hebraic-Gnostic)
Thea (Greek)
Virgin Mary (Christian-Gnostic)
Zvezda (Slavic)

Metzli (Aztec)
NuKua (Chinese)
Pax (Roman)
Spinning Woman (Native American)
Tiamat (Babylonian)
Yachimato-Hime (Japanese)

Yule Gods

All Re-Born Sun Gods
Apollo (Greco-Roman)
Balder (Norse)
Cronos (Greek)
Helios (Greek)
Janus (Roman)
Lugh (Irish)
Mitra (Aryan)
Ngau (Maori)
Oak/Holly King (Anglo-Celtic)
Ra (Egyptian)
Sol (Roman)
Yachimata-Hiko (Japanese)

Aker (Egyptian)
Attis (Egyptian-Phoenician)
Braggi (Norse)
Father Sun (Native American)
Hyperion (Greek)
Jesus (Christian-Gnostic)
Maui (Polynesian)
Mithras (Persian)
Nurelli (Aboriginal)
Odin (Norse)
Saturn (Roman)
Ukko (Finnish-Yugoritic)

Imbolg Goddesses

All Virgin Goddesses
Anu (Irish)
Arachne (Greek)
Arianhrod (Welsh)
Athena (Greek)
Audhumla (Teutonic)
Branwen (Manx-Welsh)
Brynhild (Teutonic)
Dahud (Breton-Cornish)
Frimia (Teutonic)
Inanna (Sumerian)
Laufey (Teutonic)
Selene (Greek)
Vesta (Roman)

All Flame Goddesses
Aradia (Tuscan)
Arani (Aryan)
Artio (Gaulish)
Attar (Arabic)
Blaize (Breton)
Brigid/Brid (Irish)
Cardea (Roman)
Februa (Roman)
Gaia (Greek)
Kebehut (Egyptian)
Lucina (Roman-Norse)
Triduana (Scottish)

Imbolg Gods

All Dragon-headed Gods   All Flame Gods
Bannik (Slavic)   Braggi (Norse)
Cupid/Eros (Greco-Roman)   Dainichi (Japanese)
Diancecht (Irish)   Dumuzi (Sumerian)
Essus (Gaulish)   Februus (Roman)
Pax (Roman)   Trusto (Teutonic)

Ostara Goddesses

All Virgin Goddesses   All Goddesses of Love
All Moon Goddesses   All Androgynous Deities
Some Fertility Goddesses   Anna Fearina (Roman)
Aphrodite (Greek)   Astarte (Canaanite)
Athena (Greek)   Coatlicue (Aztec)
Cybele (Roman)   Doda (Serbian)
Eostre (Teutonic)   Erce (Slavic)
Eriu (Irish)   Flidais (Irish)
Gaia (Greek)   Garbhog (Irish)
Hera/Juno (Greco-Roman)   Ishtar (Babylonian)
Iris (Greek)   Isis (Egyptian)
Lady of the Lake (Welsh-Cornish) Libera (Roman)
Madhusri (Hindu)   Ma-Ku (Chinese)
Melusine (Franco-Scottish)   Minerva (Roman)
Moon Mother (Native American)   The Muses (Greek)
Ova (Greek-Etruscan)   Persephone (Greco-Roman)
Renpet (Egyptian)   Rheda (Anglo-Saxon)
Salamaona (Middle Eastern)   Vesna (Slavic)
Vesta (Greco-Roman)   Venus (Roman)

Ostara Gods

All Gods of Love   All Moon Gods
Some Fertility Gods   All Gods of Song and Dance
Adonis (Greek)   Attis (Persian)
Cernunnos (Greco-Celtic)   Dagda (Irish)
Danh (West African)   Dylan (Welsh)
Gwali (Central African)   The Great Horned God (European)
Lord of the Greenwood (English)   Mithras (Greco Persian)

Odin (Norse)
Ovis (Roman Etruscan)

Osiris (Egyptian)
Pan (Greek)

Bealtaine Goddesses

All Virgin-Mother Goddesses
All Flower Goddesses
All Fertility Goddesses
Aphrodite (Greek)
Artemis (Greek)
Blodewedd (Welsh)
Cupra (Etruscan)
Damara (English)
Diana (Greek)
Fand (Manx-Irish)
Flora (Roman)
Hilaria (Greek)
Kaikibani (Polynesian)
Mielikki (Finnish)
Prithvi (Hindu)
Rhea (Cretean)
Sarbanda (Babylonian)
Skadi (Teutonic)
Var (Norse)
Xochiquetzal (Aztec)

All Goddesses of Song and Dance
All Goddesses of the Hunt
Aima (Hebraic)
Ariel (English)
Baubo (Greek)
Chuang-Mu (Chinese)
Cybele (Greek)
Devana (Slavic)
Erzulie (Voodun)
Flidais (Irish)
Freya (Norse)
Ilamatecuhtli (Aztec)
Lofn (Norse)
Perchta (Slavic)
Rainbow Snake (Aboriginal)
Rhiannon (Welsh)
Shiela-na-gig (Irish)
Tuulikki (Finnish)
Venus (Roman)

Bealtaine Gods

All Gods of the Hunt
All Gods of Love
Arthur, King (Welsh-Cornish)
Bel/Belanos (Celtic)
Cernunnons (Greco-Celtic)
Cupid/Eros (Greco-Roman)
Frey (Norse)
The Great Horned God (European)
Manawyddan (Welsh)
Orion (Greco-Arabic)
Puck (English)
Telipinu (Hittite)

All Fertility Gods
All Young Father Gods
Baal (Phoenician)
Beltene (Irish-Scottish)
Chors (Slavic)
Faunus (Roman)
Herne (Greek)
Lono (Polynesian)
Odin (Norse)
Pan (Greek)
Robin Goodfellow (English)

Midsummer Goddesses

All Pregnant Goddesses
All Young Mother Goddesses
Most War Goddesses
Aine (Irish)
Aestas (Roman)
Artemis (Greek)
Athena (Greek)
Banba (Irish)
Bona Dea (Roman)
Cerd (Iberian)
Chup-Kamui (Japanese)
Dag (German)
Damona (Breton)
Dana (Irish)
Dia Griene (Scottish)
Djanggawaul Sisters (Aboriginal)
Elat (Semitic)
Eos (Greek)
Erce (English)
Eriu (Irish)
Freya (Norse)
Gerd Teutonic)
Gokarmo (Tibetan)
Grian (Irish)
Hathor-Tiamet (Egyptian)
Indra (Aryan)
Isis (Egyptian)
Jord (Teutonic)
Juno (Roman)
Kali (Indian)
Keca Aba (Russia)
Kou-Njami (Siberian)
Kupulo (Russian)
Mabd/Maeve (Irish)
Marici (Tibetan)
Mitra (Aryan)
Nut (Egyptian)
Olwen (Welsh)
Robigus (Roman)
Sekhmet (Egyptian)
Shekinah (Hebraic)
Vesta (Rome)
Wurusema (Hittite)
Xatel-Ekwa (Hungarian)
Zoe (Greek)

Midsummer Gods

All Sun Gods and Goddesses
Most War Gods
Most Thunder Gods
Apollo (Greco-Roman)
Baal (Phoenician)
Balder (Norse)
Bochica (South American)
Chacol (Mayan)
Dagda (Irish)
Donnus (Irish)
Dharme (Aryan)
El (Semitic)
Hadad (Syrian)
Helios (Greek)
Hyperion (Greek)
Ganges (Indian)
Gwydion (Welsh)
Legba (Voodun)
Llew (Welsh)
Lugh (Irish)
Maui (Polynesian)
Oak/Holly King (Anglo-Celtic)
Orunjan (Yourban)
Prometheus (Greek)

Ra (Egyptian)
Thor (Norse)
Xiuhtecutli (Aztec)

Sol/Helios (Greco-Roman)
Upulero (Indonesian)
Zeus (Greco-Roman)

Lughnasadh Goddesses

All Grain Deities
All Livestock Goddesses
Alphito (Irish)
Cabria (Phoenician)
Ceres (Roman)
Damia (Greek)
Frey (Norse)
Habondia (German-Celtic)
Ishtar (Babylonian)
Kornjunfer (German)
Marcia (Italian)
Morgay (English)
Persephone (Greek)
Po Ino Nogar (Cambodian)
Robigo (Roman)
Selu (Cherokee)
Tailltiu (Welsh-Scottish)
Tuaret (Egyptian)
Zaramama (Peruvian)

All Mother Goddesses
Aine (Irish)
Ashnan (Sumerian)
Carmen (Italio-Iberian)
Chicomecoatl (Aztec)
Demeter (Greek)
Goddess of Mundus (Norse-Celtic)
Hani-Yasu-NoKami (Japanese)
Kait (Hittite)
Libera (Roman)
Mama Alpa (Incan)
Nisaba (Chaldaean)
Pirua (South American)
Qocha Mana (Hopi)
Saning Sri (Japanese)
Taillte (Irish)
Tea (Irish)
Uti Hiati (Pawnee)
Zytniamatka (Teutonic)

Lughnasadh Gods

All Father Gods
All Lovestock Gods
Bes (Egyptian)
Dagon (Phoenician)
Ghanan (Mayan)
Liber (Roman)
Llew (Welsh)
Neper (Egyptian)
Xochipilli (Aztec)

All Grain Deities
Athtar (Phoenician)
Bran (Welsh)
Ebisu (Japanese)
Howtu (Chinese)
Lono (Polynesian)
Lugh (Irish)
Odin (Norse)

Mabon Goddesses

All Grape-Berry Goddesses
Akibimi (Japanese)
Cessair (Welsh)
Harmonica (Greek)
Mama Allpa (Peruvian)
Morgan (Welsh-Cornish)
Nikkal (Canaanite)
Ninkasi (Sumerian)
Rennutet (Egyptian)
Snake Woman (Aboriginal)
Sura (Indian)

All Fruit-Vegetable Deities
Anapurna (Indian)
Epona (Celtic-Gaulish)
Lilitu (Semitic)
Modron (Welsh)
The Muses (Greek)
Ningal (Sumerian)
Pamona (Roman)
Sin (Irish)
Sophia (Greco-Hebraic)

Mabon Gods

All Wine Gods
All Gods of Fruits
Dionysus (Roman)
Haurun (Canaanite)
Great Horned God (European)
Iacchus (Greco-Tuscan)
Orcus (Roman)

All Non-Grain Harvest Gods
All Gods of Abandonment
Bacchus (Greek)
Hermes (Greek)
Hotei (Japanese)
Mabon (Welsh)
Thoth (Egyptian)

⇥ Appendix VII ⇤

Pagan Symbols

Many symbols have been used in paganism throughout its long existence. Some of them have been taken from nature, some from abstractions about the structure of the universe, and others from the ancient early alphabets of our ancestors. Hebrew, Sanskrit, Egyptian Heiroglyphs, and Native American picture writing were among the earliest writing systems—all of them either originally or still pagan cultures. The following are some of the most important, potent, and well-known symbols. Use them to carve on your magickal tools, design pagan jewelry, or to decorate your altar or Book of Shadows.

PENTAGRAM
This five-pointed star shown with its apex up is paganism's oldest symbol. It represents Spirit or Deity over matter—the four elements of water, air, earth, and fire. In the microcosm it also represents mind over matter or flesh.

PENTACLE
The Pentacle is a pentagram contained in a circle that adds the representation of infinity and rebirth to this old pagan symbol.

SUN WHEEL OR BRIGID'S CROSS

The equilateral cross represents balance and the four lesser Sabbats—the Equinoxes and Solstices. This symbol is usually seen and used at Imbolg which honors the Irish Goddess Brigid, and at Lughnasadh which honors the Celtic Sun God Lugh.

THE TRIANGE OF CREATION

The two upper corners of this symbol represent the God, or the male principle of creation, and the Goddess, or the female principle of creation. The lower point represents all creation which was made from this union.

THE TRIPLE GODDESS TRIANGLE

Each point of this triangle represents a different aspect of the Triple Goddess—Maiden, Mother, and Crone. Who is at the top point depends on either the Sabbat or moon phase being celebrated. For example, if the Sabbat is Imbolg, a day which celebrates the Virgin aspect, then the Virgin is on the top. The triangle rotates clockwise (deosil) so the next phase of the Goddess (the Mother) is placed in the lower left, and the Crone on the lower right.

SEAL OF SOLOMON

This six-pointed star which is often depicted as inter-lacing is most well-known for being the Star of David that symbolizes the Jewish faith. But before it was Jewish, it was pagan. As a pagan symbol it represents the union of the triangles of the Triple Godess and of Creation. It was also adopted by the Alchemists as a symbol of the four elements which were drawn as triangles with or without lines through them.

THE ANKH

This symbol is from Egypt and symbolizes creation. The bottom half is a phallic symbol and the top represents the great cosmic womb where all life took shape. It represents life, sex, rebirth, and spiritual knowledge. It is sometimes called the Crux Ansata.

SWASTIKA

This ancient Aryan sun wheel got a bad reputation in the 1930s and 1940s when the Nazi Party of Germany turned it backward and adopted it as their symbol. Like all Sun Wheels, it represents the power of the Sun Gods and the Equinoxes and Solstices. Notice that the corners all point clockwise, indicating its positive use. The Nazi version is going counter-clockwise (widdershins) in the manner of destructive force.

THE TRIDENT

Sea gods have carried this staff as their emblem for eons. Most well-known associations of the Trident are with Neptune, Posiden, and Lir. Since there is a Triple Goddess but no triple God, the Trident was used to impregnate the Triple Goddess using only one God.

CIRCLE

The circle is a symbol of eternity, the Wheel of the Year, rebirth, protection and containment. As a symbol of creation it represents the full womb and the opening of the birth canal.

THE TRIPLE GODDESS

The three phases of the moon represent the three phases of the life of the Triple Goddess—the waxing moon is the Maiden, the full moon (Esbat) is the Mother, and the waning moon is the Crone. Each symbol can also stand on its own to represent a particular Goddess. Sometimes a double-headed axe blade is used to represent this Triplicity.

THE SCYTHE

The rounded blade of the scythe has been long associated with the entity known as Death. It has come to symbolize reincarnation to pagans because it not only cuts down life (as in a wheat field), but provides food that sustains life.

THE EIGHT-POINTED STAR
Sometimes called an octagram, this star was used in northern and western Europe to represent the Wheel of the Year and the eight solar Sabbats.

THEBAN ALPHABET
The Theban letters have been adapted into paganism and are used for writing and decoration. This symbol is used at the end of communications and has come to mean all endings.

OGHAM WRITING
The Celts developed this writing system for carving on tools, stones, and other hard objects. The system consists of a center line with other lines representing sounds.

ANGLO-SAXON RUNES
This rune represents fertility. Runes were an early form of Germanic writing that, like the Ogham, employed straight lines to make carving easier. Like many early alphabets, it was held sacred because of the belief that writing words brought about their manifestation.

THE ELDER FUTHARK RUNES
These are the most well-known of the Teutonic runes—and they are probably the oldest. These runes symbolize fertility and beginnings.

NATIVE AMERICAN PICTOGRAPHS
The Native Americans had a rich sign
language, both written and visual. This
symbol means lightning.

This is another Native American sign
that means a mountain or insurmount-
able object.

This one means flight.

THE SHIN
Hebrew was another early alphabet with
mystical connotations. This letter, the
Shin, once represented a Triple Goddess,
though modern Judaism uses it to symbolize the glory of their God.

THE TRISCALE
A Druidic symbol that represented their
sacred number of three.

THE YIN-YANG
The Eastern Tradition's symbol of totality. It is always rendered in black and
white, each half representing polaries
such as light/dark, male/female, good/
evil.

ZODIAC SYMBOLS

The Sun   ☉

The Moon   ☽

Mercury   ☿

Venus (Also the symbol for females)   ♀

The Earth (resemblance to a sun wheel is
intentional)   ⊕

Mars (Also the symbol for males)   ♂

Jupiter   ♃

Saturn   ♄

Uranus   ♅

Neptune (A form of Trident)   ♆

Pluto   ♇

Aries   ♈

Taurus   ♉

Gemini   ♊

Cancer   ♋

Leo   ♌

Virgo   ♍

Libra   ♎

Scorpio   ♏

Sagittarius   ♐

Capricorn   ♑

Aquarius   ♒

Pisces   ♓

⇥ Appendix VIII ⇤

Cross-Stitch Guide

Yule Wreath Decoration

Symbol	DMC Color	Color
℧	White	White
X	321	Bright Red
\	520	Pine Green
Back stitch	3371	Dark Brown

Use 18-count white Aida or other evenweave fabric. Use 2 strands of floss for the design and one for backstitching. Finished design will fit in a three-inch wood embroidery hoop and can be hung on a Yule tree or wall.

Sabbat Sampler

Symbol	DMC Color	Color
•	White	White
L	211	Lavender
7	309	Deep Coral
R	321	Bright Red
h	347	Barn Red
V	353	Violet
/	354	Light Violet
P	520	Pine Green
N	645	Steel Gray

D	647	Medium Gray
G	676	Gold
C	712	Cream
M	739	Pale Beige
The Corn	743	Dark Yellow
Y	745	Pale Yellow
B	775	Light Blue
—	815	Dark Red
T	830	Brown
B.S.	844	Very Dark Gray
\	924	Deep Teal
X	934	Dark Pine
O	976	Pumpkin
g	989	Light Grass Green
W	3013	Pale Gray Green
S	3046	Wheat Gold
Z	3371	Dark Brown
Back stitch	3371	Dark Brown
⚨	3689	Pink

Use 14- or 18-count Aida ecru fabric or 14- or 18-count Fiddler's Cloth for a more rustic look. 14-count cloth will yield a finished design about eight inches square, and 18-count cloth will make a finished design about five and a half inches square.

Each square should be worked within its design square, leaving two empty spaces between each square. Fill in remainder of cauldron with 645. Fill in remainder of apple with 815. Fill in hearts at the bottom sides with 347. All backstitching is done with one strand of 3371 floss with the following exceptions. Backstitching on pentagram done in two strands 844. Yule package wrapped in two strands 321. Yule wreath bow is two strands 321. Cauldron is backstitched in one strand 844. Flames under cauldron are a blend of one strand of 976 and one strand 743. Feet on cauldron in three strands 645. Lettering in green squares done in two strands of 924. Lettering in teal squares done in two strands of 934. Corn tassels in three strands 3013. Apple stem in two strands 830. Imbolg candle wicks in one strand 3371. Lining in rabbit's ear in two strands 3689.

Yule Wreath Decoration

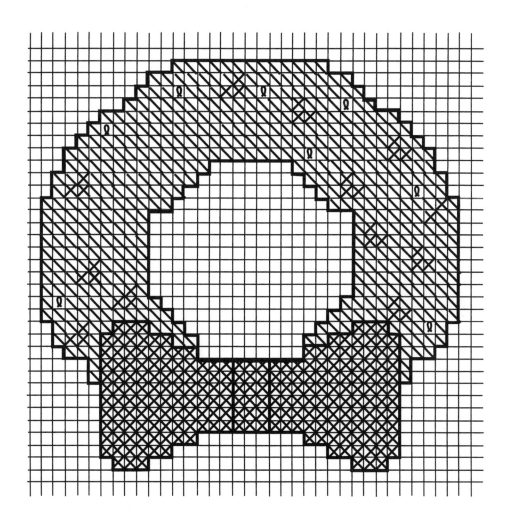

Sabbat Sampler

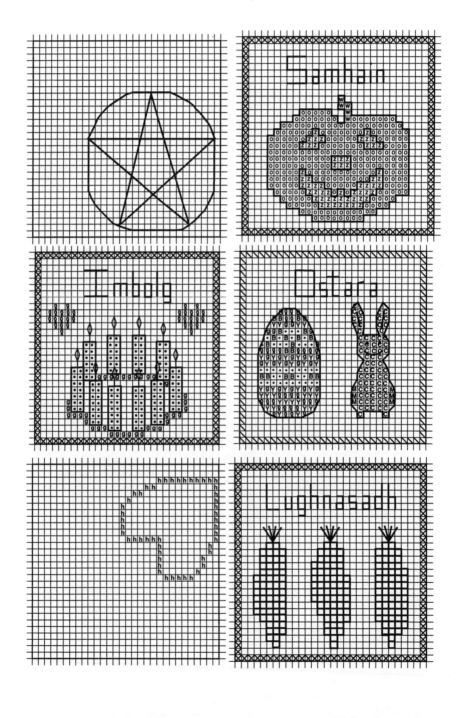

You can work each square separately as a single wall-hanging, or stitch the entire design together as a sampler. If you do stitch the design as a sampler, be sure to leave two empty spaces between each square design.

Bibliography
and Selected Readings

Below is a list of books on a myriad of pagan subjects which I recommend heartily to any pagan interested in gaining more information and insight into their religion. A few of these works constitute the bibliography that I consulted while attempting to put together the history and lore of the Sabbats, especially necessary for the times when I was working outside of my familiar tradition. Others have been cherished books on my own library shelves for many years, usually dog-eared from repeated use, and some are new books which are exciting additions to pagan literature.

The authors and books listed here will form a solid nucleus around which to build your own pagan library. But don't stop here! Read everything you can get your hands on about paganism: magick, mythology, criticism, commentary, folklore, ritual, etc. As long as you keep in mind the Pagan Rede and the wise words of teachers you love and trust (media teachers as well as personal teachers), then you cannot go wrong.

Religions evolve just as people do, so feel free to adapt and combine traditions until you find a unique approach to the old deities and old ways that are meaningful and fulfilling to you.

Adler, Margot. *Drawing Down the Moon* (Revised and expanded edition). Boston, MA: Beacon Press, 1986.

> This large compilation was the work of several years of research into pagan movements in the United States and the various traditions they follow. A good source book for eclectic pagans and for those unfamiliar with the many paths available to witches.

Beck, Peggy V., and Anna L. Walters. *The Sacred* (Fifth printing). Tsaile, AZ: Navajo Community College Press, 1988.

> This work deals with the sacred beliefs and practices of several Native American cultures, most notably the Navajo and the Dakota/Lakota.

Bettelheim, Bruno. *The Uses of Enchantment: The Meaning and Importance of Fairy Tales.* New York, NY: Vintage Books, 1977.

> This is an enlightening and intellectual analysis of why fairy tales hold such appeal for our children.

Brandon, Ruth. *The Spiritualists.* New York: Alfred A. Knopf, Inc., 1983.

Buckland, Raymond. *Buckland's Complete Book of Witchcraft.* St. Paul, MN: Llewellyn Publications, 1987.

> Precise and well-explained lessons in paganism from a Saxon-Gardnerian perspective. Contains a detailed list of common dream symbolism. Also look for Buckland's other books on practical magick, most all of them available from Llewellyn Publications.

—— *Scottish Witchcraft.* St. Paul, MN: Llewellyn Publications, 1991.

Budapest, Zsuzsanna E. *The Grandmother of Time.* San Francisco, CA: Harper and Row, 1989.

Brokaw, Meredith and Annie Gilbar. *The Penny Whistle Party Planner.* New York, NY: Weidenfeld and Nicolson, 1987.

> This team has produced excellent books on children's parties, published seasonally. All are great sources of holiday ideas for pagans of all ages.

Bulfinch, Thomas. *Bulfinch's Mythology.* Garden City, NY: Nelson Double-day, Inc., 1968 (First published in 1855 as *The Age of Fable*).

Brennan, J.H. *Astral Doorways* (Revised edition). Wellingborough, Northamptonshire, England: Aquarian Press, 1986.

Cabot, Laurie. *The Power of the Witch.* New York, NY: Delta Books (A division of Doubleday), 1989.

> A very intelligent work on basic pagan beliefs. Cabot is the founder of The Witches' League for Public Awareness which combats negative press and tackles discrimination issues. The WLPA is listed in the Resources Appendix.

Cagner, Ewert. (Translated by Yvonne Aboav-Elmquist.) *Swedish Christmas.* New York, NY: Henry Holt and Co.

Campanelli, Pauline and Dan. *Ancient Ways.* St. Paul, MN: Llewellyn Publications, 1991.

> This award-winning book on the Sabbats approaches them from a traditional "recapture the past" point-of-view.

—— *Circles, Groves and Sancutaries.* St. Paul, MN: Llewellyn Publications, 1992.

This book is packed with photos and drawings of real pagan worship sites. A good guide for great ideas on creating worship sites for newly-formed covens and solitaries.

—— *Wheel of the Year.* St. Paul, MN: Llewellyn Publications, 1989.

Campbell, Joseph. *The Masks of God: Primitive Mythology.* New York, NY: Viking Press, 1959.

Campbell was probably the most renowned mythologist who ever lived. His works are probing, insightful, and he treats nature spirituality with respect. Look in video stores and on Public Broadcasting for rebroadcasts of his mini-series, *The Power of Myth.*

—— *The Mythic Image.* Princeton, NJ: Princeton University Press, 1974.

Castleman, Michael. *The Healing Herbs.* Emmaus, PA: Rodale Press, 1991.

Chaundler, Christine. *The Book of Superstition.* Secaucus, NJ: Citadel Press, 1970.

Cole, Joanna, ed. *Best-Loved Folktales of the World.* Garden City, NY: Doubleday and Company, Inc., 1982.

Cunningham, Scott. *The Complete Book of Incense, Oils, and Brews.* St. Paul, MN: Llewellyn Publications, 1989.

All of Cunningham's books are excellent and ethical guides for pagans. In this work he gives several wonderful recipes for Sabbat ritual oils and incenses.

—— *Crystal, Gem and Metal Magic.* St. Paul, MN: Llewellyn Publications, 1988.

—— *The Magic In Food.* St. Paul, MN: Llewellyn Publications, 1991.

This large book is packed full of seasonal recipes, traditional Sabbat and Esbat foods, and lots of ideas for kitchen magic.

—— *Magical Herbalism.* St. Paul, MN: Llewellyn Publications, 1987.

—— *The Truth About Witchcraft Today.* St. Paul, MN: Llewellyn Publications, 1988.

An excellent, easy-to-read introductory guide to modern paganism for those with little or no background knowledge.

—— *Wicca: A Guide for the Solitary Practitioner.* St. Paul, MN: Llewellyn Publications, 1988.

This is an excellent primer for beginners whether they are solitaries or part of a coven.

Cunningham, Scott, and David Harrington. *The Magical Household*. St. Paul, MN: Llewellyn Publications, 1987.

Davidson, H.R.E. *Myths and Symbols in Pagan Europe*. Syracuse, NY: The University of Syracuse Press, 1988.

Denning, Melita and Osborne Phillips. *The Llewellyn Practical Guide to Astral Projection*. St. Paul, MN: Llewellyn Publications, 1987.

Dolfyn. *Shamanic Wisdom*. Oakland, CA: Earthspirit, Inc., 1990.

> Basic Shamanic practice adapted for modern, ecology-minded people. Contains many good exercises for contacting earth and animal spirits.

Dunwich, Gerina. *Wicca Craft*. New York, NY: The Carol Publishing Group, 1991.

Farrar, Janet and Stewart. *Eight Sabbats for Witches*. Custer, WA: Phoenix Publishing, Inc., 1981.

> This book, from the Gardnerian Tradition, gives some basic information for each Sabbat, and an accompanying ritual based on their tradition's practice and concept of deity.

—— *The Witches' God*. Custer, WA: Phoenix Publishing, Inc., 1989.

> An extensive list of pagan Gods from many different cultures.

—— *The Witches' Goddess*. Custer, WA: Phoenix Publishing, Inc., 1987.

> An extensive list of pagan Goddesses from many different cultures.

Fitch, Ed. *Magical Rites From the Crystal Well*. St. Paul, MN: Llewellyn Publications, 1986.

> A collection of works reprinted from the famous pagan periodical of the 1970s, *The Crystal Well*.

Froud, Brain and Alan Lee (Edited and Illustrated by David Larkin). *Faeries*. New York, NY: Harry N. Abrams, 1978.

Frazer, Sir James. *The New Golden Bough* (Abridged Edition). New York: Criterion Books, 1959 (first published in 1890 in twelve volumes).

> This classic work has some holes in its scholarship, but it is still remains one of the best all-around sources of old pagan practices in western Europe. Readers should keep in mind that it was written by someone who, though interested in metaphysics, did not view paganism/witchcraft as a "real" religion.

Gardner, Adelaide. *Meditation: A Practical Study*. London, England: The Theosophical Publishing House, 1968.

Gardner, Gerald B. *Witchcraft Today.* London, England: Rider Press, 1954.

> After England repealed its anti-witchcraft laws in the early 1950s, Gardner came out with this ground-breaking book. The first public work done on the subject of witchcraft, it has had a profound influence on modern pagan practice.

Glass-Koentop, Pattalee. *Year of Moons, Season of Trees: Mysteries and Rites of Celtic Tree Magic.* St. Paul, MN: Llewellyn Publications, 1991.

Gonzalez-Whippler, Migene. *The Complete Book of Spells, Ceremonies and Magic.* St. Paul, MN: Llewellyn Publications, 1988.

> A catch-all for explaining all manner of magickal systems. There is also an excellent introductory section on numerous forms of divination.

Graves, Robert. *The White Goddess.* New York: Farrar, Straus and Giroux, 1973 (first published 1953).

> A classic text on Goddess mythology which is used in university classes in the classics and mythology.

Gimbutas, Marija. *Goddesses and Gods of Old Europe.* Berkeley, CA: University of California Press, 1982.

Gundarsson, Kveldulf. *Teutonic Magic.* St. Paul, MN: Llewellyn Publications, 1990.

> A good sourcebook on the Teutonic Tradition.

Hazlitt, W. Carew. *Faiths and Folklore of the British Isles (Volumes I and II).* New York: Benjamin Blom, 1965.

Hole, Christina. *Easter and Its Customs.* New York, NY: M. Barrows and Company, Inc., 1961.

Hutchinson, Ruth Shepherd and Ruth Constance Adams. *Every Day's A Holiday.* New York, NY: Harper and Brothers Publishers, 1951.

Jung, Carl G. *Man and His Symbols.* New York, NY: Doubleday, 1964.

King, Serge Kahili, Ph.D. *Urban Shaman.* New York: Simon and Schuster, Inc., A Fireside Books Imprint, 1990.

> Shamanism from the Hawaiian tradition.

Langley, Jonathan, illus. *Rain, Rain, Go Away! A Book of Nursery Rhymes,* New York: Dial Books for Young Readers, 1991.

Leek, Sybil. *The Complete Art of Witchcraft.* New York, NY: Signet Books, 1971.

> Another classic written by one of the few truly hereditary witches who made themselves known after the repeal of the British anti-witchcraft laws.

Linton, R. *Halloween*. New York, NY: Henry Schuman, Inc. 1950.

Lobel, Arnold, ed. and illus. *The Random House Book of Mother Goose*. New York, NY: Random House, 1986.

Malbrough, Ray T. *Charms, Spells and Formulas*. St. Paul, MN: Llewellyn Publications, 1987.
> Magick from the Voodun tradition, New Orleans-style.

Matthews, Caitlin. *The Elements of the Goddess*. Longmeade, Shaftsbury, Dorset, England: Element Books, 1989.

Matthews, John. *The Elements of the Arthurian Tradition*. Longmeade, Shaftsbury, Dorset, England: Element Books, 1989.

—— *Taliesin: Shamanism and the Bardic Mysteries in Britain and Ireland*. London, England: The Aquarian Press, 1991.
> This work explores Anglo-Celtic shamanism through ancient poetry.

Matthews, John, and Caitlin Matthews. *Hallowquest: Tarot Magic and the Arthurian Mysteries*. London, England: The Aquarian Press, 1990.

McClain, Florence Wagner. *A Practical Guide to Past Life Regression*. St. Paul, MN: Llewellyn Publications, 1987.
> How to access past-life experiences.

McClester, Cedric. *Kwanzaa*. New York, NY: Gumbs and Thomas Publishers, 1990.

McCoy, Edain. *A Witch's Guide to Faery Folk*. St. Paul, MN: Llewellyn Publications, 1994.

—— *Witta: An Irish Pagan Tradition*. St. Paul, MN: Llewellyn Publications, 1993.

Mella, Dorothee L. *Stone Power*. New York, NY: Warner Books, 1988.

Monaghan, Patricia. *The Book of Goddesses and Heroines*. St. Paul, MN: Llewellyn Publications, 1990.

Monroe, Douglas. *The 21 Lessons of Merlyn*. St. Paul, MN: Llewellyn Publications, 1992.
> This book of teaching stories takes the reader into the world of young King Arthur and presents a comprehensive guide to the Druidic Tradition from the Male Mysteries point of view.

Montgomerie, Norah and William, ed. *A Book of Scottish Nursey Rhymes*. New York, NY: Oxford University Press, 1965.

Morwyn. *Secrets of a Witch's Coven.* West Chester, PA: Whitford Press, 1988.

> Explores the Alexandrian Tradition, combining Ceremonial Magick with Wicca.

Muir, Frank. *Christmas Customs and Traditions.* New York, NY: Taplinger Publishing Co., 1975.

Pringle, Mary P. and Clara A. Urann. *Yule-Tide In Many Lands.* Boston, MA: Lothrop, Lee and Shepard Co., 1916.

Rees, Alwyn and Brinley Rees. *Celtic Heritage: Ancient Tradition in Ireland and Wales.* New York, NY: Thames and Hudson, 1961.

Richardson, Alan. *Earth God Rising: The Return of the Male Mysteries.* St. Paul, MN: Llewellyn Publications, 1992.

> Explores the often overlooked path of men's spirituality.

Ryall, Rhiannon. *West Country Wicca: A Journal of the Old Religion.* Custer, WA: Phoenix Publishing, Inc., 1989.

St. Clair, David. *Pagans, Priests, and Prophets.* Englewood Cliffs, NJ: Prentice-Hall, Inc., 1976.

> Explores Mexican and Aztec pagan beliefs.

Sabrina, Lady. *Reclaiming the Power.* St. Paul, MN: Llewellyn Publications, 1992.

> Practical ritual for all seasons and reasons. A must-have book for anyone wishing to fully understand pagan ritual practice.

Scourse, Nicollette. *The Victorians and Their Flowers.* Portland, OR: The Timber Press, 1983.

Starhawk. *The Spiral Dance.* San Francisco, CA: Harper and Row, 1979.

Stein, Diana. *The Women's Spirituality Book.* St. Paul, MN: Llewellyn Publications, 1988.

Stepanich, Kisma K. *The Gaia Tradition: Celebrating the Earth in Her Seasons.* St. Paul, MN: Llewellyn Publications, 1991.

> A lovely vision of not only the Sabbats, but of the spirit of each season.

Stevens, Jose, and Lena S. *Secrets of Shamanism.* New York, NY: Avon Books, 1988.

> A practical guide to Native American mysticism.

Stone, Merlin. *When God Was A Woman.* New York, NY: Harcourt Brace Jovanovich, 1976.

Thorsson, Edred. *Futhark: A Handbook of Rune Magick.* York Beach, ME: Samuel Weiser, Inc., 1984.

—— *Northern Magic: Mysteries of the Norse, Germans and English.* St. Paul, MN: Llewellyn Publications, 1992.

> This is a small, but information-packed, study of the beliefs and practices of these "Northern" traditions by a much respected writer who has studied and practiced these ways for many years.

Time-Life Books, the editors of. *The Enchanted World Series.* Alexandria, VA: Time-Life Books.

Tuleja, Tad. *Curious Customs.* New York, NY: Harmony Books, 1987.

Valiente, Doreen. *An ABC of Witchcraft.* Custer, WA: Phoenix Publishing Inc., 1973.

> A good dictionary of both familiar and unfamiliar terms from all paths of paganism.

—— *The Rebirth of Witchcraft.* Custer, WA: Phoenix Publishing Inc., 1989.

—— *Witchcraft for Tomorrow.* Custer, WA: Phoenix Publishing Inc., 1978.

Valiente, Doreen and Evan Jones. *Witchcraft: A Tradition Renewed.* Custer, WA: Phoenix Publishing Inc., 1990.

> This book presents the viewpoints of a small English tradition which grew out of the Gardnerian one. For those who are interested, there is much emphasis on the Roman stang as a ritual tool.

Walker, Barbara G. *The Crone: Woman of Age, Wisdom, and Power.* San Francisco, CA: Harper Collins, 1985.

Wallis, Wilson D. *Religion in Primitive Society.* New York, NY: F.S. Crofts and Co., 1939.

—— *Women's Rituals: A Sourcebook.* San Francisco, CA: HarperCollins, 1990.

Weinstein, Marion. *The Ancient Modern Witch: The Halloween Lecture.* New York, NY: Earth Magic Productions, Inc., 1991.

—— *Earth Magic: A Dianic Book of Shadows.* Custer, WA: Phoenix Publishing Co., 1986.

> This book, by a very popular pagan personality, presents a working system from the Dianic Tradition.

—— *Positive Magic.* Custer, WA: Phoenix Publishing Co., 1978.

Wilde, Lady. *Ancient Cures, Charms and Usages of Ireland.* Detroit, MI: Singing Tree Press, 1970 (First published in 1890 by Ward and Downey Ltd. of London, England).

Index

☽ LLEWELLYN ORDERING INFORMATION

Order Online:
Visit our website at www.llewellyn.com, select your books, and order them on our secure server.

Order by Phone:
- Call toll-free within the U.S. at 1-877-NEW-WRLD (1-877-639-9753). Call toll-free within Canada at 1-866-NEW-WRLD (1-866-639-9753)
- We accept VISA, MasterCard, and American Express

Order by Mail:
Send the full price of your order (MN residents add 7% sales tax) in U.S. funds, plus postage & handling to:

Llewellyn Worldwide
P.O. Box 64383, Dept. 1-56718-663-7
St. Paul, MN 55164-0383, U.S.A.

Postage & Handling:

Standard (U.S., Mexico, & Canada). If your order is:
$49.99 and under, add $3.00
$50.00 and over, FREE STANDARD SHIPPING

AK, HI, PR: $15.00 for one book plus $1.00 for each additional book.

International Orders (airmail only):
$16.00 for one book plus $3.00 for each additional book

Orders are processed within 2 business days. Please allow for normal shipping time.
Postage and handling rates subject to change.

SPELLWORKING FOR COVENS
Magick for Two or More

Edain McCoy

Multiply the power! Here's the only book about magick for covens . . .
While there are numerous books about creating rituals for group use, and
others on how to form, organize, and operate covens, this is the first to discuss working magic in a group (of two or more people). *Spellworking for Covens*
addresses raising and sending energy as a group, the power of the group
mind, traditional ritual structure, and several types of spells.

To make it even more practical, this book also provides a grimoire containing
texts and instructions for actual spells that can be worked within the group
setting.

0-7387-0261-7
7 ½ x 9 ⅛, 264 pp., appendices, bibliography, index   **$14.95**